CONFESSIONS IN PSYCHOTHERAPY

Confessions
in
Psychotherapy

By Sharon Hymer, Ph.D.

GARDNER PRESS, INC.
New York & London

Library of Congress Cataloging-in-Publication Data

Hymer, Sharon.
    Confessions in psychotherapy.

    Bibliography: p.
    Includes index.
    1. Psychotherapy.   2. Confession.   I. Title.
[DNLM: 1. Psychotherapy—methods.   WM 420 H996c]
RC480.5.H96   1988   616.89'14   87-19623
ISBN 0-89876-134-4

Gardner Press, Inc.
19 Union Square West
New York, NY 10003

All foreign orders except Canada and South America to:
Afterhurst Limited
Chancery House
319 City Road
London N1, United Kingdom

To my mother, *in memorium*

Contents

Acknowledgments

The encouragement and friendship of many people helped me to complete this book.

My patients' courage and varied life experiences fueled much of my thought on confessions. Tony Ellison's discerning eye helped shape the progress of this book. Gilbert Hymer's extensive literary and musical knowledge enriched the illustrative framework. Dr. Barbara Rubin's presence stimulated thought and joviality. And Dr. Loretta Walder's clinical insights and enduring support were invaluable.

I would like to single out Jacqueline Beagan, Rebecca Drill, Wayne Hamilton, Stuart Wachs, and Marcus Wiener for their helpfulness as resource guides, researchers and editorial assistants. This book could not have gotten off the ground or proceeded smoothly without them.

And finally, because my mother embodied the spirit of intellectual curiosity, enthusiasm, and generous service to others, it is to her memory that I lovingly dedicate this book.

1

The Unique Nature of Confessions in Psychotherapy

The desire to reveal ourselves to others is a distinctly human characteristic. Human beings, gregarious animals, cannot thrive without communication. Our way is littered with signposts. Gestures, syllables, scratchings on rock or papyrus illuminate the long, winding path of human existence.

We know the Vikings roved as far as Istanbul because one of their number paused to carve his name on the smooth marble of Hagia Sophia. Bits of graffiti unearthed at Pompeii remind us that the ancients held remarkably modern views on love and politics. Such tracings exist quite apart from the official record. They are not the carefully weighed words of the historian but the hasty jottings of the ordinary people, hurrying to make their marks while they could.

In our time the combination of language and technology has turned the business of revealing secrets into a high-volume industry. Judging from the proliferation of psychomedia advisors, gossip columns, pulp magazines that promise ever-newer, ever-truer revelations about our favorite celebrities, and unauthorized biographies that "tell all," we seem a society obsessed with disclosure.

Humankind came to the conclusion early on that confession is good for the soul. The individual who kept too many secrets was courting a kind of spiritual dislocation. In the Egyptian *Book of the Dead*, the soul seeking resurrection enters the hall of truth and appears before the gods. Here the suppliant's heart, symbolic of conscience, is weighed in the balance. If the suppliant is found truthful and worthy, he or she is led into the presence of Osiris, god of eternity. Unless the heart is freed of secrets, the *ka*, or soul, cannot aspire to immortal bliss. A similar insistence on truth can be found in the Judeo-Christian tradition. Here, as in Egyptian theology, a clear conscience is a prerequisite to resurrection.

Our confessions are not meant for our gods alone, however. The need for another person in our confession is paramount. "Confess your faults to one another" reads the Epistle of James, while Christ's parables frequently show confession as instrumental in achieving renewal. The prodigal son squanders his inheritance, returns home, and confesses his folly to his father. But this admission brings more than absolution. The father prepares a feast and draws the prodigal son back into the family, saying to his dutiful, older son, "It is meet that we should make merry, and be glad: for this thy brother was dead, and is alive again; and was lost, and is found" (*Luke* 15:32).

Our society today is plagued by divisiveness and lack of social ties. The mercurial rise in divorce, geographical uprootedness (Packard, 1972), weakening of the family (Bronfenbrenner, 1974; Conger, 1981), urban alienation and the demise of traditional commitments (Yankelovich, 1981), render the individual impoverished in his or her accessibility to the ever-diminishing pool of intimate confessors.

This situation is sharply different from the confessional resources found in preliterate societies (Opler, 1936; Leighton & Leighton, 1941; Frank, 1963) in which the entire community shared the conviction that confession was salutary and therapeutic. Furthermore, the shaman or designated healer (in contrast to the therapist whose patients may keep their visits secret) enjoys the absolute confidence of all. Unlike the Western therapist, the shaman/confessor shares the same background and values as the confessant. As such, both historical continuity and psychological/sociocultural homogeneity promote a spirit of well-being through confessional release.

The decline in religious belief and church attendance in our culture has forced individuals to look elsewhere for confession. Gone also, for the most part, are the family doctor and the wise relative, as well as the personal servant who was often the repository of the master's secrets. With the disappearance of traditional avenues of confession, psychotherapy has arisen to provide an outlet for the confessional impulse.

In Meares' words (1976), "The revelation of secret...was the seed from which early psychoanalytic theory grew" (p. 258). The confessions proffered by Freud and Breuer's (1895) patients had primarily cathartic value, as their verbalizations and accompanying discharge of affect eliminated discrete symptoms. Yet it was not long before Freud realized the crucial importance of the interpersonal factor in the therapist/patient relationship with his discovery of transference in the Dora case. Freud (1925) was later to realize that "the personal emotional relation between doctor and patient was after all stronger than the whole cathartic process..." (p. 27).

Freud moved confessions out of the realm of sin into the domain of secular humanism. Bruner (1956) points out that Freud's view of human beings was free of both utopianism and asceticism. Freud's emphasis on our need to confess to affirm and confirm our humanness initiated a revolutionary treatment approach in which confession cemented and intensified the bond of relatedness between patient and analyst.

In dealing with his own Oedipus complex, Freud adopted the attitude implicit in the Terence maxim, "I count nothing human alien to me," that "everything I experience with patients I find here" (quoted in Bernstein, 1976, p. 404). Montaigne (1572-1580/1965), the inventor of the essay (that highly personalized genre of self-disclosure), likewise writes, "When I most strictly and religiously confess myself, I find that the best virtue has in it some tincture of vice..." (p. 368).

In Freud's nonjudgemental approach toward his own confessions, we can discern the move away from religious toward humanistic ideals. From this perspective confessions were no longer executed to obtain forgiveness; instead they became a vehicle for insight and understanding into the universality of human foibles. Tillich (1962) comments that "with the empirical rediscovery of the old philosophical concept of the unconscious, he [Freud] broke through his own moralism.... Freud showed the ambiguity of goodness as well as of evil, and in doing so, he helped to undercut Protestant moralism" (pp. 10–11).

For Montaigne as well, confession involved opening ourselves up to all sides of our nature. In his "Apology for Raymond Sebond," Montaigne explicitly stated this theme: "I am glad not to be sick, but if I am, I want to know I am; and if they cauterize or incise me, I want to feel it. In truth, he who would eradicate the knowledge of evil would at the same time extirpate the knowledge of pleasure, and *in fine* would annihilate man" (quoted in Khan, 1983, p. 14). Confessions thus make us less morally threatening to ourselves and draw us closer to others. The immediate uneasiness of confessing is invariably outweighed by the relief that comes in acknowledging a part of ourselves that has long remained underground.

From birth on we have a universal need to relate to each other that may gradually be subordinated to self-suffient aims. The work ethic and emphasis on immediate gratification have bred the "me generation" of alienated achievers who desperately crave intimacy and love, yet all too often resign themselves to the impossibility of balancing these needs to achieve "the good life." Confessions represent a shift toward such a balance. As a voluntary form of self-expression, confession enhances intimacy and relatedness and combats loneliness and alienation.

Three ingredients are vital to the confessional process in psychotherapy: a secret to be told (the confession), a teller of the secret (the patient/confessant), and someone to tell the secret to (the therapist/confessor). Our patients' secrets, no matter how many times they confess them to themselves or offer them up in prayer and meditation, remain stubbornly their own until they share them with us. It is with this thought in mind that we may now turn to the unique nature of confessions in psychotherapy.

HOW DO CONFESSIONS DIFFER FROM OTHER THERAPEUTIC INTERCHANGES?

The word "confess" has been defined as (1) to disclose something that has been kept secret or (2) to make oneself known, to acknowledge one's identity (*Oxford English Dictionary,* 1971). The etymology (Latin convariant of *cum*—together, fully; and *fateri*—to acknowledge) speaks to the interpersonal significance of confession.

To transmute Bettelheim's (1950) "love is not enough" confession in the limited sense of a one-time verbal disclosure is not enough. Confession in psychotherapy is not simply an abreaction or catharsis. Relief is a prime component, of course, but once patients have risked acknowledging their secrets (*risk* component) and experienced a degree of catharsis (*relief* component), they can begin the often arduous task of coming to terms with the disclosure as it impinges on multiple aspects of their lives in relation to self and to others (*redemption/renewal* component). In this last step, the patient is faced with possibilities for constructively dealing with the consequences of the confession (*redemption*) and thereby experiencing a transformation of self in the process (*renewal*).

Both conscious and unconscious secrets form the subject matter of confessions. In many instances patients are aware that they have been harboring secrets for months, or even years. Other patients have kept themselves in the dark about their own secrets. Freud (1925/1926) makes the distinction between conscious and unconscious secrets. "With the neurotics, then, we make our pact: complete candor on one side and strict discretion on the other. This looks as though we were only aiming at the post of a secular father confessor. But there is a great difference, for what we want to hear from our patient is not only what he knows and conceals from other people; he is to tell us too what he does *not* know" (p. 174). In general, then, confession consists not only of those secrets the patient has been consciously carrying around, but also of those unconsciously submerged secrets that emerge in the process of free association.

The confession is a special form of therapeutic disclosure with the following characteristics:

1. *Exclusivity* (or near-exclusivity). The confession has not been shared with anyone else save the analyst or has been divulged to only one or two intimate others.

2. *Affective Quality.* The patient's confession is generally accompanied by greater affect than other disclosures. Bernfeld (1951) notes that the patient often lowers his or her voice and may use gestures. Shame, guilt, or narcissistic excitement often go hand in hand with preambles to prepare the analyst and buttress the patient against feelings of vulnerability. These confessional preludes (e.g., "I never told this to anyone before" or "This is probably the weirdest thing you ever heard") underscore the dramatic quality of confessions.

3. *Changes in Self-Esteem.* The cognitive and affective intensity of confessions heralds oscillations in the patient's level of self-esteem. The patient who risks confessing a secret deemed disgusting or guilt-inducing may experience a deflation in self-esteem prior to confessing. Following confession the patient often will evince relief and heightened self-esteem for having taken the risk, being accepted by the analyst, and focusing the therapeutic lens on a major life issue to be worked

through. Alternatively the patient with repressed grandiosity often sees the confession as the moment to foster the emergence of the grandiose self. For these patients self-esteem is dramatically elevated through confession.

4. *Risk.* Patients frequently attribute a greater element of risk to confession than to other disclosures owing to self-recrimination as well as fantasized recriminations from the analyst and other internalized objects on the basis of prior confessional experiences.

5. *Identity.* Patients see a greater piece of their identity bound up in confessions than in other communications. To confess is to acknowledge one's identity *(Oxford English Dictionary,* 1971), to reveal an intimate bit of one's core self to another.

6. *Specialness.* Confessions enhance the patient's sense of uniqueness. "My secret is lurid, different, exotic, unusual" are commonly voiced descriptions. As such the confession is unconsciously perceived as a narcissistic treasure that is often split off from one's conscious feelings of guilt, shame, or anxiety.

7. *Discontinuity.* Confessions often introduce a rupture in the sometimes routinized continuity of therapy. Bernfeld (1951) mentions that after confessing, the patient resumes his or her normal manner of speaking. I have noticed that the confession's cognitive and affective aura is discrete and distinct from communications prior to and following the confession, which tend to be more mundane, less threatening, and/or more resistance-laden. Patients who begin sessions by stating, "I have nothing to say," followed at some point by the revelation of an unconscious secret, might be those who are generally articulate and forthcoming with material. Others who tend toward intellectualization or an overly withholding cognitive style may reach a phase in treatment in which the confession is forthcoming with an unexpected accompanying flood of affect. Confession thus often signals a turning point in psychotherapy.

8. *Phenomenology.* The patient's self-labeling is a crucial component of the conscious secret. Ellenberger (1966) notes that the subject matter itself is often less important than the meaning the patient attaches to the secret. The patient is aware of the momentous, or at least less than commonplace, nature of the confession, and searches for the optimal time–space–object sequence to share his or her private world. The analyst and analytic setting come to fulfill these criteria of temporal, spatial, and object constancy. On this experiential level, it is the inter-

subjective interplay of consciousness between patient and analyst that brings the confession to life and underscores its existence.

THE PSYCHOANALYTIC REVOLUTION: RELIGIOUS VERSUS PSYCHOTHERAPEUTIC PERSPECTIVES

Freud revolutionized our thinking on the meaning and consequences of confession. Psychoanalysis abjured the tenets of sin, preordained morality, and absolution.

Worthen (1974) notes that the Catholic Church offered universal ritualized procedures for absolution in which the priest, as mediating judge of conscious sin, provided the means for restitution through God's grace. In psychotherapy both the secret and the confession can derive from the unconscious. While Mowrer (1961, 1964) bemoans the failure of psychtherapy to exhort the patient to make restitution, in psychoanalysis restitution and renewal are not automatic results of compliance with superego (church's or analyst's) demands, but rather spring from the patient's ability to undertake the journey into the self and seek his or her own way of resolving the confession.

Psychotherapy has been called the new religion in the age of anxiety. Although both spheres of life have their own rituals and props, psychotherapy prescribes no axiomatic absolution, nor does it provide a universal means to deal with the consequences of the confession. The religious confession is a self-contained, time-limited ritual in which the confessant receives absolution whereas the confession made in psychotherapy is repeated in all its thematic variations in the working-through process over a period of months or years. Following the thematic working-through process, the patient remains the final arbiter of the confession's destiny, including whether or not restitution is to be made.

Exploration replaces evaluation in psychotherapy. Patients are no longer primarily accountable to their gods, but confess to set the record straight with their peers. The psychotherapeutic shift in object relations has been dramatic. The analyst/confessor is not a representative of a higher power who summarily dictates the way to resolve the confessional dilemma. The patient instead may see the analyst as a receptive listener who is concerned with the patient's problems and with trying to help the patient within the framework of an ongoing, long-term relationship.

Confessions in psychotherapy, in fact, often raise more questions to be examined and worked through. The patient starts to tread a path of self-discovery that offers no formulated solutions or promises of absolution. Benign regression (Winnicott, 1971, 1975) and dependency are often inevitable ingredients in the therapeutic process, but the patient ultimately is forced to rely on his or her own resources and judgement in confessing. The analyst, in turn, will not judge, but also will not absolve the patient.

The gratification derived from the certain diminution of guilt through compliance with religious ritual and superego institutions gave way to the analytic emphasis on the power of the unconscious actively to be revealed, accepted, and interpreted in the presence of the noncensorious analyst. In confessing the patient is engaged in an I–thou encounter (Buber, 1937) with the analyst in which no outside force—whether god or community—need be invoked.

There are, of course, certain marked similarities between religious and psychotherapeutic confessions. The auricular confession, like psychoanalysis, emphasizes the auditory. The penitent in the confessional does not view the priest, just as the supine patient cannot see the analyst.

The priest is bound by the seal of confession, even if threatened with death, never to reveal the identity or sins of the patient. While threat to the well-being of the larger community has modified our ethical purview, with some notable exceptions, the rule of confidentiality to protect the patient's privacy is a *sine qua non* of the analytic armamentarium.

There has even been notable diversity among religious groups in their stance toward confidentiality. Wesley offered spiritual discipline through the class meeting. In religious meetings of the Salvation Army and certain Pentecostal sects, individuals publicly rise and confess past sins in an often frenzied revivalistic climate. In the confession practiced by the early Roman Church, the penitent publicly confessed mortal sins to the bishop. Absolution came only after the completion of penance, and the Sacrament could be practiced only once in a lifetime.

Ritualized forms of confession and absolution were thus often public. Even the division of the confessional into private compartments only came into general use in the sixteenth century, after Charles Borromeo had created the confessional in 1576. By about 1600 A.D., public penance was almost nonexistent.

Psychotherapeutic and religious confessions represent two different levels of reality with diverse world views, methods, and goals. The religious patient need not face the agony of relinquished choice. Both religion and psychotherapy offer avenues toward redemption and renewal. It is left for each patient to choose his or her own path(s).

THERAPEUTIC ELEMENTS IN THE DEVELOPMENT OF SELF AND OBJECT RELATIONS

All too often we wear masks that hide our true selves not only from others but also from ourselves. In so doing we may avoid people who remind us too much of our hidden selves or readily discern defects in others via projection so that our own complacency can continue unscathed. Confessions force patients to remove their masks temporarily in acknowledging and expressing disavowed aspects of self. This heightening of self-awareness engenders the emergence of the true self.

The unveiling of self-deception, in turn, contributes to a more consolidated sense of self and elevated self-esteem for the following reasons:

1. The patient feels emboldened in having risked revealing himself or herself to the analyst.

2. In the process of confessing, the patient discovers an aspect of self that may engender surprise, joy, excitement, and so on; that is, confession provides gratification from the affirming analyst and from the patient's own assimilation of repressed grandiosity into a fuller, more enriched self-image.

3. Confession can also be accompanied by disgust, shame, guilt, or anguish. Even in these instances, the patient at least feels enlivened through the intensification of emotions and thereby propelled to work through these issues further. This state of strong affectivity is especially significant for schizoid patients for whom any strong emotional reaction signals a wrenching away from their habitual apathy.

4. The patient sees that both he or she and the analyst have survived the confession. The dreaded Armaggedon did not, in fact, materialize. Just as the "ruthless" baby (Winnicott, 1963) notices that his or her destructive impulses did not kill mother, so does the patient realize that, by confessing, the patient/analyst dyad triumphs as the therapeutic process is moved forward.

5. Once the true self begins to emerge without repercussions or censure, the patient feels relieved and finds the courage to begin to come to terms with the consequences of the

confession. The patient also develops the ability to risk playing out some of these hitherto internal scenarios in the transferential arena of object relations.

Confessions unfold in an interpersonal setting. The presence of the "holding" analyst (Winnicott, 1965; Bion, 1977) is crucial in the establishment of an atmosphere secure enough for the patient to risk revealing himself or herself without fearing reprisal from internal or external bad objects. The patient's confessional style underscores the struggle between dependence on and separation from the object. The enhancement of trust and intimacy with the analyst following confession can then, in time, transfer to extratherapeutic relationships. The analyst, as the often exclusive confessional object, must be fine-tuned to the nuances of the patient's discourse as it reflects the level of self-development, as well as relations with significant objects in the patient's life.

Acknowledging a secret to oneself is not enough, especially when it serves as an intellectual exercise in self-justification. The analyst's presence is needed to create and sustain the confessional pact. A patient whose mother was dying related to me how the whole family acknowledged the veridicality of this fact, but never communally brought this "secret" into awareness. "I felt intimate with my family for the first time when we all spoke about our unspoken fears. Talking about the inevitability of my mother's death brought us closer together, and also brought each of us more in touch with our innermost feelings."

Confessions can only truly take hold in the encounter with others. Sometimes the mere presence of the silent, receptive analytic "ear" is enough. At other times the analyst must be more actively engaged in affirming the patient's confessional "gift" or analyzing the resistances that block confession. In every instance the analyst should recognize the confession's phenomenological meaning to the patient, as well as how the confession fits into the historical and present object relational currents in the patient's life.

A CONFESSIONAL EXEMPLAR: THE CASE OF KYLE

Kyle, a 32-year-old engineer, was able to reveal a number of confessions to me that illustrate both the dynamic complexity and the diversity of treatment issues encountered by an analyst. Kyle's initial complaint involved a series of obsessions that made him feel crazy; they included the fears of jumping out of a window or off the subway platform and a dread of falling down when walking. These disclosures, which were made in an unemotional manner, actually concealed what the patient regarded as his "big secret", for which the obsessions served as penance to alleviate guilt. Kyle's discussions of these obsessions, while important in the overall *gestalt* of his treatment, could not be termed confessions as they lacked the required exclusivity. Kyle also told various friends about these obsessions, which he viewed as inevitable baggage in his life.

Following the seventh month of treatment, the normally straitlaced and dour patient informed me, while looking at the floor, that he had something to tell me that he had never revealed to anyone before. Slightly blushing, he proceeded: "I usually buy *Screw* magazine [a New York-based pornographic publication] and just glance at the ads. Certain ads really turn me on. I like big women wrestlers who will force me down and insist on sitting on my face. I called the number once or twice, but hung up. Last week, I actually made an appointment.

The woman was big—almost 180 pounds—and wore black boots, a black garter belt, and a black-and-white lacy mantilla around her neck. She was firm and pushed me to the ground. I told her ahead of time what I wanted. Almost immediately she sat on my face and it felt fantastic—so warm and close. I could never have the guts to ask my wife to do that, and yet I feel guilty, mostly because it cost me $100. Now I'll have to think of an excuse for what I spent the money on."

Kyle's pervasive guilt about his obsessions, his recurring dreams of being chased by police, and his "secret sexuality" *prima facie* involved oedipal concerns. Yet, as his confessions unfolded, preoedipal issues emerged that took precedence over the primarily oedipal cover.

The oedipal aspects of Kyle's history were evidenced by his strong identification with his critical father. Kyle's introduction to sex began when he accidentally discovered his father's secret collection of pornographic movies and magazines, to which he would masturbate. His father belittled him with statements such as "You can be taller than your father but never bigger." At the same time, his father wanted his son to live up to his expectations by being everything that he was not. Kyle was raised in the impossible double bind of feeling guilty if he surpassed his father and also if he did not.

The second paternal secret Kyle became privy to was that his father had sired an illegitimate son by his secretary. At that time, Kyle again identified with his father by going out with a "good woman whom I don't deserve" and another "who is out for a good time and is wild, but a lot of fun." Kyle not only felt guilty about not telling his girlfriend (later to become his wife) about the other woman, but again experienced a double dose of guilt in not telling his mother about his father's affair.

Several subsequent related confessions established the primarily preoedipal nature of Kyle's makeup. One day Kyle called in a panic and asked whether I could see him. He entered my office, shaking and hyperventilating, and poured out a description of the morning's event. "I was in a porno store and started to feel faint, wondering what would happen if someone saw me there. I became even more anxious at that thought and, out in the street, had to hold onto a truck in order to stand up."

I first soothed the panic-stricken patient by informing him that it was good that he was able to think of calling me and that he was able to make it to my office. This message calmed Kyle and addressed his ego's ability to make constructive decisions. We then discussed Kyle's fantasies regarding who would see him. "My father or even both girlfriends." I queried, "What about me?" "No, you wouldn't be there, but even if you were, you wouldn't care, because you know all about me already and are unperturbed by these goings-on." This transferential communication confirmed that the analyst was now seen as the patient's ally (the benign superego) in contrast to the other figures, who appeared to him as early preoedipal persecutory objects (Klein, 1975).

Kyle's obsessive worry that he would fall down while walking occurred again in the pornographic bookstore episode. The preoedipal nature of this symptom is evidenced in Kyle's statement, "Sometimes it is hard to stand on my own two feet. It's as if I might disappear altogether. I want someone to lead me, to tell me what to do and how to live. And when I'm falling, you help get me back on my feet again."

The patient had experienced annihilation anxiety that also recurred at times when he made love. "The other night I was in bed with my girlfriend and I got really anxious because I couldn't feel myself. The thought occurred to me that if I had touched the table with my hand, I still wouldn't feel my hand. So I told my girlfriend to hold me tight, and then I felt that I existed again."

A symbiotic hold was necessary to restore Kyle's sense of being. When he was two or three years old, he recalled, he would crawl into his mother's bed after his father had left for work, where he felt safe and warm burrowing next to her under the covers: "It was like being smothered."

To be smothered by flesh connoted a blissful union with mother in which the patient could enact a yearned-for symbiotic experience. While one might discern elements of a "forbidden" oedipal sexual union, the preoedipal need to restore oneness in order to regain a sense of wholeness is primary. In Kyle's words, "I feel warm and safe like the snuggly feeling that happens when all of that flesh surrounds you."

Kyle's confessions concerned his attempts to regain the lost paradise of symbiosis. His identifications with his father's sexuality and secrets constituted an abortive attempt to pass through the oedipal period without having satisfactorily resolved major preoedipal issues.

For patients like Kyle who are initially so well-defended, the therapeutic strategy is simply to provide a receptive atmosphere in which the patient will eventually feel free enough to reveal himself or herself to the analyst. Kyle, in time, felt sufficiently empowered to risk confessing to the analyst, who was now at least partly separated from the array of critical external and internal objects. The patient discovered that as he risked confessing and experienced relief in lieu of reprisals, he was encouraged to reveal incrementally more and more of his true self with a corresponding decrement of resistance. Initial resistance not only served to maintain the patient's characteristic defensive posture, but also represented an interpersonal communication to test the analyst's mettle in bearing with the patient and holding him through the preconfessional process. Once Kyle's confession was revealed, patient and analyst were able to explore its kaleidoscopic nature on three levels:

1. The current confession in relation to the patient's history. Kyle wavered back and forth between the preoedipal fragile self and the oedipal paternal identification.

2. The confession in relation to the patient's self-image. The patient's true self—fragile, yet resolute in its need to be interpersonally affirmed and grow—was able to find an empathic analytic arena in which to be revealed and interpretively understood in the context of annihilation anxiety and the need for symbiotic relatedness to heal the wounded self.

3. The confession in relation to the patient's objects. Confessing engendered enhanced feelings of trust and willingness to sustain intimacy with the affirming analyst. Kyle was eventually able to expand the parameters of intimate objects and eventually share his secrets with his "good girl" girlfriend, who became his wife. His need to be smothered was finally revealed to his wife, who acceded to his requests without comment. Kyle no longer has to split his objects into good and bad sexual

partners. The true self continued to flower as more aspects emerged and were assimilated into the patient's total life patterns. Kyle became able to fuse the preoedipal symbiotic mother with the exciting oedipal object without guilt or anxiety either in his marriage or in psychotherapy.

SUMMARY: THE CASE OF KYLE

Kyle's confessions are represented in some detail here to illustrate the major criteria the analyst should take into account:

1. *Object relations level.* All confessions tell a story replete with *dramatis personae,* setting and plot. The patient chooses to confess to the analyst because, in some sense, he or she has no choice. The therapeutic process cries out for confession and guarantees confidentiality to minimize the risk and maximize the gain. Confessions are played out in the arena of transference. The nature of confessions, including resistance to self-disclosure, provides valuable information about how the analyst is transferentially perceived in the interactional context of the patient/analyst match.

2. *Self level.* Confessions help the analyst discern the patient's level of self-development. Kyle required the analyst to function as a selfobject (Kohut, 1977, 1984) both to accept the patient and to enable him to merge with the analyst in order to emerge with a firmer, more consolidated self. Kyle's experience of relief in lieu of reprisal facilitated the emergence of more and more of the true self.

3. *Genetic.* The dynamic meaning of the confession in its historical context eventually enables the patient to distinguish between the danger linked to the confession in contrast to the current reality in which the patient has more resources and is thus more capable of coming to terms with the confession via the working-through process.

4. *Psychosexual.* Many patients do not display clear-cut oedipal or preoedipal issues. Kyle's confessions focus attention on how the patient oedipally sexualized a secret that masked predominantly preoedipal issues concerning the patient's attempts to repair defects in relatedness.

5. *Confessional style.* Each patient brings his or her own behavioral style to confession. The manner of disclosure or concealment is itself revealing of the patient's conflicts with his or her internal and external objects.

a. Cognitive aspects: Is the patient hesitant or overly smooth in his or her presentation? The flowing patient may, at times, be defensively trading a less relevant confession for a threatening confession more central to his or her life or avoid confessing altogether. Is the patient generally resistant to all forms of self-revelation, behaviorally manifested by silences, quick topic changes, excessive time-consuming chattiness, and so on? For such patients, resistance must be cleared away and trust built up through object constancy and the analyst's empathic receptivity before any secrets are likely to be forthcoming.

Many confessions are prefaced by phrases used narcissistically to safeguard the patient from feelings of vulnerability, such as, "You're never going to believe this" or "I'm so embarrassed, guilty, etc. I've never told this to anyone before." Other patients simply blurt out the confession without warning. The latter group is either less well defended or in a state of massive anxiety that requires immediate release.

b. Affective aspects: Is the confession accompanied by blushing, crying, anxiety, or averted eyes, or does the patient relate the confession in a relatively affectless manner? The latter patient, while more defensive, at least is willing to take tentative steps in bringing the true self into consciousness. Kyle, who at first revealed his secret in an impassive, guarded way, was subsequently able to pour out his confession in a state of anxiety. Kyle's confession initiated a process of self-transformation that enabled him to experience a fuller range of his thoughts and feelings in a new and constructive way.

Analysts often relegate redemption to the spiritual sphere. Yet redemption forms part of the critical core of confession in psychotherapy (with risk and relief rounding out the confessional triad). Once Kyle risked confessing and experienced relief, following the working-through process, he was able to transcend destructive aspects of self to achieve redemption and renewal.

2
Why Do Patients Confess?

Each of us is equipped with an inner eye which measures us against our peers. As we develop we are able to chart our growth and change by listening to our own confessions and monitoring the reactions of those to whom we confess. In so doing we are able to find our place on the human continuum.

Should our confessions meet with parental censure, we might come to feel that we do not have the right to express our innermost selves, which may then be experienced as repugnant, bizarre, or something less than human. Confessions, in such instances, are viewed by the child as dangerous phenomena to be negated or driven out of awareness.

For patients whose childhood confessions were greeted by parental disapproval, the only form of self-disclosure that might have been engaged in was the institutionalized confession exemplified by the ritual of the Catholic Church to uphold the social-familial order. Confessions for many of these patients connoted a cycle of sin, punishment, and dread of future consequences in another life. Small wonder that these patients are frequently hesitant to confess to the analyst, who may become transferentially equivalent to the punitive priest/parent/deity triad.

There is an ominous mystique pervading confessions for many patients. In addition to childhood religious confessions, such negative perceptions may arise from knowledge of the heinous tortures and demonic methods associated with the Inquisition and the witch hunts. Given a childhood legacy of dread or ambivalence surrounding confession, one might well wonder why such patients are motivated to confess at all. Still the need to reveal oneself to another who is fundamentally different from one's childhood imagoes can, in time, override the need to protect the vulnerable self.

ACCEPTANCE

To experience the emotional release of confession, the patient requires the reassurance of a listener. Like a burden shared, the confessed secret weighs less heavily on the patient. The analyst becomes a partner, a kind of surrogate who absorbs the confession and enables one to see oneself in a more forgiving light. "For now we see through a glass, darkly," writes the author of the Book of Corinthians, "but then face to face: now I know in part; but then I shall know even as also I am known" (1 *Corinthians* 13:12). By removing the obscuring glass of secrecy, patients see themselves in the analyst, and the charity they would extend to another comes back to themselves.

Patients need to unburden themselves to the analyst without being condemned. Beethoven's *Heiligenstadt Testament*, written to his brothers Carl and Johann on October 6, 1802, is a remarkable confession attesting to Beethoven's desire to be accepted and understood by others. Fearing the impending loss of his hearing, Beethoven courageously resolves to accept the challenge of fate. The composer reveals his churlishness and misanthropy as an outgrowth of his growing deafness. He writes:

> For me there can be no relaxation in human society, refined conversations, and mutual confidences. I must be entirely alone, and except when the utmost necessity takes me to the threshold of society I must live like an outcast.... Such experiences have brought me close to despair and I came near to ending my own life—only my art held me back, as it seemed to me impossible to leave this world until I have produced everything I feel it has been granted to me to achieve (quoted in Görg & Schmidt, 1970, p. 21).

Beethoven's confession constituted a plea for acceptance. Nowhere else did he so candidly acknowledge his art as the redemptive force that prevented his suicide. Alienated from the *mitwelt*—the world of social bonds—Beethoven chose to relate universally through his music. Through his art he was able to experience spiritual renewal in lieu of self-destruction.

Beethoven's moving confession reminded me of a patient who was also able to save himself through his relationship with art. While many patients report fleeting feelings of suicide, Mr. M., a 23-year-old accounting clerk, confessed that he had been on the verge of suicide when he noticed the *Desiderata* on his wall. "I read the words, "You are a child of the universe, no less than the trees and the stars, you have a right to be here.... With all its sham and drudgery and broken dreams, it is still a beautiful world.' After reading these lines, I decided to choose life over death. No matter how bad life is, in reading these words, I realized that death can never be better" (Hymer, 1983, p. 66).

I noted, "Mr. M. transformed *Desiderata* into a personal statement with profound meaning for his own life. Through his identification with the subject matter, Mr. M. was able to repair his damaged self into a future imbued with possibilities" (p. 66).

Mr. M's confession to me filled a deep need for him to be accepted for who he was despite his fantasized "crime." A product of a strict Irish Catholic background, Mr. M. needed reassurance that he was not an evil sinner. While the poem initially saved the patient by immediately infusing him with self-acceptance, Mr. M. needed to be further assured by the benign analytic superego in order to continue to weaken the hold of the internalized punitive figures of his childhood.

Tolstoy's short story *The Death of Ivan Ilyich* (1886/1975) speaks to the tragedy of living and dying without being understood by those closest to us. Many patients are able to abort this vicious cycle by finally summoning up the courage to confess and experience acceptance before it is too late. In the story Ivan Ilyich is a man who is progressively deteriorating while his entire family denies his condition. The most painful aspect for him is that his wife and children, who understand nothing, are annoyed with him for being downcast.

Ivan's confessions of discomfort meet with censure and denial. Tolstoy, aware of the solitude that develops from not being accepted after confessing to deaf ears, writes, "And he has to go on living like this, on the brink of doom, all by himself, without a single person to understand or pity him" (p. 69). Tragically, Ilyich, like the seer Cassandra, is able to foresee his own death, fully aware the he can never reveal this information to his closest kin and be understood.

In time the inevitability of Ilyich's death becomes so apparent that in lieu of ignoring his complaints or "blaming the victim," the family colludes in the great lie. Tolstoy notes, "Ivan Ilyich suffered most of all from the lie—the lie adopted by everyone for some reason, which said that he was only ill and not dying..." (p. 179).

The need to be understood and accepted is a fundamental pillar of confession. Once Ilyich can acknowledge his impending death to himself, he encounters the forlornness that ensues when his confession is not taken seriously and ultimately is negated by the family's collusion in the lie that he will recover.

Unlike Miller's *Death of a Salesman* (1957), whose tragedy lies in Willy's self-deception regarding his skills and standing in the community, Ilyich faces his inner demons head on, only to be disillusioned by his family's unwillingness to acknowledge the truth of his revelations. Only with the peasant lad, Gerasim, does he feel at ease, since Gerasim is able to understand Ilyich through the acceptance of the fact that his master is going to die.

One patient, Kathy, a 24-year-old student, related her earliest memory of a confession. "I told my grandmother that when I went to communion, I accidentally dropped the wafer on the floor. Since I didn't want to eat the dirty wafer, and also didn't want anyone to find the evidence, I trampled the wafer into the ground. When I told my grandmother what I had done, she grew very cross and told me that I could go to hell for the wicked thing I had done. I felt totally evil and condemned to ever-lasting punishment in the hereafter. Years later, after I had left the Catholic Church, at times I would still get the feeling that God knew what I had done, and that I could never escape my childhood act."

This patient sought understanding by confessing to her grandmother, and instead experienced recriminations. Her internalized sense of sinfulness was repressed, only to resurface at critical periods in her life.

Kathy was so guilt-ridden by the wafer incident that she had not revealed it to anyone else. I was not aware of Kathy's secret until about 16 months after she began therapy when she casually remarked that she had spontaneously decided to go to church one day and had taken communion. Kathy started to describe the ritual to me, and when she came to the wafer segment, her eyes filled with tears and she started to tremble.

I gently asked her what the matter was, and she responded by reticently recounting the childhood trauma of being condemned by her relentless grandmother: "I understand how prisoners feel when they are condemned to forced labor in Siberia for life. At least there you have a chance to escape, but my grandmother made me feel as though I were in a no-exit situation. But in telling it to you now, somehow I don't feel bad, just saddened at my grandmother's callousness and ignorance."

Not only did Kathy experience relief but, more important, she was able to perceive herself in a new way as a worthwhile person. By confessing in psychotherapy, she could share her inner condemned self with one who understood and accepted her. In time this patient's growing self-acceptance enabled her to successfully expel the toxic introject—her grandmother—and internalize the accepting analyst and analytic attitude.

Another facet of the desire for acceptance through confession is the need to exonerate oneself. Patients will often reveal a serious, sometimes socially stigmatizing problem to test the analyst's unconditional acceptance. Betty Ford's confession concerning her drug problem brought her sympathy from the public. David Garth, the media image wizard, utilized the confessional principle in refurbishing John Anderson's tarnished image in the Jewish community. Anderson's confession and apology to Jewish groups for his attempts to inject a Christian clause into a revised Constitution won him their increased support.

When patients are able to dredge up their most dreaded secrets, the need to exonerate themselves through the analyst's affirmation overrides the need to protect the infirm self. In sharing and exploring the dynamics of the confession with the empathic analyst, the patient is gradually able to divorce himself or herself from unacceptable deeds in a number of ways:

> 1. The patient comes to realize that the self is not equivalent to the deed: "I stole items as a child, but my core self does not comprise the makeup of a thief."
> 2. The patient may experience genuine remorse and attempt restitution (e.g., Someone who has mistreated animals may teach children reverence for animals and nature, work for the ASPCA, etc.).
> 3. The patient comes to understand the genesis of the deed (e.g., "I stole as a substitute for the love I never got"), and through a combination of analysis and positive experiences with good objects, fills in the gaps in self structure.

For patients whose confessions do not involve isolated acts but habitual behaviors such as drug or alcohol problems and homosexuality, the need to feel accepted and understood tends to be even stronger, since these issues are current, and, in the case of addictions, possibly life threatening. The biggest mistake made by the novice therapist who bears witness to such confessions is the desire to rush in and rescue the patient through a combination of advice and admonitions. Excessive activity and anxiety on the part of the analyst more often than not confirms the patient's worst fears that his or her "secret life" is truly dangerous since it can induce such intense reactions from the heretofore calm analyst.

Patients who confess in these situations want, most of all, to be accepted by the analyst. An initially silent and receptive stance signals to the patient that he or she is being acknowledged and heeded. Since such patients are often anxious or impulse-ridden to begin with, a calm, thoughtful approach on the part of the analyst serves to quell the patient's anxiety and offers the hope that the patient has finally found someone to reach out to who will reach back.

GUILT

An old French proverb reads, "Nothing is so burdensome as a secret." Many of us confess to alleviate our guilt through a prescribed ritual. By setting a sacrificial goat—the scapegoat—free in the desert, the sins of the Israelites were expelled with the goat. The prescribed atonement on the High Holy Days and the auricular confession of the Catholic Church enable followers to gain relief from their guilt through institutionalized means.

Confessional rituals both encourage the cleansing regenerative act of confession and minimize the risk factor by making confession a conventional, standardized procedure. The Japanese practice of public apology, for example, allows an individual to expiate his or her guilt by confessing *en masse*. In this way the confessant is able to apologize to those who have been wronged without incurring the risk of direct confrontation. For example, when it became known that the birth of deformed children in Minimata, Japan—sufferers from "Minimata disease"—was caused by pollution attributable to the dumping of waste into the bay by a local industrial firm, the head of the firm appeared before an assembled crowd and made a public apology.

Psychoanalysis narrows the audience to the confession to one other person, the analyst, and thereby increases the potential for risk and intimacy. The first published account of cathartic therapy was that of Janet's patient "Lucie" in 1886. Janet was able to recreate the origins of her irrational fears from a childhood fright through hypnosis and her symptoms disappeared when their origin was made conscious.

Psychoanalysis originally was concerned with the detectivelike unearthing of repressed material followed by the patient's experiencing cathartic alleviation of guilt. In Freud and Breuer's (1895) pioneering cases of hysteria, the patient's confession involved the spontaneous reliving of the secret trauma (abreaction) or the emotionally charged disclosure of the remembered event (catharsis). The confession enabled these patients to experience tremendous relief by unburdening their secret in the safety and intimacy of the analytic setting.

Jung (1933) likewise recognized the therapeutic benefits of catharsis through confession. He stated:

> I must have a dark side also if I am to be whole.... In keeping the matter private, I only have attained a partial cure—for I still continue in my state of isolation. It is only with the help of confession that I am able to throw myself into the arms of humanity freed at last from the burden of moral exile. The goal of treatment by catharsis is full confession—not merely intellectual acknowledgment of the facts, but their confirmation by the heart and the actual release of the suppressed emotions (pp. 35-36).

While treatment through catharsis has had both its advocates and detractors throughout the first century of psychoanalysis, a recent dramatic application of confessional catharsis has had surprising success with torture victims in Chile. Cienfuegos and Monelli [protective pseudonyms for two Chilean psychologists (cited in Adams, 1983)] reported that most of these patients who had developed psychosomatic symptoms, including the inability to eat and sleep, high levels of anxiety, and profound feelings of despair, experienced symptom alleviation after testifying.

The patients confessed their harrowing experiences to a therapist who made tape recordings of their sessions, which the two psychologists then repeatedly analyzed. They noted, "The mere idea of remembering the experience produced fear and anxiety...but at the same time 'telling' was the only possibilty for release from painful and humiliating memories" (p. 84). Through testimony the patients not only underwent catharsis, but also produced a self-reparative document of denunciation against their torturers.

Ferenczi embraced and extended the method of catharsis. In an important paper on neocatharis, he made the point that "psychoanalysis employs two opposing methods: it produces heightening of tension by the frustration it imposes and relaxation by the freedom it allows...On the one hand, the patient is compelled to confess disagreeable truths, but on the other, he is permitted a freedom of speech and expression of his feelings such as is hardly possible in any other department of life" (1930, p. 434). While the risk involved in confessing might initially heighten the patient's guilt and anxieties, the security fostered by the analytic setting enables the patient to find relief.

In 50 B.C. Publius Syrus said that to confess a fault freely is the next thing to being innocent of it. We know this maxim is not valid either in or out of therapy. Patients do not suddenly shed their total burden of guilt with confession, just as lovers who confess their indiscretions to each other do not automatically assuage their guilt. Nor should the aim of therapy ever be the pronouncement of the patient's innocence.

The analyst neither condemns nor absolves the patient. The patient who confesses in therapy in most cases does not do so in order to profess innocence, but rather to gain a modicum of relief from guilt in the presence of the analyst.

Camus, in *The Fall* (1956), takes a strong stand on our collective guilt: "We cannot assert the innocence of anyone, whereas one can state with certainty the guilt of all...religions are on the wrong track the moment they moralize and fulminate commandments. God is not needed to create guilt or to punish. Our fellow men suffice, aided by ourselves" (p. 110).

The need to absolve ourselves of our perceived wrongdoings in the eyes of others is a powerful motivator in confessing. The emergence of guilt with the development of the superego forces the child to face the conflict of revealing or concealing. Should the parents retaliate with harsh, punitive measures that exceed the severity of the child's misdemeanor, the child is less likely to confess, and is more apt to develop rationalizations to live with guilt. Alternatively, should the parents show appreciation for the child's honesty, and implement appropriate punishment the child is more likely to want to confess to alleviate guilt while secure in the knowledge that he or she will be dealt with justly.

Freud (1930) felt the sense of guilt to be the most important problem in the development of civilization. Although he ascribed the onset of guilt to the child's sexual and aggressive impulses toward the oedipal parents, Freud (1912–1913) further traced the origins of guilt to the mythical patricide exacted by the sons in the primordial horde.

Freud implicated the severity of socialization in fostering unrealistic guilt that impeded the flow of aggressive and sexual energies. Mowrer (1961) took exception with Freud on this point; he postulated that guilt is real in psychopathology and so the goal of confession in psychotherapy should be not merely insight, but also repentance and restitution. When analysis evolved from a treatment by suggestion to one that focused on the dynamic unfolding of the patient's life, the aim of treatment became *not* to assuage the patient's guilt via suggestion, but rather to have the patient confront the guilt and come to terms with it in the working-through process.

Freud recognized early on that catharsis and insight *in vacuo* were insufficient, as the patient's secrets would merely reappear in different contexts under new guises. Like a musical variation on a theme, the patient had to acknowledge and take responsibility for the repressed secret as it reappeared in consciousness.

Psychoanalysis has sometimes been accused of eschewing the doctrine of responsibility. Yet, in a passage on dream wishes, Freud (1925a) writes, "Obviously one must hold oneself responsible for the evil impulses of one's dreams. In what other way can one deal with them?... If, in defense, I say that what is unknown, unconscious and repressed in me is not in my 'ego' then...I shall perhaps learn that what I am reputiating not only 'is' in me but sometimes 'acts' from out of me as well" (p. 151). Freud's great existential leap was to free his patients from the shackles of theological morality in their search for an autonomous self that enabled them to take responsibility and make choices outside the grip of authoritarian strictures. Atonement and restitution thus become possibilities, not necessities.

Freud, who was a friend and admirer of Binswanger, the founder of *daseinsanalyse*, certainly concurred with many of the tenets of existential analysis. When May (1958, 1959) speaks of ontological guilt arising from forfeiting one's own potentialities, one can also see parallels in the constricting effects of neurotic guilt in which the violation of parental superego prohibitions locks the patient into the conviction of his or her badness. Some of my patients guiltily confessed to stealing cookies from the cookie jar or change from their mother's purse with a stronger feeling of self-condemnation than other patients who had been in trouble with the law. Such patients may convert their guilt connected with the original "bad deed" into obsessive-compulsive behavior that further restricts their inner self from developing.

In such instances of ballooning guilt, it is important for the analyst to greet the confessions receptively and with respect. I have heard too many therapists express a tendency to reassure patients, subtly or not so subtly, that they really should not feel guilty as they have exaggerated the gravity of their offense. Although such comments initially might decrease the patient's anxiety, the therapist has unfortunately bypassed the significance of the confession in the patient's life. A recurrence of the guilt is thus likely to take place.

The severity of the internalized parental superego at times blocks the patient's potential to grow and transform the self in creative directions. While most therapists recognize the damage wrought in replicating parental prohibitions, not enough therapists give credence to the dangers of "killing patients with kindness." That is to say, if the patient is to be freed to grow away from the restrictive climate fostered by strict compliance with parental edicts, the patient does not need a surrogate parent to dictate how to live right. Rather the patient, in collaboration with the empathic analyst, can explore the dynamics of his or her ontological and neurotic guilt with the goal of arriving at ways to confront and work through the guilt.

We often look upon guilt as a negative, stultifying emotion. It is my contention that guilt can also be a constructive force, both in the development of civilization (Freud, 1930) and in the mobilization of creativity and constructive living. Max Beckmann was an artist whose relationship to his art offered him temporary relief and ultimately saved him from suicide. Although he suffered a nervous breakdown in the German trenches in World War I, Beckmann also became aware that exorcism through art could save him from self-destruction.

During the time when he was bringing back bodies from the trenches, he wrote, "I amuse myself often with my own idiotic tenacious will to live for art. I worry about myself like a loving mother, I vomit, I retch, push, force, I must live and I want to live... I would make my way through all the sewers of the world, through all the degradation and desecrations in order to paint. I must do that" (quoted in Larson, p. 65). Art allowed Beckmann temporary respite from his suffering, which still resurfaced in Sisyphus-like fashion. Yet he chose to continue, since art provided the most suitable arena for him to exorcize his inner demons by confessionally depicting his hellish inner world.

Stasis is the antipode of creative mobility. Lifton (1979) discusses two forms of static guilt: self-lacerating guilt, in which self-condemnation eventuates in an unchanging image of evil, and numbed guilt, in which guilt feeling can be avoided altogether. Lifton alludes to the benefits of constructive guilt when he states, "An animating relationship to guilt exists when one can derive from imagery of self-condemnation energy toward renewal and change"

(p. 139). The patient who is constructively enlivened by guilt assumes the anxiety of responsibility mentioned by Freud and May that is needed to transform self-condemnation into a constructive alternative.

Louise, a 34-year-old editor, continually berated herself for the excuses she had devised to stop playing the piano, and thereby not live up to her musical potential. "I feel so guilty, because I love music and my parents spent all that money on piano lessons for nothing. My teachers all told me I was good, which only makes me feel more guilty for failing everyone." One can see here the confluence of onto-logical guilt (the patient's perception of not living up to her creative potential) and neurotic guilt (noncompliance with the wishes of authority figures).

The patient then found herself in the fortuitous situation of moving into a building filled with music students. Two roommates —a violinist and a cellist—asked her if she would like to play some chamber music with them. Louise refused at first, but then con-sented following their friendly encouragement. All seemed delighted by the impromptu results.

Louise came to her next session beaming. "I am now forced to practice a little in my spare time, but I love it. Since I don't want to be shown up by my music partners, I have to maintain at least a minimal level of competence. What used to be a dreaded chore has become an anticipated joy. What a terrific feeling."

Louise did not eliminate the original guilt that accompanied her recriminatory confessions concerning her sloth and procrastin-ation, but transformed these feelings into constructive guilt marked by a return to music making in concert with others to whom she felt responsible. She experienced a surge of renewal and a heightened sense of well-being by reanimating her musical self in the presence of affirming, like-spirited others. The patient was able to transcend her ontological guilt as her constricted self gave way to a self enlivened with creative potential.

While Freud primarily focused upon oedipal guilt, several of his followers traced the development of guilt preoedipally to oral and anal stages. Klein (1975) made the most radical departure in seeing guilt as emanating from the baby's innate proclivities initially pro-jected onto the breast. In Klein's view we come into the world with destructive propensities that make us feel guilty by as early as eight months of age for having the power to destroy the good breast.

Klein (1948) sees the essence of guilt as the conviction that harm done to the loved object is caused by the subject's aggressive impulses that derive from the death instinct. The reparative ten-dency involving the individual's wish to regain externally and internally the "omnipotently destroyed" mother also forms the basis for creative activities originating in the infant's wish to regain his or her lost objects.

While one might seriously question the validity of the death instinct concept, it has nonetheless become increasingly evident to me that the confessions of many patients have revealed an overwhelming feeling of guilt because of the belief that they had seriously injured, or even destroyed, someone dear to them through thoughtless words or deeds. One patient said that she could not help but feel that she had contributed to her mother's death from a heart attack at the age of 48. "My mother always told me that words kill and that I should learn to curb my tongue with others. Even though my mother and I had a good, loving relationship, every now and then these words come back to haunt me."

This patient was convinced that her oral-sadistic omnipotence played a role in her mother's death. Confession not only helped the patient to come to terms with both her destructive and her loving feelings toward her deceased mother, but also enabled her to attempt to make reparation to her damaged self. As the patient continued to acknowledge and accept all her feelings toward her mother—which ranged from hatred, rage, and envy to love, joy, and gratitude—she began to engage herself in the parallel process of discovering and owning an expansive self in which guilt could coexist with creativity and other reparative activities.

It was the later object relations school, especially Fairbairn and Winnicott, who placed guilt squarely in the sphere of environmental object relations. In Fairbairn's (1943) schema, the baby is *de facto* relating to objects from birth onward. For Fairbairn, guilt originates when we begin to give up our bad internal objects. Since bad objects are better than no objects (Guntrip, 1969), the child would tenaciously hold onto an abusive parent rather than be left with no parent at all.

Miriam, a 38-year-old executive, confessed how her separation from her husband brought back the feelings of abandonment she had felt when she finally left home after 18 years of physical and verbal abuse by her mother. "It's strange, but I still feel guilty about leaving my mother. I don't know why, but I love her, maybe just because she is my mother. I left her, and yet it felt as though she left me. [The patient started to sob.] I never got to see her again before she died. I don't know if I can ever forgive myself for that."

In a related vein, Alice Miller (1981) poetically draws on instances of guilt evoked in the child who attempts to be a separate person in lieu of a selfobject (Kohut, 1977, 1984) extension of a narcissistic parent. The patient who dares to risk becoming a separate being harbors guilt-inducing fantasies, such as: "My parent(s) will die" (that is, the patient is needed as a life-line for parental suste-nance). Or, "My parent(s) will abandon me" or "I will become noth-ing without my parent(s)" (separation anxiety and annihilation anxiety). One patient who had made great strides in becoming her own person poignantly related how her mother sent her a birthday card in which she wrote, "In fond memory of the daughter you used to be." The patient exclaimed, "She can never just let me be. As long as she's alive, she'll never let me forget my place as my mother's daughter."

Finally, Winnicott (1963/1965) describes the "ruthless" baby experiencing guilt over aggression directed at mother along with the development of the capacity for concern to alleviate guilt. For this benign outcome to materialize, the mother who has been destroyed in fantasy must be reliably present to give the infant the opportunity for reparation (between five to six months and two years). As the starting point of morality, the capacity for concern depends upon the mother being present as a whole object who sur-vives destruction.

The patient's reparative tendencies may be related less to per-sonal guilt then to the patient's depressed mood (Winnicott, 1948/1975). As a selfobject parental extension, the child/patient may thus assume the parental mood. Also, the child/patient who feels responsible for his or her parents' well-being experiences the reparative need to cure the parent or analyst (Langs, 1978; Searles, 1979b).

Confession to the good mother/analyst or father/analyst helps recreate the historical scenario devoid of the catastrophic dread and horrifying consequences connected in fact or fantasy to the original event. In this sense confession is a self-reparative activity in which the patient can confront and examine relationships with both the historical and contemporary transferential mother or father. Since the past is experienced as present in the transference, "to the unconscious, the analyst *is* the father and the father *is* the analyst" (Racker, 1976, p. 78).

In confessing the patient not only experiences the regaining of a lost intimacy, but also learns to see himself or herself as a person capable and worthy of intimacy with others in the present. More-over, patients who have spent their lives as compliant extensions to gratify their parents' needs often realize through the confessional process that the guilt they have assumed is not based on their own deeds but has emanated from their readiness unconsciously to assume the guilt induced in them by their parents for attempting to be themselves.

Patients who feel bound to parents who induced guilt in them for their attempts to separate often initially confess a series of events whose focus concerns their having wronged their parent(s). As the patient continues to unravel the skein of incidents in which he or she felt guilty for not complying with every parental edict, the patient begins to see his or her childhood in a new light.

Over time such patients often express rage at being a parental pawn instead of a child to be loved in his or her own right. One patient who came to feel especially betrayed vehemently confessed fantasies of killing his parents, which left him drained and subject to a new form of guilt. Like Winnicott's ruthless baby, this patient gradually developed self-reparative tendencies along with the capacity for concern for his parents.

In unleashing a gamut of rageful feelings against his parents and seeing that both he and they survived (both actually and psychically), he was able to continue to develop an autonomous self freed from the burden of parental guilt. As we examined his mother's need to control everyone, he began to realize how paralyzed his mother had felt when his grandmother was alive, and how the cycle of guilt unconsciously was passed down from generation to generation. This patient, who had always tried to "fix" whatever ailed his mother through unquestioning adherence to her demands, one day came into a session with a totally different attitude. He mentioned that his mother had been rushed to the hospital with angina pains, but had insisted on leaving the hospital and going back to work the next day.

The patient continued, "Suddenly, I realized in my gut that I was not responsible for her. She always would say, 'You make your bed and sleep in it' and I thought, 'This is what she wants to do and I can't stop her.' It's amazing how crippling guilt can be. I've spent my whole life feeling responsible for other people and somehow got lost in the shuffle."

The patient became silent for a long while, and then quietly stated, "I still love my mother. Her intent was good even when she goaded me to death. I hope she lives for a long time, but I can't do anything to help her anymore."

Through the confessional cycle, this patient was able to unveil his rage at being a parental extension and to develop self-reparative potential in separating and coming to terms with his mother's shortcomings. His capacity for concern enabled him to live with his deep feelings of love and hatred for his mother, freed at last from the shackles of guilt.

RITE OF PASSAGE

Some confessions that may appear to be trivial or banal to the outside observer are experienced by confessants as guiding lights that signal turning points in their lives. Saint Augustine, in his *Confessions* (398 A.D./1961) castigates himself over a childhood theft of pears but condones his abandonment of his family to devote himself to Christianity. This seemingly minor childhood prank became a powerful motivating force in strengthening his will to follow a life-style and ideology that called for sacrifice and endurance.

The confession as rite of passage may thus serve as a signal to herald the individual's transition from one phase in life to another. Leo Tolstoy, in his *Confessions* (1882/1983), speaks of the existential ennui and discontent he was experiencing at a time in his life when he was successful, rich, and enjoying the love of his wife and children. It was through the acknowledgment of this unnamed void that Tolstoy was able to begin the search for enlightenment that dominated the remainder of his life.

Like Tolstoy, many patients confess in an effort to find new meaning in their lives. They often reveal their deepset doubts and darkest secrets in order to risk "the courage to be" (Tillich, 1952). For such patients the courage to be encompasses the courage to be different; that is, to move out of their ossified existence and risk new modes of being that challenge the traditional internalized parental voices.

Confessions that constitute rites of passage are often perceived to be the most dangerous and difficult to reveal. Patients who enter therapy with the hope of resolving their "secret life" sometimes spend months, and even years, examining issues deemed safer to reveal. This is often the case because, even though the secret pertains to one select aspect of the self, the patient sees the integrity of the whole self bound up in the would-be confession.

A striking example of the conceal–reveal dilemma involved an attractive, sophisticated, 38-year-old vice-president of a company who, over several months, had been fruitfully working on a number of issues. One day shortly before the New Year, Liza came into my office and sat down. I noticed that her usual garrulous manner had given way to embarrassment as she fidgeted on the couch and made very little eye contact with me. Slowly and haltingly she began to speak. "I made a New Year's resolution that I was not going to go through another year of therapy without telling you the thing that's bothering me the most. And yet it's so hard. I've rehearsed telling you a thousand times and always back down. But I'm resolute, even if it takes a holiday to get up my courage. O.K. I'm getting ready. Here goes. I'm...I'm...I can't say it. I'm...I'm...a virgin." At this point the patient looked at me to get some idea of my reaction to her disclosure.

I maintain that the analyst who would hurriedly reassure such a patient, for example, that she "is not the only one," makes a serious mistake, and risks losing the patient's respect as a purveyor of the truth, since the patient well knows that she is in a statistical minority. The analyst who "objectively" empathizes (Kohut, 1984) with the patient, understands and accepts the disclosure without attempting such reassurances.

Liza wanted me to accept her for who she was so that she could summon up the courage to risk adding a sexual aspect to her self-image. She also feared the discomfort that might eventuate in her being forced to reveal her virginity to her first lover. Without going into further details of her treatment following confession, suffice it to say that Liza, who was afraid of ongoing intimacy in many relationships, was able to use the trust and intimacy built up over time in our relationship to get her over the first confessional hurdle. Although still somewhat embarrassed following confession, she did not run away from the topic, nor did she act out by canceling subsequent sessions. Concurrently with this turn of events in therapy, Liza began to notice a deepening of her friendships, and even had begun to date a man whom she felt might be able eventually to understand her "secret."

Liza unveiled her secret as a first step in integrating her sexuality into the totality of her being. In the confession as rite of passage, the patient is implicitly asking permission of the analyst either to be who she or he is or to shed a habitual aspect of self and move on to a new way of being.

The patient who moves from closeted to open homosexuality in therapy establishes a shared intimacy unfettered by societal proscriptions. A fundamental aspect of the true self shines forth, awaiting affirmation by the analyst. The homosexual patient, in this case, does not seek to alter his identity, but to be accepted in the fullest sense of his being. In risking disclosing himself to the analyst, the patient in time may decide to opt for full self-disclosure with high-risk confessors such as parents and friends.

Still, in every instance of confession in psychotherapy, the ther-

apeutic aim is not the unquestioning advocacy of unremitting confession. It is left to the patient to face the challenge and
consequences of widening the range of confessors (or not) and
examining the role of the confession as it influences changing self
and object relations.

UNCONSCIOUS GUILT

Reik (1959) viewed the need to confess "sinful" thoughts or
deeds as a desire for punishment to expiate unconscious guilt
emanating from oedipal wishes. The child early on realizes a link
between atonement for wrongdoing and the restoration of parental
love after being punished. In structural terms, Reik maintained
that, by confessing, we assuage the severity of the superego for having attained id gratification.

All of us at times experience the criminal in ourselves. We revel
in vicariously participating in the "forbidden" activities of criminals
and quasi-criminals. The popularity of such films as *Bonnie and
Clyde*, in which the "heroes" are bank robbers and murderers, and
Death Wish, in which the citizen whose wife was murdered retali-
ates by killing and wounding muggers and thugs, attests to the
symbolic value of such figures as vicarious outlets for the release of
our murderous rage.

In 1985 the real-life public approbation garnered by the New
York City "subway vigilante" Bernhard Goetz, who shot four teen-
agers when they allegedly attempted to mug him, consciously
relates to our frustration concerning our vulnerability in the face of
crime. We can hereby vicariously fulfil our murderous impulses
while consciously maintaining a stance of righteous indignation at
the impotence of the lawful authorities.

In these incidents we are saved from confessing directly by
unconsciously adopting a surrogate confessant whose deeds
become our deeds and whose destiny we latch on to as if it were our
own. In fact the analyst would do well to listen carefully to a patient's
discussion of such fictional and nonfictional criminal/hero types,
which may serve as a prelude to a "criminal" confession by the
patient.

Again, many patients feel like criminals or, via free association
or dream material, become cognizant of the existence of unconscious guilt for crimes committed or intended. In such confessions,
once the patient becomes aware of the "forbidden" thought or deed,

the conviction of guilt is the driving force that prompts confession.

Patients who enter therapy to deal with self-destructive behaviors such as anorexia, hair pulling, or self-mutilation reveal a crucial aspect of their secret through their acting-out behavior. While already punishing themselves, many secretly hope that the analyst will further castigate or admonish them for their acts.

Although the patient is often forthcoming with conscious reasons for anger, guilt, and frustration, what is least accessible to the patient's awareness is the unconscious guilt which, once brought to consciousness, produces the *idée fixe* of criminality. With regard to the anorexic, hair pulling, and self-mutilating patients, all three went through a cycle of "layered" confessions in which they first revealed what they deemed to be their shameful behavior. They next went into related self-punitive behaviors and elaborated on the genesis, thoughts, and feelings connected with each act. The final and most deeply hidden secret generally emerged in veiled fashion through dreams or via vicarious associations with popular media or fictive heroes. Each patient opted to torture herself in lieu of killing her parents.

The patient's mortification in her final revisionist account of the guilt in part allayed that guilt in that the need for punishment was partially gratified by the compulsion to confess. The very act of confession unmasks these patients' "degrading" wishes or deeds to the analyst, who may transferentially be seen as a parental figure who can punish but then forgive and love again.

Patients do commit deeds that become repressed and result in unconscious guilt. Yet, more often than not, our thoughts and wishes are equally powerful elicitors of unconscious guilt. A case in point: Nora, a 25-year-old student, had several dreams in which she was sexually involved with her brother. She confessed her attraction but was baffled by the intensity of her guilt.

What subsequently emerged was that when Nora was a teenager, she would tease her younger brother by grabbing his penis or lying on his lap and rubbing her head against his penis. Years later the patient discovered that her brother was a homosexual. After the initial surprise, Nora never alluded to either event again, until the "return of the repressed" intruded itself into her dreams.

"I suddenly felt overcome with anxiety and would wake up in a sweat. Now I think I finally know why. All this time I've believed that I caused my brother's homosexuality. Rationally I know this is ridiculous, but I still feel that I was partly responsible." This patient was finally able to examine the unconscious guilt that stemmed from her perceived incestuous actions. Her brother's homosexuality unconsciously represented the punishment meted out to her for her sororal "criminal activity."

DEMORALIZATION

Confessions can serve as a salve for the patient's state of demoralization (Frank, 1963). Psychotherapy's effectiveness resides in its ability to arouse hope through both the therapist's faith that the patient can benefit from treatment and the patient's faith in the therapeutic relationship.

Frank (1959) continues:

> Psychiatry, in its preoccupation with illness, has concerned itself almost exclusively with pathogenic feelings such as fear, anxiety, and anger. It is high time that the "healing" emotions such as faith, hope, eagerness, and joy receive more attention. Of these, the physician–patient relationship affords a special opportunity to study the group of emotions related to expectancy of help which may be grouped under the generic term *faith* (p. 39).

Faith and hope can grow in the nurturant soil of the therapeutic relationship. The patient who may have seldom, or never, been given the opportunity to open up and be heard suddenly is cast into a situation in which he or she is the focus of attention.

Patients who have seldom been listened to or taken seriously enter therapy in a state of demoralization. For many patients treated as nonentities for much of their lives, therapy becomes their last hope in a heretofore futile quest for understanding and solace.

With the gradual development of trust in the therapist and therapeutic process, these patients can finally take center stage. The confession in the presence of the attentive, affirming analyst becomes a means to enhance feelings of self-worth.

Demoralization arises from warping experiences in the patient's past history that stunted growth and inhibited or prohibited confession. Patients whose confessions are appreciatively processed over time receive the needed emotional nutrients in which the tentative self can grow.

Frank (1981) sees one of the major functions of therapy as the restoration of morale by providing experiences with a therapist who offers support in morale building and combating perceptual distortions and maladaptive behaviors. Confession serves as a major step in solidifying the patient's sense of worth. With the analyst as buffer and conduit, the confession can dramatically particularize the critical moment in the patient's demoralized past. The confession simultaneously offers hope for redemption and renewal in the patient's quest for alternative ways of being in the presence of the morale-building analyst.

The patient's confession shared with the validating analyst diminishes the sense of aloneness. Even when the patient is despairing, the therapist serves as an object who is an unswerving beacon of life and hope for the wavering patient.

May (1958) comments that the problem is that human beings have "lost their world" (p. 56). I sometimes tell very despondent patients who say that they feel lost that my office is the "lost and found." Truly, therapy does become a process of finding one's self—the true self—even when the patient becomes entangled in a morass of despair. The patient, through confession, finds the lost self. Confession offers the hope of truly being understood and taken seriously as a person with a separate, "hidden" life outside the parental sphere of influence. Hope, in turn, provides an antidote to feelings of demoralization.

NEED TO RELATE

Freud and Breuer's *Studies in Hysteria* (1895) established the object relational context for confessions. The analyst is described "as a father confessor, who gives absolution...by a continuance of his sympathy and respect after the confession has been made" (p. 328). Confession creates a bridge that connects patient to analyst. The interpersonal bond is strengthened as the confession becomes a means for the patient to dispense with the pretense of bad faith in becoming authentic with the analyst. The very act of sharing an intimate secret helps the patient combat feelings of alienation and depersonalization.

Jung (1933) understood the relational nature of confession when he wrote, "There appears to be a conscience in mankind which severely punishes the man who does not somehow and at some time, at whatever cost to his pride, cease to defend and assert himself, and instead confess himself fallible and human. Until he can do this, an impenetrable wall shuts him out from the living experience of feeling himself a man among men" (p. 34). Confession erodes the wall of resistance that cuts the patient off, not only from the analyst, but often also from his or her true self.

Sullivan (1953) once noted that the pain of loneliness was more damning than that of anxiety. The theme of confession as a means of reaching out to another in order to countermand loneliness runs through many of Dostoevsky's novels. In *Crime and Punishment* (1866/1921), the protagonist, Raskolnikov, who views himself as a superior being free to determine his own destiny, kills an old woman to prove his freedom. This freedom becomes a short-lived, tormenting chimera. He finally confesses to the doggedly relentless Detective Porfiri to escape loneliness.

The need to relate is even stronger than the need for absolution in Camus' *The Fall* (1956). The protagonist, Jean-Baptiste Clamance, having stolen a valuable art object and eluded the police of three countries, is obsessed with the idea that he could not die without confessing. "Otherwise, were there but one lie hidden in a life, death made it definitive. No one, ever again, would know the truth on this point, since the only one to know it was precisely the dead man sleeping on his secret. That absolute murder of a truth used to make me dizzy" (p. 90).

Clamance, the lawyer/thief, needs to draw himself into the confidence of others in order to justify his life. As with many patients, Clamance seeks to confess not primarily to alleviate guilt, but rather to break through the wall of solitude.

Two brief examples are cited of "high-risk" confessions proffered by patients who preferred to drive a wedge through their loneliness in lieu of continuing to exist in their uneasy cocoon. Paula was a 44-year-old schizophrenic patient who at first hesitated to speak about anything. She was distrustful of me in that she felt that any time I moved in my chair, scratched my head, or changed my facial expression slightly, I was giving her signals that I was bored or that I disliked her. She was also given to finding words in the dictionary that became ominous portents of how I might retaliate against her.

In the receptive stillness of the analytic environment, Paula slowly began to display her troubled inner world to me. At first she risked providing small bits of contemporary information pertaining to her dissatisfaction with living with her tyrannical mother and sister. Whenever I said anything, she would take issue with it, or would regard my words as interference, which caused her to withdraw. I soon learned from my patient that, in the beginning of treatment, only total silence would fulfil her aching need to be understood and accepted.

The next level of risk assumed by Paula concerned her confessions about my powers over her as manifested by my body language and dictionary language. When the patient had thus tested my loyalty as a constant object, during the 21st month of therapy, she revealed what she considered to be the most threatening confession: the existence of Zoru, her inner voice and companion, who gave her orders and criticized and taunted her. What frightened Paula the most, and the reason she had desisted from letting me in on her secret, was that she thought I would think she was crazy and hospitalize her.

Paula continued, "I first recall Zoru appearing in the window when I was seven. He has been with me off and on for almost my entire life. Even though Zoru tells me to do bad things (the patient had been given to cutting herself and pulling out her hair) and tells me how stupid and boring I am, I feel empty without him."

The need to escape unbearable loneliness in part fostered the appearance of Zoru in the first place. Yet the imaginary companion/tormentor was not enough. Patients like Paula need the analyst both as an ally to protect them from powerful inner sources and as a nurturant figure to understand their loneliness. The loneliness came from not being understood by family members and, at times, being harassed by toxic introjects perceived by the patient as autonomous inner beings with lives of their own. The desperation of being trapped in a world of strangers impels such patients to take perceived catastrophic risks in letting the analyst in on their forbidden, secret world. Gross (1951) aptly notes that the secret is seen as a potential gift in consolidating relationships. The telling itself encourages intimacy and lessens the unbearable loneliness.

Confessions, paradoxically, both enable the patient to feel larger than life and permit him or her to experience the security of common human relatedness. A patient revealed to me, with Raskolnikovian-like bravado, that when she was seven, she relished squeezing frogs' throats. "I liked to hear the sound of their croak, and sometimes went so far as to kill them." She paused and searched my face for reactions. When she did not discern the expected indications of admonishment, she was able to explore her anger at her parents' uncaring behavior and her need to vent her frustrations and be noticed for what she was doing.

When I asked the patient what she was thinking as she stared at me intently, she commented, "I wondered whether you might be disapproving of my behavior. In a way I know it was disgusting. But at the same time, I enjoyed it and thought I was the only little girl in the world who was gutsy enough to perform such daring feats."

This patient confessed her childhood deed, not primarily to alleviate guilt, but to test the boundaries of intimacy with me. She pondered whether I would still accept her after her "unconscionable" behavior. She felt the need to establish greater intimacy with me both to affirm the common denominator of her essential humanness and to convey to me her need to be special and different. "How many patients have you known who ever killed frogs?" she asked expectantly.

In Dostoevsky's last novel, *The Brothers Karamazov* (1881/1957), Mikhail confesses to Father Zossima that 14 years previously he had murdered the woman with whom he lived because she wanted to marry someone else. A servant was implicated but died in prison before he could be brought to trial. Mikhail, who is overcome with guilt, then confesses to the authorities, whereupon he falls ill and dies. On his deathbed he tells Zossima, "There was heaven in my heart from the moment I did what I had to do" (p. 287).

Mikhail finds relief, but also a sense of relatedness with God and with the human race through confession. Dostoevsky, however, also contended that the confessant is able to gain redemption only through voluntarily accepting suffering. In Dostoevsky's world suffering was essential for the expiation of guilt and ensuing spiritual rebirth.

The idea that suffering brings a better life is also part of the Mesoamerican Indians' culture. Abusive penance, including bloodletting, piercing of cheeks and lower lips, circumcision, and passing a thread through the hole all were preventive activities designed to propitiate the gods to desist from punishing the penitants with illness. Once sickness occurred however, public confession was undertaken in which the confessant accepted the blame for misfortune and directed it inward. The "sins" of which they most commonly accused themselves were theft, homicide, bearing false witness, and the weaknesses of the flesh.

Religious overtones are, of course, not integral to the confessional process in psychotherapy. When the patient reveals himself or herself to the therapist, neither God nor any higher authority need enter into the equation. The secular nature of the confession in psychotherapy enables the patient to find redemption through communion with an empathic other. Suffering is not necessary to assuage guilt. Acknowledgment of one's inner self and the will to face oneself squarely allow the patient to find redemption without recourse to self-recrimination or suffering.

Confessions in psychotherapy are a testament to the patient's capacity and willingness to relate to the analyst in a deepening, ongoing way. The need to achieve intimacy evolves in the context of a trusting relationship with the therapist, whom the patient comes to know and identify as a constant, reliable presence.

Bowlby (1969, 1977a, 1977b) sees attachment as a special form of relatedness integral to our well-being. Conversely, many forms of emotional distress, including anxiety, anger, depression, and emotional detachment, are attributed to unwilling separation and loss.

Attachment involves proximity and is an enduring bond directed at specific individuals. The child who becomes attached to the care-giver feels free to explore the environment, knowing that mother is there. Mahler's (1968) *rapprochement* subphase of separation–individuation likewise concerns the child who ventures forth into the wider world, only to return to mother for refueling, in a back-and-forth dance ultimately culminating in separation–individuation.

The care-giving analyst, like the "good enough mother" (Winnicott, 1963/1965), anticipates and accepts the patient's confessions as a way of developing intimacy and extending the newfound experience to a wider circle of caring others. The analyst welcomes the patient's desire to explore possibilities for intimacy in the extratherapeutic world. In so doing the patient demonstrates that he or she is sufficiently attached to the analyst to risk self-revelation in less secure surroundings. Patients who expand their orbit of intimate relationships fear neither censure nor abandonment from the analyst, who is seen as an available constant object.

These feelings of security both promote and enhance the confessional process. Boswell, the biographer and friend of Samuel Johnson, notes the following event in his *Life of Johnson* (1791/1981): Johnson, in speaking to Boswell about a gentleman who was running out of his fortune and quarreled with friends, who would drive him away, retorts, "Nay, Sir, we'll send you to him. If your company does not drive a man out of his house, nothing will" (p. 255). Johnson admitted he was angry at Boswell's pro-American attitudes, and when Boswell asked him why he took his revenge directly, Johnson replied, "Because, Sir, I had nothing ready. A man cannot strike till he has his weapons" (p. 255). Boswell records, "This was a candid and pleasant confession" (p. 255).

Boswell's willingness to share his hurt feelings with Johnson and Johnson's candid admission of impulsiveness enabled the friendship to endure and flourish.

Confession thus can strengthen the security base of friendship and other intimate relationships. Still, precisely because friends and lovers can constitute high-risk confessors with potential for censure, blackmail, and abandonment, the patient is more likely to initiate confession and stay in the confessional mode with the analyst exclusively for a considerable length of time.

Further, the analytic process lends itself to the transferential re-evocation of archaic love objects with whom the patient had formed attachment bonds. The patient who felt secure enough to explore his or her world as a child has greater attachment potential in later life (Bowlby, 1977a) and thus also makes for a patient who is more likely to feel sufficiently comfortable to reveal the inner self with less entrenched resistance.

For many patients who lack this secure developmental base, attachment to the analyst does not come readily. The self-sufficient narcissist or withdrawn schizoid and schizophrenic patient enters therapy with a genetic history hampered by mistrust, vulnerability, and a precariously fragile self-image. While such patients unconsciously yearn for love and concern from the analyst, they repress or suppress attachment feelings since they are terrified of intimacy and dependency. By concealing their core selves, they avoid the pain of rejection or the repetition of being someone else's confidante or caretaker.

One patient poignantly spoke to this latter issue when he said, "My mother's monologues were always so draining. From the moment I came home from school, she would sit me down and tell me how hard her life was and what a trial it was being married to my father. Only now do I realize in hindsight how much I hated her for robbing me of my childhood. While other kids were out playing, I had to sit home and listen to my mother's endless tales of woe. She never asked me anything about school or about any aspect of my life. I felt as though I was put on this earth to be there for her."

For this patient, being on the receiving end of countless confessions became a draining, endless task. As a minion for his mother's needs (Miller, 1981, 1983), this patient, during the course of therapy, became aware of his deep resentment directed at his self-absorbed mother. The patient expressed the fear (stemming from his selfobject identification with his mother) that if he started to reveal himself, he would never want to stop, and that such incessant confession would drain me.

As the therapeutic relationship developed, and this patient began to feel closer to me, his tentativeness gave way to the wish to confess to cement the loving relationship (Gross, 1951; Sulzberger, 1953). As the patient began to feel attached to the analyst who made no demands on him to exist solely for the analyst's benefit, he slowly started to realize that trust and intimacy might be attainable goals in a relationship marked by new beginnings.

To protect the vulnerable self, Coppolillo, Horton and Haller

(1981) suggest that "titrating the amount one reveals of his secret inner self to another person is one vehicle for achieving and managing varying degrees of intimacy" (p. 81). For patients who have spent a lifetime concealing their inner selves, risking the smallest revelation signals the patient's overriding need for authentic relatedness.

Further, since the desire to be cared for is a human need throughout life (Bowlby, 1977b), the patient who reaches out to the analyst via confession without repercussions can then feel redeemable. Through confession my patient took the first step in leaving the prison of his "no-exit" relationship with his mother to embark upon a life in which he and his inner contents count as important and valuable in their own right. Moreover, this attachment to the caretaking analyst is not regressive, but can be seen as a natural outgrowth of the therapeutic relationship, which promotes the continuation of lost or incompletely developed intimacy with the early parental figures.

As patients continuously confide in the analyst, they experience a renewal of trust and faith in themselves. Such revelations are accompanied by an enormous emotional release that alleviates the feelings of tension that have accumulated over months or even years. In confessing patients begin to do away with "bad faith" (Sartre, 1971) as they become by degrees more authentic with the analyst. The interpersonal bond thereby produced turns out to be one of the best ways to solidify feelings of trust and closeness between patient and analyst.

There are myriad motives for placing a precious piece of one's inner life in the analyst's hands. Alleviation of conscious and unconscious guilt, acceptance, infusion of hope, and intimate relatedness propel patients into the confessional mode. Still other patients confess to feel important, to wrestle with disavowed aspects of identity, or to transform themselves creatively. It is to those confessional realms that we now turn.

3
Therapeutic Functions of Confessions

SOOTHING

Catharsis has been viewed historically as the bedrock of confession. While early psychoanalytic notions of catharsis essentially eschewed the interpersonal influence of the analyst, later theorists, notably Kohut, emphasized the analyst's role as a tension regulator and soothing object (Kohut, 1971, 1977; Tolpin, 1971). (Refer to chapters 1 and 2 for elaboration of catharsis in the history of psychoanalysis.)

In this schema a gradual shift takes place from the patient as emitter of confessions (the prototype being Freud and Breuer's patients in *Studies in Hysteria,* 1895) to a greater reliance on the analyst as empathic elicitor of confessions. The analyst, in turn, buffers patients against indiscriminate self-revelatory outpourings that they developmentally may not be able to handle.

The analyst, in his or her soothing capacity, must know when to put a lid on confessions by more disturbed patients. Such patients can rapidly become overwhelmed in confessing "too much too fast." Particularly in the case of schizophrenics, whose unconscious is sometimes experienced as an open sore seeping into consciousness, excessive self-recriminatory confessing can result in panic or self-fragmentation.

A 29-year-old patient, Evelyn, told me that she remembered every trauma in her life and wished that she did not have such a good memory. "At night, I'm haunted by nightmares repeating my past while my days are contaminated by 'daymares.'" Evelyn implicitly was asking me to help her curtail the power of her unconscious to obliterate her. When Evelyn would recount the torment of being trapped between her nightmares and daymares, I would acknowledge empathically how scary this was and deliberately would not explore the dynamic significance of much of the confessional content.

In this way I was able to serve as a maternal shield (Khan, 1974) protecting Evelyn from the dangers of panic-induced disintegration. In concert with this nurturant-soothing process came a greater trust and willingness on Evelyn's part to risk revealing secrets in order to test the limits of the analyst's loyalty and caring. These confessions involved feelings toward me that greatly embarrassed the patient. While Evelyn, in time, revealed that sometimes she wished I were dead so that she would not feel so dependent on me, the secret that was harder for her to reveal involved her sexual feelings toward me.

Having incrementally built up feelings of security and trust in me as a person who would be there for her, Evelyn stated that she sometimes thought about me when she masturbated. I told her that when patients express their innermost thoughts and feelings to a therapist who accepts and recognizes their needs, feelings of warmth and love are likely to develop. Sometimes these feelings take on a sexual cast, but they all concern patients' needs to establish greater intimacy and contact with the analyst.

This rather extended interpretation soothed and satisfied the patient on two counts. First, by proffering the interpretation in general terms about all patients, Evelyn was made to feel that she fell into some kind of normative range. Second, the fact that I equated her sexual feelings with desires for warmth and intimacy enabled her to experience catharsis in the presence of the soothing analyst.

We can thus see a marked historical shift in the function of catharsis among selected segments of the patient population. While analysts in the early years of psychoanalysis championed the ventilation of confessions as a rapid route to move from the unconscious to the conscious, later analysts who focused on character disorders and preoedipal conditions underscored the necessity to exercise control in cases in which the patient's ego was too weak to cope with excessive self-revelation.

Spotnitz (1976) emphasized the need to build up the schizophrenic patient's emotional immunity so that the patient is ready to

confess and hear interpretations. Wilhelm Reich (1972) likewise cautioned against the advisability of the analyst's forcefully confronting
the patient's character armor prematurely. From an ego psychological
perspective, the Blancks (1974) advocate taking into account the
patient's level of ego development in deciding whether to support and
build up the ego or to confront the patient's defensive structure.

Patients with fragile selves *de facto* lack the ego strength of
Freud's hysterical patients. While many crave cathartic relief, they
nonetheless must be primed to deal with the aftermath of confession
to guard against withdrawal or psychotic regression. As the analyst
increasingly is seen as a soothing, benign superego, such patients
begin to feel free enough to risk confessing. Nevertheless, the analyst
must remain cognizant of keeping confessions within acceptable
boundaries to match the patient's level of self-development and ego
strength.

One method I have found particularly useful in managing this
aspect, without dictatorially stopping the patient or arbitrarily changing the topic, is to adopt an empathic, commiserative stance that mirrors the patient's emotional state. Evelyn once recounted a bad dream
involving being on a football field and kicking a bloody head that once
was a football. While it became clear from the story of her life that the
bloody head referred to Evelyn's feelings of both murderous rage and
victimization, such interpretations often only exacerbate current
pathology and make the patient feel "as though I were scattered in little
bits all around the room" (her description of how she felt following an
earlier premature interpretation). The role of the analyst with such
patients involves the dual task of soothing the patient to build up
defenses against the tyrannical unconscious and simultaneously pav-
ing the way for the development of sufficient trust and initiative to
enable the patient to risk confessing in measured doses to achieve
catharsis.

TRUST

Patients enter therapy with varying degrees of trust in themselves
and others. In looking at confession retrospectively, we see that the
quality and quantity of the patient's self-disclosure over the course of
therapy speak volumes about changes in the patient's level of trust
vis-à-vis others.

Erikson (1959) views the development of basic trust occurring in
the first year of life as "the cornerstone of a healthy personality" (p. 56).
Trust is a natural outgrowth of nurturant experiences with the "good

enough mother" (Winnicott, 1965, 1975) who gives the baby a sense of security that forms the foundation of later identity. Theorists who either focus on an undifferentiated stage of selfobject fusion (e.g., Kernberg, Mahler, Jacobson, Balint) or conceptualize the infant as a fragile being relating to mother from birth on (e.g., Fairbairn, Guntrip) agree that the first year of life is a critical period in the formation of trust.

For patients who did not have satisfactory early maternal experiences, an invisible wall is constructed to prevent any hurtful experiences from entering or any potentially hurtful confessional material from leaving. Reich (1972) first wrote about such character armor forming because the patient fears parental punishment. Winnicott (1975) and Guntrip (1969) subsequently ascribed the development of character resistances to maternal environmental impingements resulting in the development of either a compliant false self or a withdrawn schizoid self respectively.

Infants who have lost hope in the possibility of a healthy, growth-oriented experience with the maternal object unconsciously choose to armor themselves against further disappointments in order to survive psychically. Kohut (1971, 1977), from a self psychology perspective, sees the erection of narcissistic defenses as stemming from either understimulation or overstimulation in infancy. The overindulgent, omni-praising parent is as likely to contribute to defects in the offspring's development of healthy narcissism as the excessively critical or absent parent. The overvalued or undervalued sense of self that develops in such environments results in repressed grandiosity or oscillating self-esteem teetering between feelings of worthlessness and fantasies bordering on megalomania.

In all the aforementioned schemata, patients experience the need to armor themselves against further frustration and vulnerability. With parents who were either themselves the deprived victims of narcissistic supplies (Miller, 1981) or grossly deficient in care-taking and ordinarily expected maternal functions (Bowlby, 1977a, 1977b; Winnicott, 1965), a wholesome match was never established between infant and parent to ensure the development of trust.

Such patients yearn for intimacy, yet enter therapy with a trail of defenses that precludes the rapid development of trust as a prelude to confession. The therapist is examined microscopically by many of these patients. Kohut (1971, 1984) has written extensively about how even minor imperfections are perceived as gross flaws resulting in devaluation, particularly with narcissistic patients. The patient can find an excuse to climb back into his or her shell and continue to resist self-disclosure. The patient's armor thereby works against the confessional process. Resistances blocking confession become historically encrusted and difficult to peel away.

Most patients display some degree of guardedness during different phases of therapy. After all, the therapist must earn the patient's trust. Many patients have had hurtful experiences in which they placed their trust in another, only to be betrayed or let down in some fashion. Further, it is precisely the people to whom we become closest who have the greatest potential to disappoint us. Thus patients who enter therapy with histories involving rejection, betrayal, calumny, and other assorted disillusionments do not automatically place their trust in the analyst, even if they did experience a blissful first year of life. While the early development of basic trust no doubt is helpful in withstanding some of the subsequent "slings and arrows of outrageous fortune" (*Hamlet*, 111.i.66), these later injurious experiences are likely to jolt such patients out of their blindly optimistic and trusting views of the world.

To reiterate, even patients with positive early experiences are likely to encounter later situations of betrayal that challenge their *weltanschauung* of basic trust.

It is the therapist's task to provide an atmosphere of safety and constancy in which patients gradually can develop a sense of trust that enables them to open up to the analyst despite disappointing experiences with significant others in the past. The analyst's patient receptivity is the attitude most likely to evoke confessions.

Boss (1962) sees the fundamental categories of existence in terms of being open or closed, disclosed or concealed, expanded or constricted. The patient's willingness to risk sharing a secret with the analyst constitutes a crucial step in the direction of trust and openness to self-disclosure.

Playing implies trust, and is a special form of communication in psychotherapy (Winnicott, 1971). In Winnicott's words, "Playing is inherently exciting and precarious" (p. 52). Patients' dramatic or dangerous revelations are fantasized to be high-risk ventures that can alter the way in which the therapist perceives the patient. Nonetheless, as the patient grows to trust the therapist, the play of confessions becomes an important interpersonal test for the therapist to pass. Successful confessions are perceived as "win-win" situations in which the analytic bond is strengthened and the therapeutic process moves forward.

Even the most guarded patients wish to trust the analyst. Otherwise why would they have undertaken the therapeutic journey at all? As the analyst "passes" the patient's tests—devaluation, negative transference reactions, and a host of other phenomena—he or she ultimately earns the patient's trust as a survivor and a constant object that can weather storms.

IDENTITY[1]

Confession is one means by which patients can acknowledge and come to terms with their identity. In a classic paper, Gross (1951) emphasized the central conflict in secret keeping in psychosexual terms: "The secret tempts its owner both to surrender its content and to retain it" (p. 38). Hoyt (1978), as does Gross, attributes the conscious refusal to tell secrets to primitive castration fears, but also introduces the important concept of giving up one's own identity or "secret self."

The interpersonal trust and decision-making ability involved in *either* keeping a secret or confessing can be viewed as part of Hartmann's (1964) conflict-free area of the ego. The child's ability to exercise choices in keeping or divulging secrets lends itself to the development of self-control, which enhances the child's identity.

Freud initially recognized the value of confessions in the establishment of identity. In revealing the secret meaning of their symptoms, Freud and Breuer's patients were better able to separate themselves from the parent to whom they ministered, and thereby establish their own identity. While Margolis (1966, 1974) and Meares (1976) associate separate identity with having secret thoughts and feelings, it is likewise evident that patients who confess enhance their identity via affirmation from the empathic object. Indeed the patient who shares a secret with the analyst or group may assume a common, shared identity.

Feelings of communal solidarity are especially prevalent in group therapy or self-help groups, such as Alcoholics Anonymous and Overeaters Anonymous. In these groups all members are united by a common problem, which they must acknowledge and face. Their addiction has become their identity, thus preventing the healthy self from developing. Group members seek help in overcoming their addiction through confession so that they can get on with the business of developing an identity devoid of addictive attachments.

Similarly, the patient who shares a confession with the analyst is seeking to "bring the true self out of cold storage" (Winnicott, 1954).

[1] Major portions of the identity section are extracted from Hymer, Sharon, "The Therapeutic Nature of Confessions," *Journal of Contemporary Psychotherapy* 13:129–143, (Fall/Winter 1982).

Having established relationships with bad objects (people or addictive substances), such patients seek intimacy with the analyst as a way of reestablishing ties with lost good objects or establishing an intimate connection for the first time.

The patient's confession thereby enables him or her to affirm the self through participation with the analytic object. The patient/confessor has established a "good enough" sense of self to risk sharing a secret with the analyst without fearing abandonment or retaliation.

Erikson (1959) views personal identity as being contingent upon others' and one's own perception of one's self-sameness and continuity in time. Erikson (1968) refined the concept of identity to include a sense of personal self-definition comprising knowledge of who one is and the goals, values, and beliefs to which one is committed. Patients who confess thus signal their willingness to commit themselves to the discovery and rediscovery of who they are.

Lichtenstein (1977), like Erikson, sees the importance of the social in the subjective experience of identity when he states that "the existential structure of human identity comes into being in a social matrix" (p. 12). For Lichtenstein identity arises in the infant's preverbal relationship with the mother, who validates the infant's being through mirrored affirmation, but also conveys to the child that she is other. Thus the child is also separate. Lichtenstein further defines identity as invariance within a process of transformation, the invariant being the thematic blueprint laid down in the early mother-child interaction that is frequently based upon the mother's unconscious expectations for the child.

Both Erikson and Lichtenstein note the aspect of sameness or invariance integral to identity. Humanistic and existential therapists, notably Rogers, Maslow, and May, have talked about therapy as a process of becoming who one is (that is, retrieving and getting back to one's essential self). In Zen the feeling of continuity most often occurs during the *satori* (enlightenment) experience in which the person reaches the overwhelming realization that one is what one has always been. Individuals can thus see themselves as they really are.

In therapy the act of confessing likewise lends a continuity to the patient's life. The rupture that is the secret not only forces the patient to constrict his or her being, but also causes a rift in his or her own consciousness of the hidden self. Upon confessing to the analyst, the patient can begin to experience an integration of the ruptured self. The enlightenment that comes with acknowledgment and acceptance of the secret lends continuity and credence to the patient's identity.

In a famous passage quoted by Suzuki (1956), a Zen master remarked, "When I began to study Zen, mountains were mountains; when I thought I understood Zen, mountains were not mountains;

but when I came to full knowledge of Zen, mountains were again mountains" (p. 240). In explaining this passage, Suzuki maintains that the mountains are really mountains when they become assimilated into one's being. The secret also often remains an alien object until it becomes part of the patient's ongoing self via confession.

Loewald (1972/1980) has written that memory makes our experiences connectable by weaving them into a context. Memory activity becomes linking activity. The memories evoked in confession provide historical continuity for the patient. Confessions provide critical links in the patient's chain of being. When patients uncover traumatic secrets, they not only experience catharsis, but also may recover a select aspect of their identity that can now be examined in the light of their current state of being.

Nonverbal confessions can be especially cogent communications in helping the preoedipal or highly resistant patient come to realize select aspects of identity. Sircello (1972) illustrates such persons' dilemmas in stating, "One reason that a person may have difficulty in expressing himself is that he does not yet, and cannot yet, know what his 'self' is. Seeking to express oneself is at once trying to 'find oneself,' to discover what one's fundamental nature is. And succeeding in expressing oneself is discovering what that nature is. Patients' reflections on art (their own or others') permit access to undiscovered aspects of self in nonthreatening ways.

The more cohesive the patient's sense of self, the more the patient is able to share aspects of the "secret self" (Hoyt, 1978) with the analyst. For patients who have developed basic trust and are willing to reveal themselves, or even relish doing it, the confessional experience in therapy becomes a barometer of self-change in Loewald's sense of invariance in the process of transformation.

Many patients who experience identity diffusion by submerging themselves in an idealized other allow their true selves to unfold for the first time in therapy. What appears to be a drastic metamorphosis usually connotes the patient's retrieval, through a series of confessions, of the essential core of his or her being. In therapy patients dare to ask themselves what they want and need. Confessions enable patients to gain a sense of who they are in the presence of the analyst, who may be the first person who does not dictate who they ought to be.

INTIMACY

The word intimacy derives form the Latin *intimus*, meaning most within. The analyst becomes privy to the patient's innermost self in the sanctuary of interpersonal relation.

In achieving intimacy through confessing, the patient operates on the level of Grotstein's (1981) dual-track system of consciousness; that is, the desire for closeness and fusion exists together with the need to be a separate and autonomous individual who can analytically examine the dynamics of the confession. To this end Wilner (1982) remarks, "In all intimate relationships the presence of simultaneous connectedness and separateness is established in the requirement that individuals move beyond their own inner contradictions and differences with others in order to grasp the others' full presence through their own" (p. 23).

Levenson (1974) likewise views intimacy as a willingness to expose one's private self that characterizes the positive therapeutic alliance, and traces the shift in the meaning of intimacy from an intrapsychic to an essentially interpersonal emphasis. Relatedness is a crucial dimension in the establishment of intimacy. Patients confess when they sense that they truly have found a reliable object who respects them and cares enough about them to warrant the risk of confessing. In revealing themselves patients can once more enter the authentic world of Buber's (1937) I–thou relationship and temporarily cast off the anonymous persona ubiquitous to I–it relationships.

Even in the intimate I–thou relationships that patients establish extratherapeutically, secrets tend to be compartmentalized. Friends who unhesitatingly discuss the trials and tribulations of their sex lives often assiduously conceal financial secrets. And in our intimate relationships with others, we selectively turn such I–thou bonds into I–it relationships that reflect our insecurities and distrust of those closest to us.

The I–thou relationship established with the therapist may become the only domain of the patient's existence in which he or she feels sufficiently secure to decompartmentalize confessions. This breakdown of boundaries that marks a deepening of intimacy between patient and analyst is evidenced when, for example, married patients confess things they cannot or will not tell their spouses.

With these patients only the therapist is seen as a safe repository for all manner of secrets. Even in such instances, however, it is important to bear in mind that the establishment of intimacy in therapy is a gradual process that builds up over time as the positive therapeutic alliance develops. The patient is apt to transfer onto the therapist much of the baggage of hurt and distrust accumulated over a lifetime. Through the analysis of transference distortions, along with the patient's perceptions of the therapist's real human qualities, patients become able to utilize the uniqueness of the therapeutic relationship to overcome doubts and enhance intimacy.

Erikson (1963) sees intimacy as the capacity to commit oneself to others and maintain such commitments, even though they may call for sacrifices and compromises. While Erikson theorizes that intimacy developmentally follows identity, he has also described intimacy as "fusing of identities" (1968, p. 13).

The confession often is seen by patients as an integral yet heretofore hidden aspect of their identity. The intimacy experienced by patients in the therapeutic dyad gives them the courage to confess to the therapist. Confession, in turn, helps patients to retrieve disavowed aspects of identity and further to consolidate a sense of self.

One may well ask, "Does intimacy follow identity as delineated in Erikson's epigenetic theory of development or does intimacy precede identity and serve as a foundation on which identity is predicated?" When intimacy is defined as the revelation of one's inner self as a way to enhance closeness (Levenson, 1974; Wilner, 1982), it is clear that secrets and selective confessions are utilized by children as young as two years old (Gross, 1951). Further, many analysts who focus on the earliest mother–child interactions (prominent among these being Bowlby, Balint, Khan, Mahler, and Winnicott) have written extensively about feelings of mutual intimacy experienced in this bond. Such affective coloration of intimacy lends credence to the notion that the sense of intimacy fostered in the early mother–infant dyad provides the blueprint for the subsequent establishment of identity (Bowlby, 1977a&b; Lichtenstein, 1977).

Many patients require the emotional support consonant with the development of intimate relatedness before they are ready to explore issues revolving around their identity. To paraphrase Mahler (1968), identity for many patients concerns not so much who they are as that they are. For such patients identity emerges through the intimacy established in the symbiotic relationship with the analyst. As they sense *that* they are through the analyst's mirroring affirmation, they can move on to an understanding of *who* they are in Erikson's cognitive-social sense of identity.

Erikson reverses the aforementioned process in the developmental sequence. In Erikson's words, "It is only when identity formation is well on its way that true intimacy—which is really a counterpointing as well as a fusing of identities—is possible.... True 'engagement' with others is the result of firm self-delineation" (p. 135). A 29-year-old doctor who called himself "The Vampire" is illustrative of Erikson's developmental sequence in which identity precedes intimacy. This patient gleefully confessed, "I really feel like a vampire. All my girlfriends supplied me with traits I lacked: exuberance, optimism, and warmth. I stayed with them until I could suck those things out of them that I needed, and then I left. They were very nice, but they had outlived their purpose."

The Vampire would dissolve his relationships out of fear of permanent fussion, having never attained a solid sense of identity. The patient would utilize these unions to borrow aspects of identity, only to realize that such assimilations did not fill the void and confusion at the core of his being. It was only after several years of therapy in which the patient painfully came to terms with his own identity dilemmas that he was able to develop sufficient trust to enter into a committed relationship of intimacy that eventuated in marriage.

Erikson's (1963) conception of intimacy as a commitment to relationships after identity has been established can be seen as a developmental offshoot of the successful resolution of the earlier preoedipal intimacy–identity dilemma (Lichtenstein, 1977) described above. Once patients are able to confess in the safety of the analytic environment, they often become more resolute in risking committing themselves to other significant relationships. Having risked confessing in the intimate therapeutic bond, these patients subsequently feel freer in revealing themselves extratherapeutically.

COGNITIVE CLOSURE

One of the Gestalt laws of perception—the law of closure—pertains to the fact that we tend to complete incomplete percepts. If a circle is presented that has a space between two points on its circumference, for example, we tend to see it as a complete circle rather than as a broken figure. In a similar cognitive vein, we need to complete the disruptions in our lives that block us from moving forward. Secrets constitute such ruptures-in-being, especially when they remain unconscious and stymie patients in their creative efforts.

In his preface to the second edition of *The Interpretation of Dreams*, Freud (1900) notes, "For this book has a further subjective significance for me personally—a significance which I only grasped after I had completed it. It was, I found, a portion of my own self-analysis, my reaction to my father's death—that is to say, to the most important event, the most poignant loss in a man's life" (p. xxvi). One of Freud's most shattering discoveries in his self-analysis was his repressed hatred of his father, whom he consciously admired and respected. In this book he was also courageously revealing his death wishes toward his son.

For Freud the writing itself provided a cognitive closure function (self-analysis) and a creative impetus to redeem himself from guilt by constructing the edifice of psychoanalysis. By engaging in creative reparative activity, others would be able to profit by an interpersonal journey of self-discovery unfettered by the limitations of self-analysis.

John, an especially gifted writer, came forth with a most unexpected confession that drew smiles of recognition from both John and myself. This patient had been creatively blocked for months, except for sporadic fits and starts of work. He would periodically complain that no new revelations had been forthcoming in therapy lately and would then proceed to berate himself for his sloth and procrastination.

John began to discuss how the clutter in his apartment annoyed him and diverted him from writing. During one session he remarked, "I've decided on a new course of action. The majority rules. Since no one else seems to mind the mess, I'll just take care of my small territory on and around the desk. In fact I just straightened my desk the other day and feel much better about it."

John then started to review some of the issues he felt we had explored regarding his writer's block. He kept returning to his competition with his deceased father, who had been a writer of some eminence, and then went on to ponder why he still could not write now that his desk was in order.

I found myself overcome with an unusual feeling that can only be described as a sense of the macabre, which prompted me to ask, "Where do you keep your father's ashes?" (John had informed me that after his father died, he had carried his ashes home. Since his father's widow could not decide where to scatter them, they were still in John's apartment.)

John started and, lowering his voice, replied, "On my desk." We both smiled, having realized that a pivotal missing piece of the puzzle had now been found. The patient went on to say that while he hoped his father's daimon would suffuse him with inspiration, it seemed as though his father's critical ghost was hovering over him instead.

This kind of dramatic confession, needless to say, is not the "meat and potatoes" of psychotherapy. The patient's life unfolds in random fashion with many twists and turns in the road to self-discovery. It is consistent exploration in the context of a constant, committed relationship that fosters these cognitive leaps that prompt patients to break through habitual, stultifying patterns.

We sometimes speak of "seeing the light." Insight in therapy pertains to being in sight of the reality of one's thoughts, feelings, and existential life situation. In this sense analysis becomes a process of helping patients remove the blinders from their eyes. The patient's view can thereby be expanded to a horizon with multiple possibilities. John could not see that the constant view of the urn containing his father's ashes was restricting the field of his creative potential. The therapeutic closure illuminated by my question allowed John, like

Goethe's Faust, once again to "out of the dark aspire to light."

The analysis of confessions can be seen as a process of moving from the darkness into the light. In Plato's allegory of the cave *The Republic*, he describes a situation in which humans who live chained in a cave can only see what is directly in front of them, since they are prevented from turning their heads. A fire blazing in the distance enables them to perceive only shadows on the opposite wall of the cave.

When these individuals are liberated, and forced to see the light, they take refuge in their former safe illusions in lieu of facing the painful reality of the newly acquired external world. Plato equates the journey upward into the light with the intellect. In Descartes' (1628/1969) words, "Those who so become accustomed to walk in darkness weaken their eye-sight so much that afterwards thay cannot bear the light of day" (p. 44).

Our patients, not unlike Plato's cave dwellers, frequently remain comfortable in the dark and may unconsciously choose to remain out of sight of insight. For some patients to be "in sight of" confession is to betray the habitual shadows of their unconscious familial pact of secrecy or fixed image of their "should be" self in relation to others. Confessions enable patients to broaden their perspective to see beyond the narrow illusions of the shadows in their own Platonic cave toward a wider reality.

The maternal analyst can help transform the patient's outlook from darkness to light by literally "holding the patient in regard." In Bellow's novel *Humboldt's Gift* (1975) Charlie Citrine, the narrator, depicts the power of the image of the gleam in the eye during early life in offering renewed hope and joy at the creative possibilities that life may have in store for him. In this passage, Citrine has the following "in sight":

> I want it to be clear, however, that I speak as a person who had lately received or experienced light. I don't mean "The light." I mean a kind of light-in-the-being, a thing difficult to be precise about.... And this light...was now a real element in me, like the breath of life itself. I had experienced it briefly, but it had lasted long enough to be convincing and also to cause an altogether unreasonable kind of joy.... I knew long ago what this light was. Only I seemed to have forgotten that in the first decade of life I knew this light and even knew how to breathe it in. But this early talent or gift of inspiration, given up for the sake of maturity or realism...was now edging back (pp.177–178).

In this revelation he is able to revive the early maternal gleam in the eye by finding closure concerning a state of being in which the look of childhood approbation rekindled the creative spark in adulthood. In seeing the light, Citrine is transformed by renewed hope at the creative potential within him.

A Japanese poem, by Akahido reads:

> The mists rise over
> The still pools at Asuka
> Memory does not
> Pass away so easily.

Therein lies the patient's dilemma concerning confessions: the will to remember and gain closure is often stubbornly resisted by the desire to forget. Freud and Breuer (1895) spoke of the hysteric not wanting to know the origin of her symptoms, while simultaneously suffering from the "dis-ease" that comes with not knowing.

The historical emphasis in psychoanalysis on making the unconscious conscious (Freud's aphorism, "Where id was there ego shall be") bears a striking resemblance to the Socratic-Platonic panegyric to the intellect. The Delphic oracle's exhortation to know thyself and Socrates' belief that "the unexamined life is not worth living" are philosophies that construe problems, secrets, and all manner of life issues as potentially resolvable through the cognitive closure provided by self-discovery.

Freud (1910) compares the neuroses to fairytales in which the power of evil spirits is broken when the protagonist can tell their names which they have kept secret. The secret correspondingly no longer has its power to arrest the patient's development when it is brought to light and cognitively and affectively assimilated. A patient who was afraid to express warm feelings toward me or anyone else gave the following veiled verbal confession: "I hope you don't mind. I put my coat over yours because there were no racks left." This patient, who had been struggling with intimacy, was indirectly disclosing a readiness to move in the direction of greater closeness, and even symbiotic relatedness.

Rather than render this interpretation, which I sensed this patient was not ready to incorporate, I said instead, "That's very snuggly." The patient rejoined, "That's exactly what I was thinking. It felt nice doing that." This patient thereby received closure on her need for fusion via an empathic interpretation that enabled her to reflect further on her feelings without being threatened.

In contrast to the more gentle closure occasioned by empathic interpretations, sometimes patients get so carried away in confessing that they start to see themselves in new, surprising ways that may contribute to a fundamental change in self-image. A telling illustration of such a confession is found in O'Neill's *The Iceman Cometh* (1940). After years of marital bitterness during which Hickey made his wife miserable by his drinking, gambling, and broken promises to change, he kills her. Hickey's confession to his friends brings unforeseen results.

> So I killed her. . . . And then I saw I'd always known that was the only possible way to give her peace and free her from the misery of loving me. . . . I felt as though a ton of guilt was lifted off my mind. I remember I stood by the bed and suddenly I had to laugh. I couldn't help it, and I knew Evelyn would forgive me. I remember I heard myself speaking to her, as if it was something I always wanted to say: 'Well, you know what you can do with your pipe-dream now, you damned bitch! [He stops with a horrified start, as if he couldn't believe he heard what he had just said. He stammers.] No. I never— (pp. 240–242).

In revealing his secret to others, the horrified Hickey lifts the veil of self-deception that has distorted his true feelings. Hickey is forced to acknowledge to himself that his "altruistic" motive for murdering his wife was a gross reaction formation obfuscating his hatred and resentment. When patients commit a perceived horrific crime and do not confess, the deed inevitably strikes at their identity. Having lived a false, inauthentic existence, they finally confess to the analyst in order to reintegrate themselves into the community of fellow beings.

O'Neill's dramatic illustration of the cognitive feedback functions of confessions forces us to realize that confessions in psychotherapy do not always result in cathartic relief. In fact the patient who confesses a secret that has undergone defensive permutations may, like Hickey, at first be startled by the shocking connotations of the confession as it is now gauged in the presence of the analyst.

The surrealist movement, concerned with the dreamlike elements of surprise, focused on the evocation of unconscious secrets in art and life. Described by Apollinaire in 1917 and developed into a manifesto in 1924 by Breton, who had also worked as a psychoanalyst, surrealism tapped human reaction outside the reach of consciousness or will. The surrealist painter, Magritte, like the confessant/dreamer, defies many of our established notions of image and reality. In his 1950 painting "The Empire of Light," a house bordered by night-heavy trees is lit by a solitary street lamp. This is perfectly normal, except that the sky above is that of midday and not midnight.

In surrealist paintings the ordinary can never be ordinary again. Confessions offer many of the surprises inherent in surrealist art and serve to jolt many patients out of their constricting preconceptions.

The revelation of secrets, in setting free phantasms, allows patients to plumb the farther reaches of their imagination and open them up to further flights of fancy. While as children we looked forward to maximizing our imaginative potential through play and stories, as adults we all too often shy away from the variegated dramatic and emotive storehouse of material that is waiting to be released from our unconscious.

In surrealism to defy reality was to come to a clearer understanding of its interstices and paradoxes. Magritte's juxtaposition of a nighttime scene against the backdrop of a light sky underscores the element of surprise that catapults patients into greater reaches of self-awareness following confession. The patient who experiences creative incongruities is forced to confront the self in a new way, untrammeled by the myopia inherent in ossified perception. Further, the more therapists accept the surrealistic in themselves, the greater is the likelihood of their welcoming the paradoxes in their patients' confessions.

A colleague recounted the following confessional incident.

> When I was a school counselor, I developed a close relationship with a patient. One day, she reported the following dream: "I was in the den when all of a sudden I heard noises and saw that my wrists were bleeding." As the therapist I saw a recurring vision of Christ. The following sentence spontaneously emerged: "Forgive them, Father, for they know not what they do." The patient became frenzied and confessed that she was planning to go to France and kill herself. Choked up, she blurted out, "How did you know that I was an artist who only painted the head of Christ?"

After this confession the patient was never again suicidal. Having felt fully empathically understood by the therapist, the patient realized that she did not have to bleed alone. The therapist was able to entertain his own surrealistic imagery in such a way that the symbols of his waking unconscious coalesced with those of the patient's dream life. The resultant relief and cognitive closure saved the patient's life.

Patient and therapist together were able to forge a picture of a crucial aspect of the patient's endangered existence. In creatively "playing" with the emotional-laden imagery, the therapist helped the patient recast her hopeless self into a self transfused with potential.

In contrast to O'Neill's Hickey, who stopped dead in his tracks once the dreaded truth of his murderous self no longer could be denied, many patients reveal themselves not only to tie the past event into the present reality, but also to facilitate further free associations that spur on related or unrelated insights. A 37-year-old Viet Nam veteran jumped at the sound of a door slamming in an adjacent office and alarmedly asked, "What's that noise? It sounds like bullets."

I inquired, "What about bullets?" The patient replied, "Today is Memorial Day." The patient started to weep and continued softly, "A lot of my buddies died in the war. I saw my buddy wounded and I had to flee. I couldn't take him with me. He was my best friend over there. After that, I killed, sometimes just for the heck of it. I remember shooting 30 bullets into one man. He was dead after the second or third bullet. I don't know why and I don't know why I'm telling you now. Except that slamming door brings it all back."

The patient started to hyperventilate, then continued to cry for several minutes. This interlude not only provided affective release, but also served as a prelude to the evocation of a still more difficult confession. "I was filled with rage when my best buddy was killed. I felt helpless and yet knew I had to do something. I spotted this dog standing peacefully on the road. (The patient began to shake.) I shot it over and over again until I was exhausted. I love animals, but something came over me. I just couldn't help it."

This patient's disclosure, initially triggered by the slamming door, was able to stimulate a series of heretofore concealed secrets that had resulted in symptoms characteristic of posttraumatic stress disorder, including depression, guilt, insomnia, and anxiety. While his other doctors had pointed out the connection between the war and its psychological aftermath, the patient had never before confessionally associated a series of traumatic events with his current jumpiness at sudden noises. Such specific cognitive closure not only produced symptom relief, but also helped the patient to see the threads of his Viet Nam experience woven into the tapestry of his life two decades later. The patient no longer had to live with the specter of unnamed dread. Through confession the past had come back to liberate rather than haunt him.

NONVERBAL CONFESSIONS IN CREATIVE EXPRESSION

The patient's/artist's creative products constitute confessions to the audience—the "universal other." The patient who particularizes such confessions chooses the analyst as the pivotal other to transform these revelations into individual, intimate terms.

The creative patient who engages his or her audience finds a creative outlet for repressed secrets. Sachs (1951), in fact, alludes to Reik's concept of unconscious guilt, in noting, "He who commits the deed in fact or in wishful thinking, alone and in isolation, is a criminal; but he who acts together with his brothers or in their joint interest, becomes a hero" (p. 56).

Janacek's second quartet, "Intimate Pages", is a confessional corroboration of his secret love for a woman 38 years his junior. In a letter to Max Brod, Janacek asks, "Tell me, is it possible to say openly in which person my motifs are crystallized? Has any writer ever told the public? With the painters, it is no secret. But a composer? Would it be taken badly if this spiritual relation, this artistic relation was openly admitted?" (Vogel, 1962, p. 378).

The patient who behaviorally confesses through creative channels not only finds a nonthreatening format in which to risk self-revelation, but also quenches a need to relate to the universal other. Sachs (1951) goes on to say, "The creator transfers the expression of his strivings and perversions, together with his expectation of narcissistic satisfaction, from his own person to the things he produces" (p. 220). While the risk incurred in creative confessions is not commensurate with that of direct confession to the analyst, the patient is nonetheless exposing himself or herself to critical scrutiny and narcissistic vulnerability.

Greenacre (1957) likewise described the talented person's creative output as an object relationship. "It seems unlikely that the artistic performance or creative product is ever undertaken purely for the gratification of the self, but rather that there is always some fantasy of a collective audience or recipient..." (p. 58). She subsequently coined the term "collective alternate" (1958) to refer to the establishment of such cosmic emotional relationships.

In a recent paper (Hymer, 1985), I defined absorption as the temporary loss of self through immersion in an object that eventuates in self-enhancement. I noted that patients who become absorbed in such relationships with Greenacre's collective alternates are better able to cope with a variety of problems and experience a heightened sense of well-being. Patients who are willing to risk becoming absorbed in the human or nonhuman environment are most likely to rediscover meaningful life experiences and repressed secrets as they recognize that to strengthen the individuated self one must temporarily surrender the self.

In that same paper, I mentioned Maureen, a 25-year-old patient with Jacksonian seizures who was convinced that orgasms were dangerous since she equated them with her seizures. Maureen accordingly would stop herself from having orgasms. The patient, who was an actress, while rehearsing a role one day at home, draped a red cloth over a mirror and suddenly burst out crying. "It felt good to cry. I was really feeling, not just drumming up phony emotions from the surface."

In staring at the prop, Maureen was able to conjure up a long-repressed memory of her drunken father who one night came into her bed and fondled her. The patient's absorption in the cloth and her scene enabled her unreservedly to abandon herself to her craft, which prompted the unexpected resurfacing of a secret central to her existence.

Godwin (1983), writing about diarists, maintains that many diarists do write for some form of audience. "This audience may be God, it may be a friendly (or unfriendly) spirit,...or it may be one's future self (at thirty-eight, Virginia Woolf wrote in her journal that she was hoping to entertain herself at fifty) or...in many cases, more often than we may care to admit...we write for some form of posterity" (p.29).

The act of confession, even through nonverbal creative efforts, thus cannot be divorced from the interpersonal sphere. The generational pull of the interpersonal in the nonverbal confessional mode found expression in Orville, a 36-year-old art editor whose deceased mother was well known in the art world. Orville one day remarked, "I was looking through my mother's books the other day and came upon a biography of an artist she particularly admired. I was struck by how many sentences were underlined, with my mother's initials affixed adjacent to many passages. I then realized that many of the misgivings and insecurities that beset my mother went unrevealed with her to her grave."

Orville pointed out that his mother was able to identify with many of the artist's world views and personal experiences, and that he felt, in eavesdropping, that his mother had established a peculiar, intimate relationship with this book. "I find myself doing the same thing," Orville mused.

Some patients are able to transform the reading (or writing) experience into an outlet through which they secretly confess, unencumbered by the risks attendant to public exposure. After all, how many of us have kept or still keep diaries in which we safely store our inner selves and keep track of our histories?

The need to confess is so pervasively human that even individuals who feel too timid or vulnerable to reveal themselves to someone else seek relatedness with nonhuman sources. Via vicarious identification patients can transform books into no-risk confessors devoid of the human connection. The anonymity and lack of feedback integral to such confessions often propel patients to own up to, and thereby own and reclaim, disavowed aspects of self in the presence of the analyst. For catharsis and closure truly and enduringly to take hold, the interpersonal relationship is needed to offer the constancy and reassurance absent from the patient's relationship with the nonhuman environment.

Philo, at the beginning of the Christian era, wrote, "Unfailingly, works of art make known their creator, for who, as he looks at statues and pictures, does not immediately form an idea about the sculptor and the painter?" (quoted in Wittkower & Wittkower, 1963, p. 281). Such an all-encompassing statement, of course, is not true of all art. One cannot, for example, look at the beatific madonnas in Fra Fillipo Lippi's paintings and discern that Lippi ran off with a nun and was given to carnal excesses.

While creative products often constitute indirect, relatively safe avenues for confession, expressionism prided itself on direct revelation of inner secrets through the medium of art. Expressionists revealed their own terrors and triumphs in their paintings. What mattered in art was not the imitation of nature, but the expression of intense inner emotions often connected with pathos, violence, or morbidity. Beckmann wrote, "What I want to do in my work is to show the idea hidden behind reality, to penetrate the invisible world by means of the visible" (quoted in Canaday, 1964, p. 438). Beckmann, as an expressionist, used his personal emotional experience as a confession transfigured through his art into universalized expression.

The expressionists exteriorized their inner feelings, projecting their emotional conditions onto canvas. Abstract expressionists such as Pollock, Gorky, and de Kooning also thought of their paintings as being inseparable from their autobiographies. Never before had the artist's creative output so mirrored the inner self. Secrets were paraded in paintings that themselves became the confessional medium for such tortured souls as Van Gogh, Beckmann, and Ensor.

These painters' inner torments and lack of personal connectedness to others resulted in striking paintings that sometimes became the sole outlets for their encapsulated trauma. Munch summed up his art by saying, "I hear the scream in nature." Dogged by death and anguish (his mother and sister died of tuberculosis), his paintings reflect human alienation and vulnerability to misfortune. In Evers' words (1970), "Munch tried to free himself from his early childhood sufferings by drawing 'his situation'" (p. 179). Many of his paintings, with such symptomatic titles as "Anxiety", "Separation", "The Death Chamber", and "The Sick Child", become transformed confessions of his inner despair.

For some artists/patients, close to a one-to-one relationship exists between their outer creative products and their inner selves. To know and understand their work is to hold a mirror to their true selves. For such patients verbal utterances sometimes actually obscure their fundamental nature, which is contained in truer fashion in their art.

Unlike the expressionists, who reveled in the confessional nature of their output, for many patients the arts frequently serve as indirect means of confession. The veiled, codified possibilities inherent in art are nowhere more apparent then in Alban Berg's "Lyric Suite." The composer's compulsive interest in numbers culminated in this work, constructed according to some hidden code revolving around the numbers 10 and 23. The composition turned out to be a secretive, rapturous love offering to Hanna Fuchs-Robbetin, a married woman. For some undisclosed reason, those were "their numbers."

Berg's despairing love is augmented and exalted through his creative expression. No one exists to whom he can confess all. Secrecy pervades the substance of his "Lyric Suite" lest his secret passion be discovered by his audience.

The frustrated artist who feels that he or she cannot risk the possible destructive results of confession at least finds a way partially to express the secret through art. The world becomes the ultimate beneficiary of such veiled confessional largesse.

Patients who dread the risk of verbal confession are able to make considerable strides in that direction when they display or discuss their creative work with the analyst. The attuned analyst who sees such material as tentative confessions rather than resistance can monitor the developmental sequence in which patients confess.

Patients who are highly resistant to self-disclosure may use nonverbal confessions displayed to the therapist as a less threatening entrée to self-disclosure. For many patients the act of discussing or showing their art during therapy allows them painlessly to relinquish their defensive posture by risking a safer, veiled confession.

One such patient was Miss A. Of her I wrote, (Hymer, 1983):

> Miss A. brought to therapy a collection of cartoon caricatures she had worked on for months, depicting her relationship with a man who had rejected her. Without commenting, Miss A. handed me the drawings. As I leafed through the pictures, I was immediately struck by the wealth of information they contained that had previously never been discussed. Miss A. was then able to communicate the sado-masochistic nature of the relationship with the aid of the visual prop as buffer. In so doing, she was able to reparatively elevate her self-esteem, both by cathartically sharing this experience and by simultaneously receiving narcissistic gratification in exhibiting her work to me.
>
> Miss A., who had been an abused child, at first rarely would make eye contact with me. Yet she kept all her appointments and slowly began to reveal her secrets through her art. At times Miss A. would refuse to elaborate verbally on her artistic productions, and I did not press her to do so. In time this patient augmented her level of trust to the point where she unflinchingly would verbalize her thoughts and feelings that were evoked as we looked at her paintings together.

To reiterate, patients' creative products are often veiled forms of confession. These nonverbal confessions are particularly useful forms of communication with preoedipal patients who sometimes feel at a loss in verbalizing confessions. Such patients may be more comfortable in processing their secrets through right-brain artistic channels that have not yet been fully integrated with their logical, linguistic left brain.

Patients who fear being retraumatized by revealing, and possibly reliving, their traumas risk considerably less by projecting these secrets onto their creative work instead of confessing directly. The analyst who remains attuned to the confessional riches to be garnered through the patient's paintings, writings, readings, and songs can thereby help the patient recognize the value of such nonverbal confessions in the creative transformation of the self.

4
Narcissistic Elements in Confession

$\mathbf{G}$uilt has long been considered the dominant motive that propels patients to confess.[1] Yet for many patients with narcissistic problems, shame is the critical affect that locks them into an intense struggle between the desire to confess and find acceptance and the desire to conceal and thereby avoid the fantasized loss of the loved or idealized object.

Indeed we find in some patients a narcissistic "compulsion to confess," which, in contradistinction to Reik's (1959) theory of unconscious guilt, involves an overwhelming need for verbal discharge and hoped-for narcissistic supplies from the mirroring, affirming analyst. Patients who compulsively tell all may be trying to gain recognition in the only way familiar to them. Confessions may be loaded with teasing and ambiguous details by patients who desperately attempt to hold the spotlight by fantasies of entrancing the analyst.

This chapter explores the many faces of the narcissistic confes-

[1]See Lewis (1971) and Morrison (1983) for discussions of the nature of shame and guilt in psychoanalysis.

sion as it contributes to the emergence of the grandiose self, and what I have termed the "inverted grandiose self"—namely, the grandiose self in those patients who engage in sexual perversions and other acting-out behaviors in order to hold together a sorely fragmented self at all costs. Another line of narcissistic confessions pertains to the emergence of ideals and idealization. Through these latter confessions, patients start to realize their own values and goals.

I wish to mention two caveats before launching into the many ramifications of narcissistic confessions.

● Shame is *not* an essential or inevitable resistance in every narcissistic confession.

Some patients have long harbored suppressed or repressed secrets integral to the grandiose self that sometimes emerge in a burst of excitement or bravado. The more stable the narcissistic transference configurations the patient has established, the more apt the patient is to confess even the most repugnant aspects of self, since the therapist, as selfobject extension, is perceived as a safe and trusted repository for such material. Neurotic patients who have developed a working alliance with me have also, over time, been able to confess historically humiliating experiences, which undergo transformations during analysis. These transformations often involve a shift from a repressed grandiose self to a grandiose self revitalized with burgeoning pride and the desire to shine in front of the analyst.

In Oscar Wilde's *The Picture of Dorian Gray* (1890/1964), Dorian mockingly states, "The only way to get rid of temptation is to yield to it" (p. 24). The narcissistic appeal of having a captive audience as a receptacle for one's secrets prods the patient to dispense with forbidden fruit that is fast becoming rancid in the solipsistic vacuum of the patient's self. What was once deemed shameful or mortifying can become sufficiently neutralized in the accepting analytic environment to enable patients to prepare themselves for confession.

Over time the patient tends to reveal, with a dramatically different tone, the same incident whose content remains essentially unaltered. A mortifying experience that was, at first, haltingly related may later be recounted with relish. This kind of confessional transformation tends to occur only after the patient has established a relatively cohesive self and a solid, trusting relationship with the analyst.

Some patients may even laugh or take pride in hitherto dreaded childhood secrets. Humor, once described by Freud (1928) as an inflation of the superego, can also be seen as the triumph of the grandiose self that now emerges unscathed to further strengthen the patient's self.

> ● The reductionistic equation linking guilt with confession, and shame with concealment, ignores the complexities of the patient's plight.[2]

The reveal–conceal dilemma is present in *both* shame and guilt. While the integrity of the self is felt to be at stake in shame, Kohut (1977) has cogently argued that guilt in the oedipal drama concerns not only castration anxiety, but also defective self structures arising when the child's sexual and assertive needs are unempathically greeted. The nature of the self is thus of vital importance in both shame and guilt.

Resistances block confessions in shame and guilt. The dynamic content of the confession (that is, how threatening to the self the patient perceives disclosure will be), along with the historical reactions of parental figures to childhood confessions, enter into the patient's willingness or reticence to confess. In short not all patients are driven by guilt to confess. Several patients, in fact, have prefaced their confessions by stating that they fully intended to have certain wrongdoings go with them to the grave. Some of these patients experience so much guilt, and sense the confession to be so intertwined with their character, that facile revelations are not likely to be forthcoming.

Once such patient who was plagued by guilt was Margie,[3] a 27-year-old teacher, who had a series of dreams in which she was being violently killed or was murdering faceless others. Margie experienced frustration with these dreams in which she was unable to make any meaningful associations to the material.

The patient became so tortured by these nightly "confessional visitors" that she finally came to therapy one day, and started the session with a minor confession as a fillip to her major secret. She began by saying, "When I entered therapy, I decided to tell you everything but this one episode. Even now, I am only telling you because I

---

[2]For a separate discussion of guilt as a major motive in confession, see Chapter 2.

[3]Margie's case is discussed at greater length in my paper "The Therapeutic Nature of Confessions," *Journal of Contemporary Psychotherapy* 13:129-143, (Fall/Winter 1982).

feel that I have no choice. My dreams will not let me rest. So it is time for me to break my vow and let you in on the one incident that has clouded my life with guilt to this day."

This is the synopsis of the major confession. When Margie was nine, her mother asked her to bring her a pair of shoes. Upon bending to get the shoes, the mother lapsed into a coma as the result of the eruption of a cerebral aneurism. During the mother's stay in the hospital, Margie's older sister never tired of blaming her for "killing her mother." Margie also overheard the doctors talking about her mother's impending death.

Margie felt like a murderer the moment her mother became unconscious. So guilt-ridden was the patient that she would go to the hospital every day to sit with her mother, hold her hand, brush her hair, talk to her, and sing to her. The patient went through the same daily routine for ten months until, one day, her mother opened her eyes and said to the astonished nine-year-old, "Is that you, baby doll?"

After her mother recovered, the ten-year-old Margie "selflessly" took on all of the household duties and continued to chauffeur and run errands for a variety of people thereafter. Her "sweet" disposition and tireless devotion to her mother and father, as well as to anyone else who was likely to ask a favor, masked the murderous rage she felt toward her parents and her older sister—rage that surfaced continuously in her dreams.

In Margie's case guilt drew her toward concealment. When the patient described her feeling of guilt about causing her mother's coma, I made the following interpretation: "From all that you have told me about your ministrations and caring daily presence in the hospital, it was you who saved your mother's life." The patient brightened in the light of this empathic yet verifiable intervention that bolstered her faltering self-esteem.

Margie's confession elucidates three major issues in confession:

1. Confessions motivated predominantly by guilt do not invariably facilitate confession. Guilt, like shame, can serve as a prime resistance in therapy.

2. Guilt can involve both drive factors (e.g., Margie felt like a would-be murderer consonant with Reik's [1959] theory of unconscious guilt) and self factors (i.e., the patient felt depleted of self supplies and thus instituted compensatory "altruistic" activities in an attempt to repair her damaged self-esteem).

3. The analyst's interpretation, "you saved your mother's life," served as a bridge between drive and self aspects of guilt;

that is, the intervention incorporated the fact that Margie in fact, was the opposite of a murderer—a redeemer, and that the guilt-ridden self could now begin to be transformed into a proud grandiose self.

SHAME, IDEALIZATION, AND THE EGO IDEAL

Kohut (1977) conceptualized the establishment of a firm identity in the narcissistic patient as being contingent upon the development of healthy ego ideals growing out of modification of idealized parental images, and the development of normal self-esteem and ambition arising from transformations of the archaic grandiose self. Shame—the emotion that penetrates to the very core of the self—is often the last layer of confession dealt with by the patient. While patients are known to shy away from these confessions, the relentless nature of shame can actually promote the confessional process in which the patient moves from self-consciousness (the heart of this resistance) to consciousness of self.

Lewis (1971) and Morrison (1983) view shame as a narcissistic reaction involving the self's failure to live up to an ideal. Morrison (1983) maintains that shame develops when the self "is experienced as defective, inadequate, and having failed in its quest to attain a goal. These goals of the self relate to ideals internalized through identification with the 'good' (or idealized) parent" (p. 298).

Shame thus is concerned with the patient's perception of narcissistic defects. The self that is experienced as having failed to live up to the ego ideal goes into retreat. The patient's reluctance to reveal the shame-filled self presents a serious resistance to confession. As the analyst assumes some of the idealizing functions of the lost or disillusioning archaic parental figures, the patient begins to feel that he or she may have another opportunity to overcome reservations by being protected or even exalted by the idealized analyst. In such idealizing transferences or idealizing intervals with neurotic patients, the analyst can become the fantasized Pieta-like embodiment of an all-embracing love that offers unconditional acceptance.

Kohut (1966) describes the two faces of shame: the inhibition or repression of the grandiose self and the inability to live up to one's ideals. Beginning with Freud, who introduced the term "ego ideal" in his 1914 paper "On Narcissism," a number of different meanings have accrued to this concept, all of which have important implications for shame-based confessions in psychotherapy. Freud (1914a) conceptualized the ego ideal both as stemming from the infant's primary narcissism (underscored in the 1921 paper in which the ego ideal was termed "the heir of the original narcissism") and as a derivative of parental idealization.

Yet, in that same 1914 paper, Freud mentions class, nation, and other external sociological factors that enter into the creation of an ego ideal. In his 1933 paper, Freud returns to the notion of perfection attributed to the parent by the child. Hartmann and Lowenstein (1962) retain much of Freud's original thinking in embracing an ego psychological perspective in which early forms of self-idealization and object idealization make up the ego ideal. With this all-too-brief summary, I return to Kohut (1977), who sees goals and ideals emerging after the grandiose self has been formed in relation to idealized, empathic selfobjects.

Because the ego ideal has been portrayed in a number of different and sometimes conflicting ways, the therapist concerned with the roles of shame and the ego ideal in confessions must find a way to simplify and integrate this important concept into the therapeutic armamentarium. Ego ideals, in fact, can be viewed as having an impact on the patient on three levels.

1. **Macro level**. When sociologists and analysts (Freud, 1914a; Erikson, 1963; Blos, 1974; Morrison, 1983) speak of values and goals deriving from admired mentors, subgroups, ideologies, class, etc., one can see how many of the patient's ideals and idealized figures emanate from his or her later environment, especially with the recrudescence of narcissism (A. Freud, 1958) and the identity crisis (Erikson, 1959) that are hallmarks of adolescence. One common form of confession occurring at this level is that in which the patient reveals a favorite hero or heroine in the context of his or her own goals and values. While patients wax poetic about these figures' glowing attributes, at some point the patient will insert the "tragic flaw" in which the hero was exposed either voluntarily (e.g., a celebrity signing into a drug abuse center) or involuntarily (e.g., a celebrity found dead from a drug overdose). Patients' identification with idealized figures, whose confessed shame-ridden problems humanize rather than denigrate them, encourages them to face their own shame in confessing to the analyst.

2. **Familial level**. Freud (1914a, 1933) spoke of the child's idealization of admired parental figures. Kohut (1977) subsequently introduced the bipolar self concept, in which children who were unempathically responded to during the earlier period of maternal caretaking could receive a second chance to consolidate the self by

merging with the idealized parental selfobject. The empathic analyst can provide yet another opportunity for the patient to elucidate and develop his or her ego ideal through confessions, which thrust the fledgling ego ideal into consciousness.

Patients who confessed to excessively self-absorbed, critical, or indifferent parents saw their ideals devalued and slowly disappear. Again, in certain families, broader sociological factors, such as religious values, reinforce excessive modesty. The continual battering of the child's confessed ideals leaves the child bereft of idealized parental selfobjects, and sometimes too disheartened to fall back on self-idealization. Such children either retreat in anger from all ideals or refrain from further goal-directed activities. As punitive aspects of the superego predominate in lieu of the loving superego (Schafer, 1960; Jacobson, 1964) or wish-fulfilling propensities of the ego ideal (Lampl-de Groot, 1962) these patients, as children, found their budding ego ideal steadily eroded.

The realization that the patient and analyst can accept shameful confessions in itself becomes a therapeutic factor. Morrison (1983) suggests that the analyst should work with the patient in modifying perfectionistic ideals and establishing more realistic ideals. While this treatment approach certainly should be considered, I have found that examination of the confession in the empathic analytic milieu should initially enable the patient freely and fully to explore the possibilities of daring "to dream (and live) the impossible dream." In other words, patients should be encouraged to explore any and all of their ideals unimpeded by the "voice of reality" reminiscent of parental rebukes and constraints. It is only after patients verbalize and explore the maximum breadth and scope of their confessions that they themselves begin to entertain notions of modifying their goals and values by identifying rather than complying with the empathic analyst.

Patients with histories of negative confessional outcomes can, in time, thereby confess to the analyst, who gives them another chance to merge with an idealized selfobject. In the process patients rediscover their own lost ideals, which then again become valued attributes.

3. **Self level**. Freud (1914a, 1921) linked ego ideals to primary narcissism, while Hartmann and Lowenstein (1962) spoke of self-idealization. On the level of self relations (White, 1980), patients hope to be reawakened to their earliest lost ideals through acceptance by the empathic analyst. Reevaluation of the genetic incident in concert with the idealized analyst eventuates in the gradual repair of self-defects.

The analyst functions as an idealized object in accepting the confession, helping the patient integrate the secret into his or her life, and allowing an idealized merger to develop, thereby placing the patient in contact with the revived archaic idealized objects. This merger or "supermerger" with two or more archaic idealized objects along with the analyst intensifies the patient's pride in the historical continuity between past and present idealized figures. These idealized models/mentors give the patient a sense of belonging and acceptance both in the nuclear family and in the extended family of humankind.

Erikson's Views on Shame

Erikson (1959) refers to his second epigenetic conflict as autonomy versus shame and doubt, and relates the growing child's dilemma to the development of upright posture during this period. As children realize their vulnerability to falling down and getting hurt, they lose their sense of omnipotence. If a child's parents manage to establish a balance between the child's need to be willful and the need to have limits set, the child can attain self-control without loss of self-esteem. Parents who are arbitrary or inconsistent at this stage contribute to the child's feelings of shame and self-doubt.

Many patients reenact this battle of the wills in therapy. The patient who had to struggle to develop a sense of autonomy with willful, narcissistic parents who could never accept the child's secrets has trouble confessing to the extent that the analyst is seen as the archaic parent(s).

Confession can function paradoxically to strengthen the patient's sense of autonomy. The role of confession in the evocation of both shame and autonomy is illustrated by this short vignette from the case of Harriet. Harriet was a 29-year-old editor whose husband's expanding business concerns prevented him from giving her the attention she craved. While Harriet explored how, as a "good girl," she had always acceded to her parents' requests and how she and her husband had vowed always to remain faithful to each other, she exultantly confessed her desire to "be bad and have fun for once." When she did not discern any verbal encouragement from me, Harriet became self-conscious and blushingly accused me of being like her self-righteous parents.

The idealized analyst was now equated with the persecutory parents who were perceived by Harriet as "breaking my will the way a proud stallion is broken into submission." Harriet went on to say, "That you are not openly encouraging me to have an affair makes me feel that you are in my parents' corner opposing me. I feel like going out and having an affair, just to show I have the guts to do it."

When we started to explore whether my silence might mean anything else, the startled Harriet remarked, "I just realized that I put you with my parents. That you did not say anything really means that I get a chance to decide without your telling me what's good for me." After the patient's initial shame reaction, she began to experience her confession as a stimulant to her growing autonomy in which she was empowered to make her own decisions.

Whether shame or autonomy holds sway in a patient's confessions depends both upon the patient's ability to examine the self critically *even* when faced with self-consciousness and upon the transferential relationship with the analyst. In Harriet's case her attainment of a relatively cohesive self enabled her to augment her sense of autonomy and transcend her feelings of shame as the meaning of her confession was examined and worked through in the context of the transference.

Mahler's Practicing Subphase

Mahler, like Erikson, underscores the narcissistic significance of the child's development of motor skills as the environment expands dramatically with locomotion. Children experience elation with their own bodies as well as with the objects in which they are narcissistically invested. Amsterdam and Leavitt (1980) point out that children become painfully self-conscious if they are restrained or directly punished for exhibiting their bodies or playing with their genitals. The body thereby becomes an object of shame.

In both Erikson's and Mahler's theories, the significance of the erect posture, when patients can hold their heads up high and walk tall, is in marked contrast to the shame-ridden body in which such physiological symptoms as blushing, minimal eye contact, and stammering give the analyst clues about the shameful secret that is being preliminarily expressed through the patient's bodily demeanor.

All too often analysts are reticent to make interpretations, or even to ask questions about the patient's physical self, despite the fact that such interventions might make it easier for the patient to begin to talk about the secret. Although therapies such as Gestalt and bioenergetics[4] directly utilize patients' bodily cues to divulge

[4]Numerous integrative therapies now exist that combine physical interventions with verbal disclosure. An excellent summary of these proliferating therapies is found in Herink, Richie (ed.), *The Psychotherapy Handbook* (New York: Meridian, 1980).

underlying conflicts, analysts sometimes are remiss in including the body as an indicator, and even a valuable elicitor, of confessions. *Mutatis mutandis*, the analyst can therapeutically utilize the patient's stance and gestures to cut through resistances that block self-disclosure.

The self-scarification wrought by bodily shame manifested itself in couple therapy with Hal and Lucy. Hal complained that if Lucy did not feel that he was totally passionate and accepting, she would become furious and cut off sex in midstream. Lucy's earliest memory involved a scene with her father in which he called her names and struck her for not being clothed. Lucy commented, "I was so mortified that I felt like dying. Since then I have always felt not quite right about my body. When Hal doesn't seem to be 100 percent into sex with me, I fantasize bashing his head in with a rock."

Lucy also expressed contempt for her mother for not protecting her from her father. This dynamic coincides with Kohut's (1977) description of shame and rage as disintegration products brought about by the breakup of the original close tie to the maternal object. Lucy did feel secure enough in the maternal analyst's protective presence to risk confessing her rageful fantasies to Hal without fearing a recurrence of her father's venomous retaliation.

THE EMERGENCE OF THE GRANDIOSE SELF

Mirrored Affirmation

As early as 14 months of age, babies show a range of affects, which include both embarrassment and "showing off," as a result of being the focus of attention (Amsterdam & Leavitt, 1980). Both shame and exhibitionism become major forms of self-expression, often before the infant can talk. One reason for the onset of shame is that the delightful experience of self-awareness converges with a newfound awareness of the self as perceived object, signaling the emergence of self-criticality.[5] The abovementioned patient, Lucy, underwent a painful shift in self-esteem as the joy-filled exhibitionistic self proudly presented itself to her father, only to be coldly scrutinized and deflated by critical, unempathic paternal rejoinders.

---

[5]For a cogent existential analysis of the self objectified by the other's look, see Sartre, J. P., *Being and Nothingness* (New York: Citadel Press, 1971).

Cultural sanctions also contribute to patients' reticence in disclosing aspects of the grandiose self. Pride is one of the seven deadly sins, and children are often rebuked for boasting or bragging about themselves. Our legal system considers genital exhibitionism a crime, while simultaneously refusing to address the widespread availability of provocative, exhibitionistic pictorial displays in all the mass media. We are thus faced with a bewildering array of contradictory messages that condemn or condone exhibitionism.

How does the welter of sociocultural/legal viewpoints affect patients' perceptions concerning whether or not to confess their secret ambitions and varied narcissistic fantasies of greatness, immortality, superhuman powers, and so on? I reiterate the argument made earlier in this chapter that broad social forces cannot be divorced from the patient's family history.

This broad range of sociological forces is initially filtered through parents whose own body language (e.g., ease with their own bodies and pleasure or displeasure in their children's bodily displays) sets the stage for the repression or emergence of healthy narcissism. Kohut (1977) has described the development of the grandiose self in relation to mirroring affirmation from the empathic selfobject. The elaboration of ambitions resonates from these early approving responses from selfobjects. Should the patient fail to gain self-affirmation from early selfobjects, who may respond with disgust or excessive modesty as a result of puritanical religious and social beliefs, the patient is likely to view any hint of grandiosity or exhibitionism with fear or disdain. Such patients, whose grandiosity has never developed at a phase-appropriate time, eschew and deride displays of exhibitionism, while secretly yearning to divulge their own grandiosity and be accepted.

One such patient was Mary, a 27-year-old administrative assistant, who could never fully relax and enjoy sex because "part of me is always scrutinizing myself, hoping my partner won't notice my body's bulges, and checking myself to see if I am doing everything right." Mary's self-conscious examination masked a secret desire to shine and be admired, bulges and all.

In the early development of psychoanalysis, shame was associated with forbidden libidinal wishes and sexual exhibitionism (Fenichel, 1945; Morrison, 1983). In patients' reconstructions of shameful childhood secrets, the reaction of the object appears to be the critical factor in invigorating or humiliating the patient's budding sexual self.

In line with the importance of the affirming object in eliciting shameful confessions, it became clear that while Mary would spend a great deal of time discussing her weight and the mortification connected with being sexually exposed, she was able to confess the origin of her sexual qualms only after several months of empathic interpretations and validation from the analyst.

Here is a synopsis of Mary's confession: "When I was five, my friend and I used to 'play nun.' Since we figured nuns were supposed to suffer, I suggested we put twigs in our underwear. Much to my surprise, it felt good. But when my friend's mother noticed the twigs when my friend went to the bathroom, she told on me. Her mother called me a bad and dirty little girl. I was so humiliated, I just wanted to crawl into a hole and disappear."

So severe was Mary's shame that she never again did anything sexual until the age of 18, when she met her husband. After she had finished her story, I remarked how difficult it must have been to listen to her friend's mother's tirade against her, and how lonely it must have felt to live with this unexpressed secret for all these years. This empathic intervention brought forth a flood of material pertaining to how the patient, as an only child, felt isolated from her parents and was ashamed to ask them anything personal for fear of disapproval or retaliation.

When the 11-year-old Mary asked her father what the word "fuck" meant, he slapped her across the face and told her never to say that word again. Mary incessantly was made to feel that adults were the authorities and that children had no rights, even the right to know. Like Kafka's (1915/1971) Gregor Samsa, who turns into the lowly, despised cockroach in *The Metamorphosis*, such children are often made to feel invisible or expendable.

These feelings contribute to the grandiose self's going into hiding for a protracted period of time. After Mary revealed the twig incident to me, along with the related genetic memories of shame and loneliness, I commented that the nun game seemed to be a creative use of play. The delighted patient said that she never expected me to say that and was half fearing reproval.

Such interventions, when they emanate from objective empathy (Kohut, 1984), are perceived by patients as growth-promoting affirmation rather than as contrived "pats on the back." One way that the analyst can discern which of these holds true is to monitor whether the patient uses that statement (in this case, that the twig game was creative) as an anchor onto which to tack further related genetic material, the revelation of which facilitates the grandiose self's further emergence.

Specialness

The grandiose self develops and flourishes in relation to empathic responsiveness from mirroring selfobjects. Patients whose parents substituted rebuke, humiliation, or self-directed narcissistic tributes for mirroring enter therapy with a legacy of repressed or distorted grandiosity. In the therapeutic environment, a steady accretion of empathy from the analyst rekindles a yearning to be special and affirmed.

Many patients care less about the dynamic decoding of the contents of confession than about the affirmative response forthcoming from the analyst or audience. The very young Sartre (1966) muses, "Am I therefore a Narcissus? Not even that. Too eager to charm, I forget myself.... Happily, there is no lack of applause. Whether the adults listen to me babbling or to the "Art of the Fugue," they have the same arch smile of enjoyment and complicity. That shows me what I am essentially: a cultural asset" (p. 25). The need to fascinate, seduce, or otherwise entertain the analyst may result in grandiose confessions that are embroidered, shaped, and otherwise transmogrified to make patients more interesting to the analyst and, by extension, to themselves as well.

Confessions that emerge from the revival of archaic grandiose needs sometimes pertain to immortality or some aspect of greatness expressed with a quiet earnestness that belies the "dramatic conceit" of these revelations. Norris, a 24-year-old graduate student in the humanities, confessed in a matter-of-fact manner that it had struck him that he was a better writer than Freud, and could probably surpass Freud in his field of study.

It is vital that the analyst be cognizant of these types of confessions in which the patient at last allows the grandiose self to emerge uncensored. Because I accepted Norris' confession without countertransferential exclamations of surprise or shock or educative attempts to correct his alleged distortion of reality, he was able to exhibit and examine his grandiosity without shame.

The exploration of maternal empathic failures in childhood, along with the narcissistic blow of his father's untimely death when Norris was seven, revealed that Norris procrastinated in order not to surpass his father. Once the patient was able to acknowledge his desire to outdistance Freud (his idealized father), it became progressively easier for him to reveal his envy and resultant disillusionment in his real father, whose premature death left the patient bereft of an idealized selfobject to offset his mother's lack of empathic mirroring.

Secrets and confessions are often viewed as something special that contributes to the child's "autonomy function" (Greenacre, 1954). A child often invents a secret, some harmless imagining that allows him or her to feel separate and special. At a moment of his or her choosing, the child bestows the secret upon a friend or parent with all the flourish of a monarch taking a commoner into confidence.

The specialness attributed to confessions by patients is often evidenced by the manner in which the subject is introduced.[6] Jane, a 27-year-old writer, started a session by saying, "I'm going to tell you something I never revealed to anyone else in my life, because it's so shameful. Off and on, for the past few years, I have eaten food and sneaked off to the bathroom, where I vomit. My father once pointed out a woman who was as skinny as a pin. Even though I think he was using her as a negative example, I nonetheless have continued to throw up food furtively."

Jane's confession enabled her to share her secret self with the analyst. In so doing she was able to experience some relief by sharing her secret with an affirming object. The act of verbalization itself in a nonevaluative atmosphere allowed the patient to reassess the self in a more favorable light.

Other confessions are related with pride and bravado. Jim, a 22-year-old veterinary student, recalled, "My earliest memory involved me lying in a crib with a bottle filled with juice. My parents must have been having a party downstairs and were ignoring me. I gleefully threw the bottle over the side of the crib. It made a tremendous crashing sound. My parents rushed upstairs to see what was the matter."

Such secrets become narcissistic nuggets that make the patient special and different from others. The sought-after attention that the patient received at the magically perceived invocation of his parents underwent a repetition in the analytic setting in the presence of the affirming analyst. In these narcissistic confessions, "the secret operates as an adoring possession and value of the personality" (Simmel, 1950, p. 313). While the secret becomes a hallmark of one's importance, the therapeutic confession operates in a similar vein.

Since the analyst is perceived by patients like Jim as an extension of self, the confession here becomes the *raison d'être* for

[6]Major segments of this section are derived from my article "The Therapeutic Nature of Confessions," *Journal of Contemporary Psychotherapy* 13:129-143, (Fall/Winter 1982).

the emergence of the grandiose self. In Jim's confession the grandiose self is allowed to shine in the glow of the analyst who mirrors the patient's delight in his fantasized omnipotence. The confession hereby becomes an arena not only for self-expression and acceptance, but also for the development of the grandiose self.

I will close this section with two cases that reveal how the grandiose self can emerge in waking life and in dreams, and how the patient's transferential reactions, in concert with the analyst's empathy, can help repair the defective self.

The Case of Ruby

While many analysts maintain that secrets about money, not sex, are the most difficult for patients to reveal, I have found that many patients still shy away from discussing sex. Religious upbringing and sexual trauma in childhood leave many patients with feelings of shame and repressed grandiosity.

Ruby was a 29-year-old graduate student with superego constraints that made her feel that she was too "kinky" and a secret grandiosity that contributed to her feeling of being special because she was kinky. Ruby told me that even though she knew she should be discussing sex, she was shying away from it. When I asked her if this might have something to do with her feelings toward me, Ruby replied, "That question made me think of my mother. Strangely, my mother was not moralistically evaluative, but she was intrusive. She had to know everything, including the details of my sex life. She once even asked me what percentage of times I had orgasms with my boyfriend, and I told her it was none of her business."

Ruby remembered me inquiring about her sex life. I gently reminded her that I asked her whether there was anything she would not tell me about, and Ruby unhesitatingly mentioned sex. The patient laughed in recognition and said, "You're right. The funny thing is, I have brought up sex before in dreams, and even told you how, as adolescents, my friend and I fondled each others' breasts. I guess this time the difference is that I remembered that you initiated the discussion, and that felt intrusive.

"You see, my sex life is my only secret from my mother. Yet, since I broached the subject last week, I noticed that I had great sex with my boyfriend this weekend. It's like my boyfriend is loosening me up physically and you are mentally."

Ruby felt that sex was the only sphere of activity in which she could totally separate from her intrusive mother. At the same time, she sincerely wished to reveal her sexual self to me, since she had misgivings about the appropriateness of her sexuality.

Blake (1793/1974) wrote that shame is pride's cloak. Confessions initiated in the analytic atmosphere of empathic receptivity can be transformed from shameful secrets to narcissistic snowballs that grow larger as the patient's excitement and enjoyment increase. The grandiose self, set free, elatedly expands as it gains momentum.

Ruby, in a breathless anticipatory manner, proclaimed, "O.K. Here goes. My boyfriend bought me a vibrator on Saint Valentine's Day. He also buys me porno magazines every month. Even though I love it, I wonder if my girlfriends use these props, but don't dare expose myself to them."

In this narcissistic snowball effect, the confession not only demontrates the patient's increasing elation, but also embodies the thrill of disclosing a forbidden, special deed or thought to the mirroring analyst. Further, once the confessional snowball gets rolling, other related confessions (in Ruby's case, other sexual deeds) that become associated with the original confession are expressed to enhance euphoric feelings.

The Case of Bert[7]

Many patients' ambitions, hopes, and dreams are sealed so tightly in a container of repression that the only way that the grandiose self is capable of revealing itself is through dreams. Few patients display the effervescent grandiosity of a Dali (1904), who confessed that at age seven he wanted to be a Napoleon and that his ambition had been growing steadily ever since. Freud (cited in Jones [1953]) also demonstrated the adaptive value of mirroring in the development of greatness when he revealed, "A man who has been the indisputable favorite of his mother keeps for life the feelings of a conquerer, that confidence of success that often induces real success" (p. 5).

Bert was a 39-year-old composer who fell on the opposite end of the grandiosity continuum from Freud and Dali. For many years he remained in his famous father's shadow and was unaware of his own grandiose needs. Bert reported the following dream: "I am playing King Lear and I am marvellous. The audience is looking at me and breaking into loud applause, marveling at how fantastic I am. During intermission my father comes through a fence, only he is now a black adolescent. Instead of praising my performance, he mentions a gift he is going to give me."

[7]This case was first discussed in my paper "The Multidimensional Significance of the Look," *Psychoanalytic Psychotherapy* 3:149–157,(1986).

With this dream Bert realized that in order to succeed, he must separate from his father. He does so by devaluing his father, who is then transformed into a black teenager. Most important, this dream heralded the emergence of this patient's secretive grandiose self—a confession coinciding with a spurt in Bert's creativity.

The "being on center stage" aspect of grandiosity is nowhere more apparent than in Sartre's startlingly candid autobiography, *The Words* (1966). "People read *me*, I leap into the eye; they talk to *me*. I'm in everyone's mouth, a universal and individual language; I become a prospective curiosity in millions of gazes. I exist nowhere, at last I *am*, I'm everywhere" (p. 122). Sartre's sense of his own specialness derives from his work and from the universal other's approbation of his creative output.

In Bert's dream he, like Sartre, is appreciatively applauded. Bert was able to disclose his grandiosity to the analyst who, in interpretively validating these feelings, enabled this patient further to extend and utilize the grandiose self productively. Through the medium of the dream, Bert was able to be doubly affirmed: first, by the audience—the collective others in his life whose approval and admiration he desperately craved; and second, by the analyst, whose interpretive validation of the emergence of the grandiose self enabled the patient to acknowledge and look at his own hitherto repressed grandiose self in a new esteem-enhancing way.

The Inverted Grandiose Self: Sexual Exhibitionism and Other Acting-Out Behaviors

In the previous section, I outlined how the grandiose self as the repository of the patient's ambitions and shameful/joyful deeds and dreams finds expression through confession. I have found it conceptually useful to differentiate those aspects of the grandiose self from what I have termed the inverted grandiose self. Patients with inverted grandiose selves struggle for the emotional survival of the self through drive discharge. Such acting-out behavior constitutes a desperate attempt to control the self through manipulation of the selfobject. Acting-out behavior, such as sexual exhibitionism, often leaves these patients feeling persecuted (or indeed prosecuted) rather than applauded, ignored rather than appreciatively admired.

Patients who act out rather than verbalize their confessions engage in daredevil feats to free the understimulated self from its depression and thereby convince these patients that they are alive. Patients who gamble, take drugs, or engage in compulsive sexual activities mask their secretly depressed or enfeebled self while revealing an aspect of their secret through these behaviors. These compromise behavioral confessions may be enacted to impress the therapist and add excitement to a depleted existence.

While perversions and other acting-out behaviors were once thought to be primarily defenses against castration anxiety (Fenichel,1945; Siegman, 1964), recent analytic theorists (Reich, 1960b; Kohut, 1971, 1977; Stolorow & Lachmann, 1980) have veiwed perversions as attempts to stave off feelings of emptiness and self-fragmentation in order to restore self-esteem. Stolorow and Lachmann (1980), in particular, emphasize the patient's quest for substitute selfobjects to offset the trauma experienced at the hands of parents who were absent or unresponsive to the patient's needs for attention and admiration during early childhood.

A colleague related the countertransferential problems she was experiencing with one of her patients, who was given to bragging about her thievery. The patient, who had embezzled $3000, once brought to therapy $300 worth of shoes that she had just stolen.

Such patients present acute dilemmas for the therapist, whose own condemnatory or envious countertransference reactions may result in a stalemate or premature termination. Further, whether the analyst theoretically views the inverted grandiose self and its resultant behavioral manifestations as a defense against dependency and envy (Kernberg, 1975) or as a severe developmental deficit (Kohut, 1971, 1977) will, in turn, guide how the analyst treats such behavioral confessions.

I have observed that many acting-out patients crave confession to the analyst as a desperate bid for attention and redemption of the fragmented self. The surprising nature of such "in-house" confessions may so confuse the analyst that he or she is unable to decide what to do next.

Here is another brief vignette presented to me by a colleague as an example of how confessions emanating from the inverted grandiose self can result in positive therapeutic gain.

"After several months in therapy, a teenage patient admitted that he exhibited himself in situations that put him in great danger. He would, for example, exhibit himself in front of a truck driver, who would chase him.

"During one of our sessions, he played out his exhibitionism by whipping off his clothes in 30 seconds flat and displaying himself to me. In looking back on the incident, I realize that I may have overstimulated the patient by asking him whether he entertained any fantasies about me. Because this patient wanted immediate gratification and I wanted to analyze his acting out, the situation was never really resolved. The patient became angry when I did not respond, but his acting out had a short-term positive effect in that he saw that he would not be castrated by the powerful therapist/father."

While a primary therapeutic aim with such patients does involve the establishment of impulse control and subliminatory potential (Kernberg, 1975), it is also important to discover and explore the historical circumstances of empathic deficiency that framed the patient's need to attract attention at any cost in order to feel alive. This patient's sexual exhibitionism itself became a confession, revealed through distorted, nonverbal channels, of the trauma experienced by the inverted grandiose self. The analyst who firmly instructs the patient to cease such activity both contains the patient's impulsiveness and offers the patient an alternate, growth-promoting verbal mode of confession.

Once limits have been established, these patients can begin to tell their stories in which sexual trauma, and/or unempathic parents who never applauded or even paid attention to them, left them deadened and bereft of ambition.

The therapist's empathic responsiveness and firm control over the patient's impulsive behavior further encourage the patient to substitute verbalization for acting out. These patients achieve two major goals in learning to verbalize confessions:

1. While the process of examining traumatic childhood secrets can be painful and arduous, the patient does learn to experience genuine self-empathy in lieu of instant gratification that can further fragment the already enfeebled self (as in the case of the patient who was chased by the truck driver). The patient who is listened to with concern and caring realizes over time that he or she can become involved in an ongoing relationship in which confessions are greeted with empathy rather than disdain or withdrawal. Through this process the mirroring analyst helps transform the inverted grandiose self into a grandiose self that no longer needs to seek outrageous, precarious outlets for its fulfilment (Kohut, 1977, 1984).

2. Once these patients have developed the ability to verbalize confessions and explore with the empathic analyst the historical moments that twisted the grandiose self into its present inverted form, they are better able to withstand interpretations that focus on the rage and dependency manifested in the transference (Kernberg, 1975).

Once the self has attained a greater degree of cohesiveness through empathic interpretations and validation, the analyst can then explore and interpret the patient's need to exert power and to regain omnipotence by fascinating the analyst (Fenichel, 1946; Siegman, 1964). Through the interplay of projective and introjective mechanisms, sexually exhibitionistic patients attempt to gain mastery over the object in order to counteract the object's ability to arouse envy or awe in the patient.

The patient's self that has become strengthened by the analyst's empathic mirroring becomes increasingly able to hear interpretations that focus on rage and envy as defenses against underlying needs for dependency and love from objects (Kernberg, 1975). The patient learns that he or she can hold the analyst's attention through verbal confession, and thereby achieve narcissistic satisfaction in gaining mastery over impulses.

The patient no longer has to put his or her fragile self on the line by resorting to acting out. A transformation of self begins to develop in the process of converting acted-out confessions into words. Through verbal confession the inverted grandiose self is transformed into a more robust, nascent grandiose self.

Confessions as Indicators of Oscillating Self-Esteem

Many patients who are overly dependent on approval from external sources have problems with regulating their self-esteem. Narcissistic disturbances involving grandiose self-inflation alternating with an utter sense of worthlessness can constitute attempts to stabilize self-esteem (Reich, 1960b; Jacobson, 1964; Kohut & Wolf, 1978).

Because these patients often are given to splitting the self and object into good and bad representations, their confessions reflect these splits. Patients whose confessions reveal their emerging grandiosity later may lapse into painful self-consciousness as the analyst, in turn, alternates in fantasy between the accepting, empathic object and the persecutory, retaliatory object. The difficult task faced by the analyst once confessions are forthcoming is to help the patient regulate self-esteem.

Sulzberger (1953) notes, "We are a communicative, vain and grandiose species and therefore, paradoxically, the psychic energy that we must invest to keep a secret develops into the pressure that pushes us to uncover it" (p. 39). The push-pull of the narcissistic element is dependent upon the patient's perception of whether or not confession will contribute to the maintenance or elevation of his or her self-esteem.

"It is the ridiculous and the shameful, not one's criminal

actions, that it is hardest to confess," remarks Rousseau (1781/1977, p. 28). To this end it is instructive to note patients' prologues to confessions. Comments such as "You'll probably find this ridiculous, but...," "I'm beginning to blush just thinking about it," and "What I'm going to tell you will probably seem absurd to you" serve as narcissistic defenses to ward off unempathic responses from the analyst and thereby offset the patient's vulnerability. In relating to the analyst in this manner, the patient is able to lessen the risk of confessing by setting a contextual climate in which patient and analyst can accept and work with the confession without any onslaught on the patient's self-esteem.

Confession ironically both hinders and facilitates the establishment of more or less evenly balanced self-esteem (Jacobson, 1964). Why does this state of affairs exist in such patients? For one, patients with self-esteem problems habitually utilize face-saving techniques to protect themselves from any untoward exposure that might upset the sensitive self. Confession presents a shock to a self system habituated to hiding as a way of life.

Alternatively, confession, once it does take place, may overstimulate the patient's grandiosity and feel like a transfusion of adrenalin from the empathic analyst, only to be followed by a routine return to the hidden self. Confessions that produce too strong a feeling of euphoria thereby may result in compensatory withdrawal. Reich (1960b) and Kernberg (1975) describe patients with problems in self-esteem regulation as manifesting abrupt mood swings in which castigation and self-abnegation alternate with grandiosity.

I have observed that patients' confessions can serve as a barometer monitoring oscillations in self-esteem. Three basic narcissistic patterns occur with some regularity:

1. *Confessions in which the self is presented as overinflated.* Many patients make confessions in which the self is aggrandized to fuel the grandiose self that feels enlivened only when self-esteem is at its zenith. Some of these patients have dreams in which they are always linked to a celebrity or great person. Others offer confessions in which they are applauded for being the greatest, or the best, or were named "the likeliest to succeed" in their college yearbook.

The Oscar Wilde epigram "to love oneself is the beginning of a lifelong romance" parodies the depletion of self experienced by these patients. The vicissitudes of narcissistic confessions provide valuable information concerning how the patient may, in time, shift from precarious pseudo-self-love to genuinely positive self-estimation.

Patients who overinflate the self in confessions often feel that to be accepted, or for the self to exist as a cohesive entity, they must overwhelm their audience (the collective selfobjects), and themselves in the process. These patients come from families in which either nothing they did or said would gain the attention of narcissistic or depressed parents, or only excessively grandiose events (e.g., winning the top award in school, saving someone's life) would be affirmed by parents, who would utilize the child's disclosure to bask narcissistically in their offspring's accomplishments.

In the latter instance, one major resistance arising from these patients' confessional histories is that they may, in fact, fabricate confessions as a way to bolster their sagging self-esteem. The analyst would do well to accept these confessions that may have the flavor of a Paul Bunyon saga as a reflection of a narcissistic need to attempt to repair defective self-esteem.

Interpretations that link the current function of these narcissistic confessions with faulty parental empathy help the patient understand the dis-ease that comes with feeling that grandiose confessions constantly must be forthcoming in order to maintain even a semblance of self-esteem. As further genetic material emerges, and the patient comes to experience empathic responsiveness from the analyst, confessions of Herculean proportions are transformed into simpler authentic confessions in which the patient can feel special and accepted regardless of the confessional content.

2. *Confessions in which the self is constantly demeaned or diminished as a way of camouflaging the grandiose self.* Rousseau's (1781/1977) "humbling" confession, in which he admits to falsely blaming the young cook, Marion, for his theft of a pink and silver ribbon, masks a certain self-congratulatory stance. In Rousseau's words, "I have been absolutely frank in the account I have just given, and no one will accuse me, I am certain, of palliating the heinousness of my offense.... I think also that my loathing of untruth derives to a large extent from my having told that one wicked lie...I have little fear of carrying that sin on my conscience at death"(I,2).

Miller (1984, p. 91) wryly notes, "Here is a unique brand of spiritual vanity...." The reader/confessor indeed can sense that Rousseau may, in fact, be attempting to regulate his self-esteem by confessing to a misdeed that seemingly lowers his self-esteem. In his "humbling" confession of guilt to the world, Rousseau also shows the smugness of a man who wants everyone to acknowledge and remember his moral superiority.

The false confession that appears to diminish self-esteem may consciously be made in order to offset an even greater narcissistic injury. Jack, a 31-year-old anthropology graduate student, recently confessed that his previous confession was a lie. "I don't really have an ulcer. I just get terrible panic attacks accompanied by a queasy stomach and racking pains. The reason I said I had an ulcer was that I believed I was mentally healthier if I had a physical symptom. Now I realize this way of thinking is foolish and I'm only hurting myself by not giving you the whole story." This patient's true and false confessions were both disclosed so that the patient unconsciously could hold on to a victimized status consonant with his habitual feelings of low self-esteem.

3. *Confessions in which self-esteem oscillates between feelings of grandiosity and feelings of worthlessness.* Coleridge (1977), in a letter to Thomas Poole, dated October 9, 1797, reveals the dilemma of a great writer whose lifelong oscillations in self-esteem had already become manifest at age eight. "And so I became very vain, and despised most of the boys that were at all near my own age, and before I was eight years old I was a character. Sensibility, imagination, vanity, sloth, and feelings of deep and bitter contempt for all who traversed the orbit of my understanding, were even then prominent and manifest" (p. 221).

In actuality the only person for whom Coleridge generally expressed contempt was himself. Although he was attempting to be humorous in this letter, there is evidence that along with his feelings of being the "great disappointment," there existed an awareness of his prodigious talent and separation from ordinary people. His self-disparaging comments, in tandem with his boastful remarks, underscore the experience of patients who suffer from severe oscillations in self-esteem. Coleridge's hypochondriachal symptoms, along with his confessions of a slothful nature, were esteem-diminishing devices that existed in marked contrast to his having read for eight hours a day for three years. Kohut and Wolf (1978) have pointed out that the fragmented self represented by the fragmented bodily feeling found in hypochondria disappears in patients when empathy with the understanding selfobject has been developed or reestablished.

In this third aspect of confession, the patient exhibits "yo-yo" self-esteem, as the self oscillates between grandiosity and self-abnegation. Kohut (1966) attributes such oscillation between overestimation of the self and feelings of inferiority to traumatic onslaughts on the child's self-esteem that resulted in repression of the grandiose self.

Confession brings an aspect of the secret grandiose self out of hiding. Since the grandiose self often is suffused with an admixture of shame, megalomania, and bizarreness, the patient initially may disclose a kernel of the grandiose self in the form of a more innocuous confession. The patient's disclosure of the secret content of the grandiose self becomes the ultimate confession that gradually brings about exploration and realignment of the patient's shifting self-esteem.

Narcissistic issues often figure prominently in confession. While patients may zealously hold on to their secrets to save face, narcissistic factors likewise can prompt patients to confess as a way of enhancing self-esteem. To this end patients confess in order to feel special and appreciated; to risk shame in order to gain acceptance; and to rediscover their lost ambitions and ideals. Confessions disclosed and examined in the empathic analytic relationship provide an arena for the grandiose self to emerge and grow.

5

The Confessional Process: Risk–Relief– Redemption/ Renewal

Confession is not an isolated act but an extended process that involves three phases. Patients consciously or unconsciously weigh the need to confess against the fear of consequences. When fear proves stronger than need, confession is aborted or postponed. The patient has seemingly resolved the dilemma, but only temporarily. The internal tug-of-war soon resumes.

Confession may be postponed again and again, for months or even years. But when need outbalances fear, the patient is ready to risk confession. Briefly, the three-step confessional process consists of:

> 1. *Risk*. Patients fear that their secrets will render them foolish, prideful, unworthy, or unlovable to others. The greater the intimacy with the confessional object, the larger looms the possibility of repercussions, such as betrayal, abandonment, or loss of love. The non-normative nature of friendship and romantic or familial involvement does not ensure the confidentiality and acceptance integral to the analytic relationship. As such the analyst often becomes a trusted low-risk confessor.

2. *Relief.* The act of sharing and working through one's secret with the affirming analyst in time results in cathartic release. Not all confessions immediately, or indeed inevitably, relieve patients. Some patients may experience an exacerbation of shame or guilt following confession. Others may initially withdraw and erect a system of defenses and other resistances that make further analytic work with the confession come to a sudden halt. Yet no matter what affects and cognitive styles first emerge following confession, I have found from my clinical observations that, in most cases, the end result of the working through of confession produces genuine relief.

3. *Redemption/Renewal.* Patients confess in order to save themselves from the darker, ominous side of their own nature. In risking the analyst's disapproval or censure and obtaining the opposite results, patients can see themselves as capable of achieving greater intimacy and moving closer to self-integration. Patients return to the archives of their past both to master the situation and to refurbish a self strengthened by the assimilation of past and present secrets into a richer, more meaningful existence.

Let me caution the reader that while all confessions do begin with the evaluation of risk, the next two phases—relief and redemption/renewal—are far more complex and do not inevitably follow the verbalization of secrets, nor are they always the only paths that complete the confessional trail. I have devoted Chapter 7 to the potentially destructive outcome wrought by the injudicious use of confession.

The present chapter explores the nature of this three-pronged confessional process presented as a model that I have found to be clinically useful and generalizable to the hundreds of confessions I have documented, both from my own practice and from the clinical cases that my colleagues have generously shared with me.

RISK

When the patient's need to confess conflicts with a perceived loyalty, the business of self-disclosure can seem as dangerous as a game of Russian roulette. Even when the secret does not indict those to whom the patient owes allegiance, the hazard of consequence remains.

At all phases of our lives, confession begins with an evaluation of risk. Individuals who wish to test the waters of honesty may begin by making confessions to those who do not play a large role in their lives. Confession can be placed on a continuum, as follows:

Low Risk			Moderate Risk			High Risk		
1	2	3	4	5	6	7	8	9
stranger (e.g. cab-driver)	clergy (e.g. priest)	therapist	hair-dresser	bartender	co-worker	friend	parent	lover

I will begin with a brief description of the confessional possibilities offered by low- moderate- and high-risk confessors to provide a sociocultural context for the emergence of confession in psychotherapy.

Low-Risk Confessors

The anonymous, substitutible cab driver and the stranger one meets during one's travels are ideally safe confessors. Unburdening one's secret to such captive audiences entails the security of never seeing the person again, along with the knowledge that approval or continuity is not the uncomfortable prerequisite that "comes with the territory" in ongoing, intimate relationships.

Confession to members of the clergy guarantees absolution; however, the priest or minister is not always a substitutible stranger, and may, at times, be a parental or friendship figure, particularly in smaller parishes. In these latter situations, the personal ongoing relationship with the priest or minister renders confession more risky.

Confession is an expected and accepted phenomenon in therapy. Moreover, the nonjudgemental stream-of-consciousness atmosphere of the therapeutic setting facilitates confessions. Why, then, do some patients perceive therapists as high-risk confessors? Because the "neutral" therapist transferentially comes to assume the emotionally overladen roles of father, mother, siblings, lovers, etc., patients may behave against their own best interests and knowledge of the therapeutic contract in concealing the secrets that may have brought them into therapy in the first place.

Moderate-Risk Confessors

Hairdressers and bartenders appear midway between the low- and high-risk confessors. With these confessional sources, no rules exist that guarantee acceptance and confidentiality. Since hairdressers and bartenders become "the ear" to many regular clients, the possibility of gossip spreading increases. Also, some of these "familiar strangers" (Milgram, 1970) eventually become friends and make the acquaintance of the client's other friends, and so the risk of confessing to them increases. Nevertheless, the prudent, tight-lipped hairdresser or bartender who relates to clients on a regular basis remains a fairly safe confessional ally. And since tips and referrals depend upon the confessor's discretion, such confessors are called upon by many with few qualms.

Co-workers often become privy to confessions, since they are perceived as less risky than family or friends, and yet more cognizant of the situation (and thereby more valued sources of feedback) than strangers. Still, many workers are reticent about confessing to each other, especially when such information later might be utilized by an unscrupulous co-worker/confessor as competitive leverage in the work arena.

High-Risk Confessors

People actively seek therapists and "lay confessors" precisely because of their reticence in sharing their secrets with friends who might reject them or not keep their secret. Whereas Sulzberger (1953) maintains that only a friend can really act as a trusted confessor, in many situations, precisely because the friend is a high-risk confessor, the stakes involved in confessing (e.g., abandonment, inadvertent leakage, and blackmail) often outweigh the benefits. In general the greater the anonymity and objectivity of the confessor, the lesser is the risk in confessing.

Since many of us consider friends, parents, and lovers to be our three most vital relationships, an enormous risk is incurred in confessing to such significant others. The fluidity and lack of specified norms in these relationships endanger the status quo position of the confessant, and may even threaten continuity. Children who confess to parents that they are homosexuals, for example, run the risk of being disowned. Lovers who confess their infidelities to each other may forfeit the relationship in return for such disclosures.

The Therapist as Low-Risk Confessor

Sir Henry Harcourt-Reilly, the stranger and psychiatrist of the missing wife of the host (Edward), in T. S. Eliot's *The Cocktail Party* (1950), discloses to Edward that to approach him "is to invite the unexpected, release a new force/Or let the genie out of the bottle./It is to start a train of events/Beyond your control" (p. 28). The revelation of secrets, even to therapists, carries risks—not only from the censorious confessor (although the therapist may be so transferentially perceived by the patient), but also from the patient's divided self that is now impelled to continue moving inexorably forward outside the controlled confines of secrecy.

Again, the transference is perhaps the major resistance that impedes the analyst's role as a low-risk confessor. Freud (1912a) comments, "It must become peculiarly difficult to own up to any particular reprehended wish when the confession must be made to the very person with whom that feeling is most concerned. To proceed at all in such situations as this necessity produces would appear hardly possible in real life. This impossibility is precisely what the patient is aiming at when he merges the physician with the object of his emotions" (p. 111). Yet for patients who risk confessing to the therapist, the confession itself becomes a potent vehicle in facilitating the separation of the therapist as a here-and-now "new object" (Loewald, 1957/1980) from the patient's past archaic objects.

Throughout the confession and the subsequent working-through process, the patient notices not only that the fantasized retribution did not materialize, but also that the analyst becomes a helpful, willing partner in the process of making this material work for the patient in a new, functional way (*renewal* aspect of confession). A relatively dramatic type of confession, which I term the "jinx confession," cogently illustrates how risking confession changes both the dynamic meaning of the secret and the patient's evaluation of self. Several years ago a colleague related to me how an old, wealthy Hungarian dowager patient confessed, in hushed tones, that she had a recurring dream in which her jewelry sank into the ocean. This patient had been on the *Titanic*, and had lost all of her jewelry. Twenty years later she found herself on the *Andrea Doria*, to be saved again, but also again to experience the loss of her jewelry.

This patient told my colleague that the reason she had resisted disclosing these incidents to anyone for all these years was that she held the conviction that she somehow had jinxed these ships, while simultaneously being endowed with the power to save herself. She had felt guilty about being saved when others died, but also experienced shame (and hidden grandiosity) at the thought of her repeated powers to survive against stringent odds.

The act of risking confession in itself brought a measure of relief to this apprehensive patient. Moreover, when she discovered that the analyst did not rebuke her in the manner of her tyrannical father, she was able to summon up the courage to explore further the nuances of the secret without feeling the need to anesthetize the past in order to curry the favor of the father/analyst. As these incidents were explored, the patient was able to see her role in the events in a different light. Through the process of discovery, exploration, and working through, she was able to relinquish her *idée fixe* of having jinxed these ships, while learning to appreciate her resourcefulness in surviving. Through the analyst's mirroring responses and empathic interpretations, this patient was able to increase her self-esteem in reevaluating her role in these events in the context of the current confessional bond with the analyst.

To risk confession is to risk judgment (fantasized or actual). The lawyer/thief in Camus' *The Fall* (1956) speaks to this issue when he states, "I was wrong, after all, to tell you that the essential was to avoid judgment. The essential is being able to permit oneself everything, even if, from time to time, one has to profess vociferously one's own infamy" (p. 141).

Confession in psychotherapy allows patients to risk opening themselves up to the full gamut of human possibilities. Once patients risk confessing, they can begin to live their lives in richer, less constricting ways. Khan (1983) addresses the existential choice inherent in risking confession when he writes, "A person can *hide* himself into symptoms or he can *absent* himself into a secret. Here, the secret provides a potential space where an absence is sustained in suspended animation...the secret carries a hope that one day the person will be able to emerge out of it, be found and met, and thus become a whole person, sharing life with others" (p. 105). Patients are emboldened to risk sharing their secrets when they allow their private space to be transformed into a shared forum of caring affirmation in which the true self can emerge.

Emerson's (1841, p. 305) apothegm to the effect that "people wish to be settled; only as far as they are unsettled is there any hope for them" describes the dilemma that patients experience prior to confessing. The unsettling nature of confession presses patients to stir up long-buried or suppressed secrets that force them to wrestle with disavowed aspects of self. Thus, in confessing, not only do patients risk evaluation from others, but they also often find themselves in the throes of self-evaluation in facing shameful or guilt-ridden aspects of the self.

In sum, the likelihood of a patient risking confessing in therapy depends on three major factors:

1. The patient's world of introjected objects and history of confessional outcome. For patients with histories of punishment and retaliation from toxic objects following confession, confession in psychotherapy is only likely to be forthcoming following the discovery, exploration, and, finally, expulsion of the toxic introjects. These early objects that play a critical part in the patient's confessional history comprise not only parents, but also clergy and teachers. In fact, a large percentage of patients mention humiliation or criticism experienced at the hands of extrafamilial objects that inclined them to shy away from subsequent confession. Conversely, the more benign and loving the past significant objects, the more likely the patient is to experience satisfaction and enhanced intimacy through confessing.

2. The therapeutic relationship. To the extent that patients establish a working alliance with the therapist, confessions are likely to emerge in time. The establishment of neurotic transferences produces ambivalence regarding confessing insofar as the analyst becomes equated with parental representations. Patients who develop stable narcissistic transferences (mirroring and idealizing) may initially be more prone to confess than their neurotic counterparts, in that the analyst, as selfobject extension, is not consistently perceived as a separate other outside the realm of the patient's power. As such, many of these patients perceive confessing as sharing their inner contents with a "second self."

3. Level of self-cohesiveness. The more cohesive the patient's self, the more the patient is likely to risk confessing. Patients with a cohesive self are less likely to view confession as a dangerous experience with such possible catastrophic outcomes as fragmentation, annihilation, or irrevocable self-deflation. Schizophrenic patients are especially resistant to confession, both because of an impoverishment of inner structure and because any secrets are enviously guarded lest the analyst steal or destroy the few inner possessions the patient can call his or her own.

RELIEF

I present the thesis that relief tends to be the ultimate emotional end point of confession;[1] however, relief is not the only emotion that follows confession, nor is it an inevitable emotional outcome.

Once patients confess they may display a number of cognitive and affective reactions, including denial ("I didn't mean what I said; it didn't really happen that way") or rationalization ("I was young and foolish then; he/she made me do it; it was like I wasn't myself"); anxiety and guilt arising from tranferential fears of retaliation from the analyst/parent; or schizoid withdrawal in which patients overcompensate for their confession by adopting cold, puritanical "prim and proper" attitudes and behaviors in and out of therapy. Once patients risk confessing, all of these potential reactions must be explored and worked through before relief can finally be experienced.

Bohart (1980) notes that the simple expression of emotions, such as anger, is not sufficient to reduce anger. Relief likewise is not an automatic outcome of confession. Only when the patient both shares a secret with the low-risk analyst/confessor and assimilates the reinterpretation of the situation that undergoes neutralization in the empathic therapeutic milieu does relief ensue.

The Temporal Factor in Relief

Whether or not the patient comes to experience immediate or delayed relief depends upon whether the confession is conscious or unconscious, and also upon the patient's perception of the analyst's receptivity. Freud and Breuer (1895) noticed that cognitive recovery of a memory did not result in symptom removal unless an emotional abreaction also took place. The importance of Breuer and Freud as elicitors of confessions and transferential objects was initially ignored. With the advent of object relations theory, we can view relief as being dependent not only upon drive discharge, but also upon the analyst's ability to help patients free themselves from the confines of transferential distortions.

[1]For simplification, the word "confession" is utilized as a shorthand equivalent for the verbal or written revelation of material; however, it is important that the reader bear in mind that confession, as an extended process, pertains to risk, relief, and redemption/renewal.

If a confession is conscious and volitionally offered, patients often experience relief, since they can control, to some extent, the timing and their presumed readiness to divulge hitherto suppressed material. I have observed that even patients who have harbored what they consider to be the most heinous or shameful offenses (e.g., incest, stealing, prolonged virginity, torturing animals, etc.) experience marked relief when they finally choose to confess, although such relief is frequently intermingled with feelings of guilt, shame, and so on.

Alternatively, if the secret is unconscious and emerges unexpectedly in the process of free association, confession may give rise to essentially unaltered repetitions of those emotions initially attached to the past event. Should the patient experience the confession as a relentless repetition rather than as a reparative reconstruction, he or she may actually undergo a heightened sense of anxiety, shame, or guilt, especially if the therapist is equated with the critical parents or toxic others from the past. Even in these latter instances of repetition, relief and gratitude may ensue once patient and analyst undertake the work of sorting out the past experience from the present reality and assimilating the past secret into the patient's present consciousness to curtail future unconscious repetitions.

Thus far I have indicated that once patients risk confessing, relief is not the only emotion that inevitably results. Patients can experience a variety of emotions from the past and present at the same time. The neurosurgeon Wilder Penfield (1959) was surprised to discover that when the temporal lobes of certain epileptic patients were electrically stimulated, these patients were able to remain aware of their present circumstances on the operating table while simultaneously abandoning themselves to a past experience that was being revivified in the present. A woman in her 60s relived the details of her birthday party at five; a male patient revived all the sensory excitement of a live orchestral concert.

Such "creative time distortion" in which conventional temporal boundaries become collapsed as past and present are experienced simultaneously has been exhibited by patients when unconscious confessions emerge. Like Penfield's patients, some therapy patients can coexist in two times and spaces during confession. For those patients who experience confession as a repetition of the earlier event, the knowledge (albeit intellectual) that the analyst is a new object, even though he or she is emotionally equated with the archaic objects, allows the patient to garner a measure of relief from the awareness of the present context in which the confession appears.

Cognitive and Affective Aspects of Relief

Bibring (1954) drew attention to the fact that abreaction does not simply have a one-step therapeutic effect. Once the emotionally charged secret is verbalized, not only is the disturbing effect of the secret weakened, but it is also accessible to corrective influence by evaluating it against reality.

In effect, once the secret is disclosed, it can be worked through further both cognitively and affectively. The release through confession is not simply emotional, but also cognitive, in that the patient is now free to explore this material further and integrate it into his or her life. The confessional release also may facilitate the patient's engagement in actions that previously were inhibited by the guilt- or shame-inducing secret. As an example of the disinhibiting behavioral possibilities inherent in confession, in Chapter 4 I described patients whose shame- or guilt-ridden sexual secrets from childhood prevented them from sexual activities of any kind until later years.

Forster's (1924/1950) *A Passage to India* offers a striking illustration of a false confession followed by a true confession that provided relief to the confessant, Miss Quested, through cognitive and affective reappraisal of the incident in question. Adela Quested, an awkward, priggish woman who has an "understanding" with Ronny, the magistrate in the city of Chandrapore in India, goes on an expedition to the Marabar Caves. Just before entering a cave, she indicates for the first time, sexual interest in Dr. Aziz, her Indian guide. Once inside, upon hearing an echo, she runs out in panic, and accuses Aziz of attempted rape.

The prosecuting attorney's questions in court force Miss Quested to retrace the events cognitively; this results in a retraction, followed by relief. She finally can be released from her hysterical symptoms of echoing in her ears reminiscent of the cave's echoes. In saving Dr. Aziz, Miss Quested also is able to be redeemed from the ignominy of an existence predicated on a lie.

Jung (1933) wrote, "It is only with the help of confession that I am able to throw myself into the arms of humanity freed at last from the burden of moral exile. The goal of treatment by catharsis is full confession—not merely intellectual acknowledgement of the facts, but their confirmation by the heart and the actual release of the suppressed emotions" (pp. 35–36). Only after Adela Quested confesses is she able to reintegrate the cognitive circumstances with the emotional turbulence of her repressed sexual feelings, and thereby gain relief.

The Nature of the Object in Relief

How the object responds to the confession is a crucial determinant of whether or not the confessant experiences relief. Bibring (1954) noted that if confession was met with sympathy, acceptance, and affirmation from the analyst, relief was likely to follow. Apfelbaum (1965) reiterated this notion in maintaining that successful abreaction depends largely on the experience of a favorable response from the object; conversely, negative reactions might provoke anxiety and guilt. The patient's confession is not simply verbal discharge, but rather an attempt to recast the secret in a new time and place with the analyst as a confidante and guide helping the patient utilize the confession to move out of a constricted existence.

Although so many patients feel stymied in pouring out their hearts to each other outside therapy, the presence of the analyst often suffices in providing a safe "holding environment" (Bion, 1977) in which confessions can emerge without catastrophic consequences. These patients feel heartfelt relief as they experience the self-deception and other-deception marring their existences transformed into authentic relatedness in the presence of the analyst.

REDEMPTION/RENEWAL

Many of us, in and out of therapy, believe that we can be "saved" by confessing. The religious confessant who atoned was assured of temporary or permanent relief. The concept of redemption is prevalent, as well, in those who seek nonreligious confessors. In psychotherapy patient/confessants are aware, implicitly or explicitly, that they hold the key to their own salvation. Moreover, should they choose to keep their secrets locked up within themselves, they may be engineering their own destruction.

Once patients have confessed or engaged in a series of confessions, they come to experience themselves in a new way. Each confession undertaken by the patient serves as a constructive building block and catalyst for subsequent confessions. Through such interactions with the analyst, patients learn to take more risks in extratherapeutic contexts with other people who slowly come to be seen as less threatening and more benign. As the transferential deadlock is broken, the "new," less distorted relationship with the analyst increasingly takes hold and generalizes to the patient's wider social circle. By putting themselves and their confidantes "to the test" through risking confession outside psychotherapy, patients reassess their social relationships by discovering who can be trusted, and who will unconditionally accept and love them.

Redemption: The Integration of the Divided Self[2]

The redemptive nature of confessions allows individuals to transcend destructive aspects of self. Literary characterizations provide striking examples of the polarity between self-redemption and self-destruction. In both Wilde's (1890/1964) *The Picture of Dorian Gray* and Poe's (1839/1965) *William Wilson*, the good and evil aspects of self emerge as separate and distinct *personas*; in both cases the evil eventually swallows and destroys the good. Neither protagonist confesses his crimes to another, not only out of fear of censure, but also because of the possible legal consequences of his deeds.

The choice between salvation and self-destruction constitutes a central theme in Stevenson's (1886/1925) *The Strange Case of Dr. Jekyll and Mr. Hyde.* Confession, or even coexistence, of the two identities becomes impossible, because Mr. Hyde's crimes make him a wanted man and Hyde (the destructive aspect of self) gains ascendancy over Jekyll. Since the two aspects of self cannot be integrated, self-destruction or public destruction at the gallows is inevitable.

Dr. Jekyll's power striving in his scientific work, along with the *deus ex machina* of the imperfections of subsequent potions, assure self-destruction. At the end of the story, neither the Jekyll nor the Hyde aspect of self can be reconciled with the other, so that when the confession is finally made, salvation through integration becomes impossible. The evil Hyde, heretofore the weaker side, is now the dominant character, to the detriment of the whole self.

Unlike Stevenson, who depicts the parts of the divided, unintegrated self as different personifications both physically and morally, Poe, in *William Wilson*, introduces the idea of the divided self as

---

[2] Major segments of this section were extracted from my paper "The Therapeutic Nature of Confessions," *Journal of Contemporary Psychotherapy* 13:129–143 (Fall/Winter 1982).

alter-ego twins. The main character—the narrator—is the "evil" one, harrassed by "the good William"—his conscience. Poe depicts the self-destructive and redemptive aspects of self constantly struggling for ascendancy and interchangeable within the same *persona*. As in Wilde's *Picture of Dorian Gray*, the "evil" Wilson, in murdering his conscience, also murders his pleasure-obsessed wicked self.

Confessions made during psychotherapy enable the patient to acknowledge the thought or deed and thereby render it less alien by rescuing it from the realm of the self-destructive "not me" (Sullivan, 1953). Because they constitute part of our universal human experience, both analyst and patient are able to tolerate and accept the most recreant confessions. In Stevenson's (1879/1925) words, "To begin to understand is to begin to sympathize, for comprehension comes only when we have stated another's faults and virtues in terms of our own" (p. 168).

In confession the darker side of the self has been exposed and rendered less powerful. No longer forced into a Jekyll–Hyde dichotomy, the patient again begins to see himself or herself as a whole person. Like the phoenix that rises from the ashes of its own destruction, the patient is freed to embark upon a new, less constricted phase of existence.

What further can happen if we choose to bury our ominous deeds? Hawthorne's *The Scarlett Letter* (1850/1962) underscores the destruction that results from the nonrevelation of a secret. The Reverend Arthur Dimmesdale, who had an adulterous relationship with Hester Prynne after her husband disappeared, finds out that she has borne his child. Hester, who refuses to reveal the father's identity, is exposed for two hours on the pillory, and sentenced to wear a red A on her breast for the remainder of her life.

Dimmesdale is dissuaded by Hester from confessing, and carries on with his ministry, while suffering intensely from guilt. *The Scarlett Letter* deals with the destructive potential of secrets that can torture the nonrevealer even to the point of self-denunciation and death. This novel exposes the personal and social tragedy of the protagonists trapped in the mores and legalities of a society in which neither confession nor concealment can ever offer redemption.

Confession here becomes not only a highly risky venture, but also an almost impossible one, should the participants desire to remain where they are. Only in exile is there a chance for them to redeem themselves and seek a renewed existence away from the collective societal eye.

Today confession can truly constitute a redemptive experience.

Low-risk confessors facilitate the disclosure of secrets within the shared domain of interpersonal relatedness. Psychoanalytic therapy provides fertile soil for the establishment of such confessional bonds. The confidentiality, acceptance, empathic receptivity, exploration, and interpretation built into the therapy relationship frees the patient to take more risks and experience redemption through his or her own efforts, in conjunction with the analyst as guide.

Redemption as Transformation

Redemption is not a concept that many therapists readily translate into therapeutic terms. Yet redemption can be a powerful aspect of confession in psychotherapy.

In examining the nature of secular confession, I am reminded of the sharp contrast between the paths chosen by Saint Augustine (398 A.D.) and Rousseau (1781). Saint Augustine moved from confession of his sins—nonbelief in God, sexual lust, and stealing pears in adolescence—to a leap into faith and redemption through religious fervor. Rousseau, while upbraiding himself for his theft of ribbons, appeared secretly to laud himself for his "humbling" disclosure (Miller, 1984). Yet Rousseau, unlike Augustine, never truly atoned for, or even acknowledged, the severity of many of his confessions (particularly the placement of his five children in an orphanage).

Since redemption through self-reflection, atonement, or restitution was nullified by Rousseau, he instead projected his own unacceptable thoughts onto others. By the end of his life, Rousseau feared plots against him by women, kings, various countries, and even his own dog.

Like Rousseau, if patients choose to do nothing to relieve the perceived heinousness of a thought or deed, guilt or shame revolving around the secret tends to escalate rather than diminish. Only through the erection and maintenance of an elaborate system of defenses and subterfuge can such individuals unconsciously maintain the continued submergence of disowned aspects of the self.

The inability or unwillingness to confess, in extreme cases, can lead to suicide. Flaubert's *Madame Bovary* (1856/1965) epitomizes the disastrous consequences that befall a woman gripped by romantic malaise, the need to live in dreams, and the failure to accept life's realities.

In brief, Madame Bovary, married to a dull country doctor, and consumed by sensual-romantic longings, takes a lover and is deserted by him; takes a second lover; and falls hopelessly into debt.

Finally she kills herself. Confession was impossible, precisely because Emma could not face the tragedy of her existence. Instead she resorted to escapism by engaging in impulsive buying and illicit affairs.

Unlike Freud and Breuer's hysterical patients to whom she bears some resemblances, Emma could not confess. In the absence of a benign confessional object to accept her and contain her behavior, Emma slowly was destroyed by the elaboration of lie upon lie, the buildup of debt, and blackmail. With the breakdown of her illusions, and the accumulation of unbearable realities, her destruction became inevitable. Since she could not confess, and thereby redeem herself, she chose suicide instead.

Destruction, however, is not always the direct antithesis of redemption. At times the destructive principle is a prerequisite in the movement toward redemption. Mythological and religious examples abound in which destruction heralds the reemergence of a self redeemed and renewed in the process.

The Janus-like face of destruction and redemption forms part of our collective religious heritage, and especially becomes manifest in the symbolic nature of the Trinity in many of the world's religions. The Western world is conversant with the idea of redemption and resurrection through corporeal destruction, but the contiguity between destruction and redemption is also prominent in Hinduism. In the Divine Triad of Hinduism (Brahma, Vishnu, and Siva), Siva literally means "the blessed one." Although Siva represents the destructive principle in life, in Hinduism the power of restoration is involved in destruction.

While patients proceed through therapy with the conviction that the secularization of confession can facilitate redemption through human relatedness, therapists cannot ignore or view as resistance patients' discussions of religious themes, along with certain universal, archetypal symbols that enter into consciousness. The analyst should thus be prepared to welcome and explore all religious subjects that enter into the patient's discourse, since from early childhood, such material forms an integral part of many patients' unconscious and conscious values and perceptions.

A clinical illustration from the life of Wilhelm Reich illustrates how other-destructiveness can result in a life devoted to redemption and transformation. At the age of 14, Reich discovered that his mother was having a secret affair with one of his tutors. When Reich reported the infidelity to his father, his mother killed herself. Reich appeared to be acting out an identification with his father's sexually repressive values, and experienced severe guilt at the suicidal outcome.

Reich underwent redemption by struggling with his own sexual repression, which culminated in a theory devoted to the enlightening aspects of freedom and the nonrepression of sexuality. Stolorow and Atwood (1979), who view Reich's theory as an offshoot of his phenomenological life themes, see his atonement for his betrayal taking the form of utter commitment to a theory based upon the "eradication of all those values and ways of thinking which had motivated him" (p. 121). In radically transforming his own mores and inner convictions, Reich's creative expression was able to touch and transform others as well.

For many patients confessing can involve a transformation of hidden aspects of self into creative expression. Many patients undergo experiences not dissimilar to those of Reich, in which energy previously channeled into repression of material or obsessive ruminations can be transformed, following confession, into growth-promoting activities. Jeanie, a 42-year-old schizophrenic woman, referred to her "bad" self as Jeanette. "I can tell you all about Jeanette, because she's a devil through and through. If she wants to, she can slash through Jeanie, she can be so strong."

After several months of therapy, a strong voice emanating from the hitherto self-effacing Jeanie told me that she hated me because I made her attach herself to me. Jeanie called me and apologized profusely for "the other one" who came through, informing me that Jeanette had done many bad things and was capable of doing more.

In subsequent sessions I encouraged Jeanie to let out and thereby let go of the deeds and thoughts inside her. Jeanie confessed that she wished that she could kill her sister, and that she had tried to kill herself with a sliver of glass that she carried in her purse.

These confessions were followed by a flood of invective against me for "making her give up her secrets." The sharing of these much guarded secrets, along with the release of long-repressed rage, freed Jeanie to pursue some of the intellectual and esthetic interests that had become blocked. In confessing Jeanie came into contact with a darker aspect of self. The acknowledgement of this material enabled her to begin to develop a less fragmented self.

The theme of confession and its aftermath of destruction evolving into redemption and transformation appears in sharp focus in Reich's life. Yet, following sef-disclosure, many patients experience redemption without destruction as a precursor. I am here reminded of Schönberg's "Transfigured Night," composed in 1899, which was based on a poem by Richard Dehmel. The music itself mirrors the content of the poem as it moves from dark to light, guilt to innocence. In the poem, as a woman walks through the woods, she confesses to her lover that she is pregnant with another man's child, and resignedly notes that life now has its revenge, since she has met her lover too late. The man consoles the woman and exhorts her not to burden her soul with thoughts of guilt. He describes the special warmth flowing between them that will transfigure the child and make it his kin.

Both the poem and the music reflect the redemptive and transformational possibilities inherent in confession. The woman risks confessing her pregnancy to her lover, who reassuringly accepts her. The woman gains relief and is redeemed through her lover's acceptance. The two are luminously transformed through the confessional bond established between them. The child will be a living testimonial to the woman's redemptive experience and to the couple's renewal.

Speaking of Luther, who, as a novice, went through the ceremony of lying before the altar with his arms spread away from him like Christ's on the cross, Erikson (1962) notes the prior's concluding words, "Not he who began, but he who persists will be saved" (p. 130). Confession in psychotherapy is the first step in a gradual therapeutic process that requires faith on the part of both patient and therapist that, through persistent and sometimes painstaking effort, the patient will develop a sense of redemption through human endeavor. It is this persistence that is so often missing in a world in which magical beliefs and "quick fix" approaches intrude on virtually every aspect of life.

Renewal: The Novel Connection

In the ancient world, patients suffering from mental disorders were taken to the sacred island of Cos. After ritual preparation they were submitted to a flooding experience, "the experience of the God," involving hypnosis combined with shock and terror. The patient was then renewed, and a new life began. Many patients, then and now, are willing to undergo psychic or physical ordeals in order to emerge freed from the impurities of the primordial yoke.

The novel therapeutic bond promotes renewal. Newirth (1982) notes that the therapeutic relationship itself can be seen as restitutive or reconstructive. In *Constructions in Analysis* (1937), Freud maintains that the analyst's interpretation need not be identical to the historical event, but rather is a construction through which patient and analyst can view the current situation in the context of a past concatenation of events. In this sense the analyst, in part, offers a new cognitive and affective structure for the patient (Newirth, 1982).

The analyst's interpretations transform the patient's secret into the present field of lived, shared experience. Many patients then are equipped with greater psychological and emotional resources to cope with the ramifications of the confession.

Confession enables the patient to assimilate and view the secret in a new light. The patient is able to feel redeemed and renewed *both* because of the development of insight and because his or her relationship with the analyst has real and new components that the patient learns to differentiate from transferential projections. Moreover, even the patient who is in the midst of a strong transference (positive or negative) often is able to risk opprobrium in knowing, on some level, that he or she will be accepted and redeemed by the safety features built into the therapeutic contract (Langs, 1978).

Freud (1914b) alludes to the therapeutic relationship in both the elicitation of the past as present (repetition) and the differentiation of the past from present (working through). In an important passage, Freud writes, "This state of illness is brought, piece by piece, within the field and range of operation of the treatment, and while the patient experiences it as something real and contemporary, we have to do our therapeutic work on it, which consists in a large measure in tracing it back to the past.... Repeating, as it is induced in the analytic treatment according to the newer technique...implies conjuring up a piece of real life" (pp. 151–152).

Erard (1983), in alluding to this passage, points out that the analytic task is no longer simply the recovery and ventilation of repressed memories, but also involves helping patients become aware of the connection between immediate present conflicts revived in the transference, and in everyday life, and their origins earlier in life. Erard (1983) summarizes, "In other words, the agent of therapeutic change no longer consists in simply recalling the traumatic origins of the illness, but in establishing, in effect, a new kind of connection between the patient's actual, contemporary experience and earlier life events of which it is a repetition" (p. 64).

It is through the interpretation of such transference distortions that the patient increasingly comes to see the analyst as a new object. Loewald (1957/1980) elaborates, "And this not primarily in the sense of an object not previously met, but the newness consists in the patient's rediscovery of the early paths of the development of object relations leading to a new way of relating to objects and of being oneself" (p. 229).

Patients who risk confessing frequently perceive the analyst as an object at the crossroads between archaic objects and new, benign objects. Such mixed perceptions facilitate the emergence of transference and simultaneously offer patients hope that they can work through and thus resolve their secrets in a unique relationship that both engenders the repetition of secrets and provides patients with an empathic arena for the working through of such dilemmas with the new object.

Renewal: The Past Reconstructed

Sedler (1983) speaks of the disjunction of past and present selves brought about through remembering and self-reflection. "Remembering makes it possible both to *own* those thoughts and feelings engendered in the past as they were originally conceived and to *distance* them from the present situation. In this way, the living present comes to be less distorted by the unconscious past; the present comes to be what it is, namely, *new*. ... Past and present are distinguished even as they are linked by remembering" (p. 95).

Patients come to experience themselves in new ways through confessions that are transformed in the process of remembering and working through. The forgoing of resistances that mask the patient's guilt-ridden or shameful self signals a change in the direction of greater strength, tolerance, and the ability to deal with the former repressed secret self. By discovering, uncovering, and owning the past, patients are on their way to autonomy in the present.

Tertullian's (1521/1931) and Nietzsche's (1885/1967) notions of "eternal return" do not signify a return to a static sameness, but to a past mastered and transformed in the light of present awareness. Nietzsche especially extols the renewal experienced as a recreation of the exuberance and joy of life.

Proust transports us into the realm of renewal over and over again in *Remembrance of Things Past* (1913–1927/1981). Marcel experiences inexplicable pleasure from reminiscences in which chronic depression and inertia are transformed into sudden feelings of self-worth. Splitter (1980) comments, "This return of an unconscious memory allows him to recover and repossess his own past self, making him feel there *is* a permanent identity which transcends temporal discontinuities" (p. 386). *Mutatis mutandis*, repressed secrets may sweep over the patient in such a way that the less-than-blissful past is now revivified as an elated present moment in which the strengthened, more cohesive self triumphs.

The renewal aspect of confession was especially striking in the case of Jim, a 32-year-old graduate student in physics, who vehemently railed against the strictures of the Catholic Church that "won't let a person live." These discussions, which were conducted in a highly intellectualized fashion, took a turn when the patient unexpectedly proffered a long suppressed shame-inducing confession.

"When I was 13, I brought a little girl of six into the house to play. I told her that I would get her some artificial flowers, but that in the interim I would have to tie her up so that she would not get lost. She agreed and I bound her hands. When I returned, I gave her the flowers and she left. Although I did nothing to her sexually, she told her parents and the story reached most of the neighbors. My mother never let me live down the shame. Even though I did nothing to molest her sexually, I still feel I'm evil because I later conjured up that scene when I masturbated."

While the patient voiced his conviction that this confession confirmed his evilness, the act of sharing his secret with the none-valuative therapist enabled him to begin to reexamine his attitudes and actions predicated on his still strongly internalized Catholicism. Although Jim acknowledged that a difference existed between sexual fantasies of bondage and the deed itself, he reminded me that the Catholic Church considered such thoughts to be sinful, as well. Through his confession Jim began to realize how much his life still revolved around the tenets of the church that he had outwardly forsaken.

For Jim the process of confessing initiated a series of therapeutic changes. By freeing himself from the yoke of self-deception, Jim gradually was able to evolve new cognitive and behavioral options that redeemed him from his perception of sinfulness and realigned his sexual priorities.

Jim, who had been physically and verbally abused by his mother, was recreating a "benign" revenge fantasy in which he had control over the female victim. This insight was accompanied by a consciously willed effort to avoid "playing the victim."

More important, Jim adopted restitutive action toward himself. By altering his fantasies, Jim was able to alter his perception of himself. He began consciously to will fantasies of sexual intercourse in tandem with the bondage fantasies.

Jim's self-image, bolstered by my acceptance and further exploration of his confession, enabled him to share his secret with his girlfriend. Since they have enacted both intercourse and bondage fantasies to their mutual enjoyment, Jim no longer views himself as a sadistic monster beyond redemption.

Patients like Jim who confess return to the scene of the "crime" or trauma both to master the original situation and to utilize the episode to build a renewed self. Bartlett's (1932/1967) finding that memory not only is reproductive, but also productive, reinstates the patient as an active agent in adopting and interpreting the past event to meet the contingencies of present life circumstances. Because the past is constantly reconstructed by the present, the patient is freed to transform rather than relive the past through the radicalizing (literally, returning to one's historical roots) process of confession.

Renewal: Rebirth and Ritual

In the previous sections, I described how patients' confessions bring the past into the present so that they can differentiate and integrate their role in select historical events to achieve renewal. Another way that patients come to terms with their repressed or suppressed selves is by bringing the present into the past in a reversal of the Proustian temporal process.

William James introduced the concept of second birth that was fruitfully adopted by Erikson in his psychohistory of Luther. James, in his *Varieties of Religious Experience* (1902/1963), differentiated the once-born from those "divided selves" who search for a second birth that will convert them in their "habitual center of...personal energy" (p. 199).

Although James' illustrations almost exclusively concerned adolescents and persons in their early 20s, it is apparent from the biographies of the famous, as well as from the confessions of our own patients, that the confessions that promote redemption/renewal occur for people of all ages. A common confession made by patients that heralds the onset of a second birth concerns their sense of only feeling free creatively and/or emotionally after a parent has died. I recall one patient who at age 60 began to dance and paint, after her aged father died.

Erikson (1962) speaks of a "second birth" as the resolution of an identity crisis. Should individuals not find fertile ground for the establishment of their own identity, they may instead succumb to intense commitments to ideological movements or charismatic leaders that result in a forfeiture of individual identity. Therapy can be seen as another kind of ideological endeavor that encourages patients to find their true selves without being swallowed up in the service of the larger group, system, or ideology.

Confession places issues of identity squarely back on patients' shoulders. As a by-product of patients' own histories, confession forces patients to return to a crucial piece of their lost or disowned identity. Confessions thereby enable patients to reclaim their own histories.

Other analysts (e.g., Lichtenstein, Balint, and Winnicott) conceptualize benign regression as a process that permits patients to return to much earlier preoedipal periods as a way of reclaiming the past in a new, less traumatized fashion. Balint (1979), for example, describes the possibility of experiencing a new beginning in the glow of the analyst's empathy.

I am reminded here of Ben, a 27-year-old sophisticated graduate student, who blushingly confessed that he was afraid of going to his doctoral defense, even though he knew it was a formality. When I asked Ben to imagine his committee members in detail (who they were and what they were doing), he unhesitatingly revealed that they were carbon copies of members of his persecutory family, who "did not give a damn about me and gloated when I failed." When I gently asked Ben what he would like to say or do to these fantasized examiners, he stuck out his tongue and, with his thumbs in his ears, made digital gestures with his fingers. He also called them bloodsuckers and vermin, and said he was going to succeed despite them.

After this episode of benign regression, the patient momentarily looked startled, but then adopted a relaxed posture, and sheepishly smiled for the first time in months. He exclaimed, "I guess I acted a little silly, but it felt so good. I never confronted those vultures then, and I felt so powerful when I told them off now. For the first time, I can actually see the difference between the examiners, who really like and respect me, and my family."

In the safety and empathy of the analytic environment, Ben was able to return to a battle-scarred past to face his persecutory objects as a nonvictim. By confronting and triumphing over his archaic objects, Ben was able to see his examiners in a new, benign light.

The constancy of ritual prepares the patient for renewal. One patient found that he was able to curtail his cycle of procrastination by taking a bath before writing. The act of bathing, with all its soothing, womblike connotations, engendered the security and relaxation necessary to invoke a ritualized past cleansed of its procrastinative debris. By repeating the benign ritual, the patient became sufficiently mobilized to press forward in creating his future.

The ritualized aspects of therapy likewise accord the patient the courage to move forward. In therapy the patient/confessant, over time, establishes an equilibrium between the anxiety-provoking change set in motion by confession and the reassuring discovery of repetition. The very predictability of the props (e.g., spatial and temporal features of the office setting), along with the reliable presence of the analyst, recharges the patient in such a way that return (benign regression) and renewal become expected, and even welcomed, phenomena.

I end this chapter with the confessions from du Maurier's novel *Rebecca* (1938), which underscore the jubilation that confessions can bring in transporting individuals into the higher realms of redemption and renewal. The story turns on a sequence of revelations. Brought home to the estate of Manderly, the second Mrs. de Winter is haunted by the image of her deceased predecessor—the beautiful, sophisticated, adored Rebecca. The new bride ruminates that surely her husband's brooding preoccupation stems from his inability to forget this magnificent woman or his love for her.

But when the unhappy bride at last confesses these suspicions, her husband makes a startling confession of his own. "You think I loved Rebecca? I hated her!" He goes on to reveal the cause of his preoccupation—he himself had brought about Rebecca's death. These twin confessions provide a new and stronger basis for love and alliance. Freed of their burdens, the de Winters prepare to begin a new life.

Confessions, in and out of therapy, furnish patients with a foundation for the rediscovery of their histories. Benign regressions that may accompany confession fuel patients who are now less encumbered by the past to move into new ways of being and relating. In owning the past and integrating it into the present, the patient can see an ever-widening view of his or her reowned self in relation to old and new objects.

6
Childhood and Adult Confessions

The choice to conceal or reveal, in childhood and adulthood, forces us to face a moral quandary. The young child has already internalized notions of good and bad with the formation of the superego—a process that Klein (1975) theorizes may already be present in rudimentary form in the first year of life. Since many of our secrets incorporate a good-bad dimension, patients may be especially reticent to reveal adult secrets of recent vintage, inasmuch as fantasized and/or real moral repercussions cannot easily be obscured by the veil of time and "childhood innocence."

We lack the comfort of set rules in our confessions. The child who is severely punished for a revealed naughty deed may internalize the notions that not only what he or she did was wrong, but also that he or she is intrinsically bad. The adult may thus feel compelled to repress or strenuously suppress subsequent secrets, since the relentless parental superego leads the patient unconsciously to anticipate similar condemnation from later objects, including the therapist.

Alternatively, adult confessions (confessions that concern secrets emanating from adult thoughts, feelings, wishes, or deeds) carry somewhat different moral concerns. Illicit or quasi-legal activities that may endanger the larger community, such as child abuse or intended murder, have already resulted in legal rulings that have weakened the "rule" of confidentiality that historically had been sacrosanct. The landmark Tarasoff case in California, in which a therapist was held partially accountable for his patient's confessions of intended murder, connotes that *both* patient and therapist must be more wary about such adult confessions.[1]

This chapter examines childhood and adult confessions viewed retrospectively by adult patients. While *all* confessions contain childhood antecedents, adult confessions from the more recent past manifest additional features involving a wider social continuum in which political, legal, and economic concerns figure more prominently.

Ellenberger (1966) was one of the few analysts who attempted to delineate some of the major categories of patients' secrets, including: thwarted love or jealously, hatred, and ambition; physical illness; moral offenses (e.g., petty theft); sexuality; and painful remembrances of traumatic events. Norton, Feldman and Tafoya (1974), who looked at secrets among students, found that students share more secrets about sex and failure than about any other topic. The secret rated riskiest to reveal was: "I have had incestuous relations."

Norton et al. discovered that the range of secrets was considerably greater for students who were in psychotherapy. While the authors obtained their data comprising 359 secrets through an encounter group exercise, the temporal constraints, demand characteristics of the exercise, and relative anonymity of the participants beg the issue of studying confessions as they emerge in the therapeutic dyad in the context of the patient's life history. An objective typology thus can never satisfactorily capture the patient's phenomenological experience of what constitutes a secret.

CHILDHOOD CONFESSIONS

The Case of Kitty

Childhood confessions can be operationally placed on a continuum ranging from two years of age to adolescence. The earliest secrets that patients reveal are characterized by a predominance of self-related concerns. The young child of two to seven years of age

---

[1] These ethical issues and their broader ramifications are extensively dealt with in Chapter 11: "Ethical Dilemmas."

operates substantially on egocentric principles (Piaget, 1966/1977). As captive within his or her own viewpoint, the object is taken into account only insofar as the child fears repercussions from external authority figures.

Among the most common secrets from this period that emerge in psychotherapy are petty theft, cruelty to animals, bullying another child, lying, bodily control issues, sexual experimentation, school pranks, and chicanery directed at parental and pedagogic authority figures. Even the most straitlaced patients note the discrepancy between the feelings connected with the revelation of secrets (accompanied by some guilt or shame) and those experienced at the time of the event. One patient succinctly illustrated her childhood egocentric perspective when she stated, "I really loved to tear the wings off butterflies. It never occurred to me at the time that they felt pain. I only knew how engrossing I found this activity to be."

The young child may engage in forbidden, fun-filled activities that have unforeseen consequences. Kitty, a 25-year-old computer programmer, revealed the near-catastrophic consequences that befell her when, as a five-year-old, she discovered that a family of bees resided in a telephone pole. Her cousin had made her a bow and arrow, and as her first target she aimed at the telephone pole. In Kitty's words, "All of a sudden, a swarm of bees descended on me and I ran for dear life. I did get stung, but not as severely as I might have. It never occurred to me that the bees would fight back."

Kitty, caught up in her enjoyment, could not switch perspectives and anticipate the bees' reaction. The visible bee stings forced her to tell her parents, who severely reprimanded her for her stupidity. It was only in retelling the incident 18 years later that Kitty expressed remorse and shame at what she had done. The childhood secret had been reevaluated in the light of greater cognitive and emotional awareness.

The Case of Lucy

Many of the childhood confessions that patients relate involve striking instances of the patient as victim (e.g., confessions involving humiliation at the hands of parents or other adults) rather than the victimizer. Lucy, a 24-year-old administrative secretary, reported feelings of dissociation and diffuse anxiety that made her feel as though she were going insane.

At first she avoided any mention of her childhood, and would deflect the topic back to her current symptoms and life circumstances. Then she finally blurted out, "I can't spend one more session avoiding the recurring event that I am afraid may have damaged me for life.

"My father, who was six feet, four inches tall and a corrections officer, used to get into fits. When these came over him, he would pull my hair and bang me against the wall. Sometimes I would lose control and urinate. That would make him even more furious, and he would start to kick me and scream obscenities at me.

"Each time this happened, I believed I was going to die. Sometimes I would even pray for death to come and take me out of my misery. Even though he would attack me for no reason, he apologized to me only once, when my mother threatened to leave him. Yet my father would always make me apologize to him, since he said I deserved what I got."

Having adopted a self-blaming stance, Lucy would apologize for everything, including her confession that betrayed the collusive family secret. During the course of analysis, Lucy was able to see how this overwhelming childhood event pervaded her entire life. It contributed to her fear of intimacy (intimacy unconsciously being equated with violence); anxiety, especially in closed spaces like the subway (involving feelings of being unable to escape a situation of impending doom); and depersonalization (harkening back to her wish and defense in which she was no longer integrally there to submit to her father's brutality).

The expression and exploration of the childhood secret enabled Lucy to acknowledge a still more deeply hidden secret: her hatred of and murderous feelings toward her father. As she began to see herself in a new light, as a person who did not have the power to control her father's tirades, she was able slowly to integrate the realization that she was not to blame. Further, Lucy's bonding with a new benign object enabled her gradually to expel the toxic paternal introject in tandem with the gradual internalization of the analyst. Lucy's secret virtually paralyzed her during most of her life. While her symptoms (anxiety and depersonalization) immediately began to diminish following confession, the rebuilding of self and object relations has been a slower process. Still, the temporal distance and wider array of cognitive tools available to the adult patient enabled Lucy to face, and ultimately master, a traumatized past, secure in her relationship with the maternal analyst.

The Case of Brigitte

I have introduced the idea that many childhood secrets involve children being manipulated as passive pawns in their parents' power maneuvers. With regard to physical violence and incest, children often recognize their positions as passive victims trapped in no-exit situations. Even more insidious are those secrets in which the patient unconsciously has become a direct victim of a parent's machinations.

One such patient was Brigitte, a 37-year-old fashion coordinator who, in revealing her secret in a noncommittal manner, was at first unaware of the devastating impact that these events had had on her, then and in the present. Brigitte began, "When I was ten years old, my mother dressed me in maternity clothes and sent me on errands. Everyone would say, 'Poor child. Only a child and already pregnant.'"

Brigitte's mother, who was then 30, was ashamed that she was pregnant, as her husband was a womanizer and came home only to visit. Her mother subsequently neglected the patient's baby brother, who would go unfed and fall out of the crib. Brigitte recalls having to rush home from school to take care of her brother and next younger sister.

Brigitte continued, "All my mother would do was sew. Even though she wouldn't take care of her own kids, she would have friends and neighborhood kids visit and converse with her." When Brigitte made these series of confessions, she was apologetic for her mother's conduct, and was compliant or martyrlike regarding herself.

When I asked Brigitte how her mother made her feel, she replied, "I felt that she wasn't totally bad. After all, I never really expected anything for myself. Even to this day, I don't want much." I rejoined, "That's why it's good you came to therapy. You got something just for yourself."

Brigitte then opened up with a flood of memories in which she assumed the Cinderella-like mother role, her childlike mother having abnegated almost all of her duties. She summarized her dilemma by saying, "It wasn't just that I felt I didn't deserve more, but also that I had so much responsibility that I could never get away and just be a kid with my friends."

Brigitte's childhood secrets and subsequent confessions underscore two fundamental issues that are vital for the therapist's understanding and treatment of confessions:

1. Patients like Brigitte, who are unconsciously locked into a dynamic of serving as a parent's selfobject extension (in this instance, as mother to her own mother, as well as siblings), are often given to expressing extremely dramatic secrets in an understated manner. Paradoxically, the more severe the child-

hood trauma, the less emotive the patient may be, since the patient who is an unwitting "prisoner of childhood" (Miller, 1981) dares not, or cannot (due to developmental deficits or defenses), acknowledge the helplessness and rage felt toward the parent.

Confession of such childhood events in therapy facilitates cognitive clarification, eventuating in the reevaluation of self and object relationships, past and present. The working through of the dynamic content of such childhood secrets in time results in the uncovering of the even more repressed secret—namely, the hidden affect (in Brigitte's case, murderous rage)—that is generally cut off from the original confession.

2. Brigitte's confessions contained the kernel of an ongoing life motif involving responsibility for others, holding back, and self-denial. Since these themes sweep into the present as enduring entities, patients' current life issues frequently provide cues that help pry loose long entrenched resistances that conceal the historical secret.

Since the present circumstances are often viewed in a more matter-of-fact way by such patients, exploration of current material can be a valuable first step in the unearthing of telescoped, repressed events. Brigitte, for example, reported that she would often hold herself in all day and not go to the bathroom, because she had so much work to do. When I asked Brigitte if she held herself in in other areas of her life, she at first shrugged off the question and looked blank. As the theme of self-denial appeared repeatedly in a variety of current contexts, I would gently repeat my question.

In time Brigitte herself laid the groundwork for the disclosure of her secrets by discussing her life themes as separate from their more threatening historical context. The relief afforded by these confessions enabled the patient to take steps in the direction of greater risk, as she continued to cut through the primary transference resistance in which the therapist was equated with her punitive parents.

Brigitte also experienced greater self-worth, beginning with her recognition that being listened to was a new, esteem-enhancing experience. In such instances the childhood secret signals the onset of a continuous life theme. This motif can be completely overturned only by the discovery and acknowledgement of the original set of secrets in order to create a rupture in the insidious legacy of the past.

Sexual Experimentation

Young children between the ages of four and eight often play "doctor" and similar games that become integrated into their developmental repertoire. Many patients recall being caught by parents who treated such activities as shameful, disgusting, or even criminal. For patients of Catholic origin, such parental reactions were subsequently reinforced by religious instruction at school, so that these pleasurable activities became transformed into shameful and/or guilt-ridden secrets to be buried at all costs.

Nadine, a 37-year-old teacher, confessed the following episode: "Between the ages of five and nine, all the children in our neighborhood were caught up in the game of doctor. After a period in which only members of the same sex would engage in 'pulling down pants' and other such fun-filled pursuits, we graduated to the next stage, in which boys and girls examined each other. I remember getting hold of a pair of pink plastic toy scissors. Chip, a six-year-old boy, and I (also six) decided to play surgeon that day, and I was to be the surgeon.

"We were standing under the overhang of the garage, and I recall having his penis in between the legs of the scissor. Just then my mother came out on the balcony to hang clothes, and, upon looking down, let out a piercing scream. I dropped the scissors, I guess in the nick of time, and wonder what would have happened had my mother not appeared when she did."

This childhood confession again illustrates that young children frequently do not take into account the consequences for the objects involved. While we can clearly note the oedipal-castration components (see chapter 8), for our purposes at this time, it is important to realize that because Nadine's mother took the time to explain the potential consequences of the act, and did not continue to castigate the child or make her feel disgusting or unworthy, this secret did not herald the onset of a life in which sex would be viewed with trepidation or loathing. Only when Nadine became a teenager and started to assimilate the concepts of castration and its aftermath, did she first experience guilt about the event, and make it a secret.

The reevocation of this secret years later in therapy took place around Mother's Day when the patient, who was having sexual problems with her husband, spontaneously felt tears well up at the memory of her mother, who treated her with kindness and patience in the face of a potentially explosive incident. The benign reception of a secret by the childhood object facilitated the revival of that moment in the positive transference.

Preadolescence

During this period the individual may be more reticent to confess, because of changes in the perception of self in relation to the parental object. The parent is now differentiated and seen, to a much greater extent, as an external source of power and retribution, as well as the purveyor of internalized values and outlooks. Further, the person who possesses a secret now also takes into account other objects who may be implicated by the confession.

Sullivan (1953) refers to the same-sex "chumships" of preadolescence. In these friendship groupings, the communal nature of endeavors frequently results in secrets that involve more than one person, in contrast to many secrets of the early years in which the child's deeds are primarily self-related or selfobject-related.

Common confessions from the chumship years subsequently divulged in psychotherapy concern group issues, such as "peeing contests," in which boys vied to see who could urinate the farthest (such secrets related years later in therapy often are told with a mixture of bravado and shame); communal stealing, akin to Saint Augustine's confession of stealing pears; and assorted pranks at the expense of siblings or parents to enhance one's standing in the group.

These secrets frequently are concealed in order to protect the other secret-sharers whose self-esteem is strongly rooted in such activities, and to maintain a sense of collective identity experienced as bound up in the communal secret. In Twain's *The Adventures of Huckleberry Finn* (1885/1940), Huck's harboring of the slave, Jim, concerns a collective secret in which Jim's very life course is at stake. The secret life adopted by the dyad also provides Huck and Jim with an identity as freedom-loving fugitives outside the societal order in which confession would destroy their collective destinies and ideals.

My patient Andrew, a 31-year-old insurance salesman, haltingly confessed that he had been raped by a group of neighborhood boys when he was nine. Andrew commented, "The reason I never told anybody up until now was that I both feared my father's reaction and was afraid that once the word got out about what had happened, these boys would continue to take their revenge on me. They did rape me more than once, but the fear of even more dire consequences happening to me if I should tell made me keep my mouth shut until now."

Without further elaborating on the dynamics of the case, let me point out that the expansion of object relations in preadolescence and adolescence makes confession a risky venture. Should the bond of secrecy be broken, the confessant risks either ostracism by the group or spiraling revenge by the group that is already extracting a toll on one's self-integrity. As such, confessions from this period frequently are revealed many years later in psychotherapy when the patient no longer is involved with the group, yet feels compelled to confess in order to be free from the burden of these internalized albatrosses.

Adolescence

To the adolescent the parental object is frequently seen as a foe or competitor. Adolescents may, in fact, relish revealing secrets to their parents, either verbally or through their actions, as a way of asserting their autonomy or rebelliousness.

Patients have reported the following types of adolescent secrets that speak to these issues: drinking all the liquor in the parents' liquor cabinet; taking drugs under their parents' roof; standing in picket lines protesting against a parent's cause or occupation; and becoming a groupie or a follower of a religious or social cult that is strictly antithetical to parental values (Erikson's identity diffusion).

Since the secrets of adolescence are frequently flaunted before parents, one can well wonder why these issues recur as confessions in therapy years later. While the adolescent acts upon his or her thoughts and feelings in order to get a reaction from parents, the "real secret" involves the underlying dynamics between the patient and the patient's parents.

Thus an adolescent who spitefully confesses to his parents that he drank all their liquor is only revealing the surface secret. Imbedded in this communication may be the adolescent's desperate need to be paid attention to and be different and special. Should such incidents not result in the expected parental reaction or change the adolescent's life in the desired direction, massive disillusionment and esteem deflation may ensue.

It is these internalized thoughts and feelings that constitute the more profound secrets that are obscured by the acting-out behavior. The more deep-seated secrets impel adult patients to dredge up these adolescent incidents in order to address the incompleted parental battles that now arise in the transference.

Summary of General Issues in Childhood Confessions

Childhood confessions present the therapist with a host of issues that contain the following important elements:

1. While the earliest secrets are primarily self-related (White, 1980) and egocentric (Piaget, 1923/1977), as the child passes through separation-individuation, the object is increasingly taken into account as an internalized entity. The object is initially viewed as having retributional power. The patient can subsequently use the object to assert his or her own autonomy via "acted-out-secrets" that may be willingly relayed to parents as a way to establish the adolescent's growing sense of empowerment.

2. Childhood secrets may constitute either discrete, discontinuous episodes (e.g., stealing a candy bar one time) or recurring life themes (e.g., cases of parental abuse—Lucy and Brigitte). In these latter instances, the disclosure of the secrets resulted in the first break in a repetitive pattern of unsatisfying, complacent "no-win" relationships.

3. Childhood secrets frequently have a cognitive-educational function that promotes growth either during the original disclosure or later in psychotherapy. The patient Nadine's mother was able productively to utilize Nadine's potential "surgical operation" on the boy's penis to teach her about the consequences of such actions without demoralizing her in the process. The patient thus did not play this incident out in her later sexual encounters or thoughts, since she was able both to assimilate her mother's teachings and to internalize her mother's benign attitude.

Moral Considerations

Confessions invariably involve a morality dimension. How the child (and later patient) processes secrets depends upon historical experiences with introjected parental objects (Freud, 1923), level of moral development (Piaget, 1932, 1966; Kohlberg, 1969), and sex differences in moral outlook (Gilligan, 1982).

I have already outlined how our earliest secrets are primarily self-related. From a self psychological perspective, one can readily discern how the young child would wish, above all, to protect the integrity of the nascent self, especially before this fledgling self has fully achieved separation-individuation. While most confessions take place in an object relational context, the young child in the grips of a confessional dilemma is rarely relating to the object *qua* individuated object. Allegiance to the self through the maintenance of self-congruity becomes the major conceptual concern.

Both Piaget and Kohlberg theorize that as we develop, morality increasingly becomes directed inward. Because we are expected to have developed a higher level of morality by adulthood, current secrets may be considered more risky to reveal. The length of time that has elapsed since the action that constitutes a childhood secret occurred, along with the rationalized greater naiveté of early life, contributes to many patients' greater willingness to disclose childhood secrets. Resistance is often greater in adult confessions because patients may feel more responsible for the incident, and also because they may have realistic fears about the legal or ethical consequences of confession. If a confession concerns illegal or quasi-legal intentions or activities, the rule of confidentiality may be overruled by the therapist's duty to protect the larger community. (See Chapter 11 for further discussion of these issues.)

Further, even should the confession not involve illegal or community-endangering activities, because the secret is current, the patient cannot temporally mute the event, nor can he or she facilely protect the identities of the players, who may be recent "accomplices" to the secret. Because the act or thought is of recent vintage, the patient cannot hide behind the youthful shields of inexperience and lack of knowledge.

Gilligan (1982) has demonstrated sex differences in how women and men conceptualize morality—differences that also enter into the confessions revealed by male and female patients. In Gilligan's words, "The moral imperative that emerges...with women is an injunction to care.... For men, the moral imperative appears rather as an injunction to respect the rights of others..." (p. 100).

Whereas male conceptions of morality involve a more autonomous "hands-off" ethos, women's responsibility for care includes a connection with others. It is not surprising, based on Gilligan's findings, that many confessions presented by female patients concern protection of abusive parents. This form of morality, in which the care of others is paramount, accounts for why patients such as Brigitte and Lucy were reticent for most of their lives to acknowledge, even to themselves, the extent of their mistreatment. To confess, in this nurturance-oriented morality, is to hurt the parental abuser and the self, who remains inextricably intertwined with the object.

I have observed that many more female patients consciously conceal childhood secrets in order to protect others who were involved. Gilligan's (1982) observations that in women the notion of care is at first self-critical, rather than self-protective, relates to my clinical findings that female patients, more often than male patients, initially blame themselves and protect the parent in their confessions.

For all patients by far the most disturbing secrets concern those unconscious manipulations perpetrated by parents "for the child's own good" (Miller, 1983). These patients spend much of their lives defending against, rather than protecting, parental pathology.

Confessions herald a shift in moral outlook as patients are forced to examine and cognitively reappraise a given episode or series of episodes. In the case of unconscious secrets that spontaneously emerge during psychotherapy, cognitive reappraisal begins with the recognition of material as a secret. Once the labeling process takes place, patients are primed to see themselves in a new light. For patients who protected their parents at extreme cost to themselves, the realization that they were not to blame results in a closer scrutiny of their parents' morality. The patient Brigitte, whose mother orchestrated a situation in which the neighbors thought that Brigitte was pregnant at ten years of age, came to realize that the rationalizations she had developed to protect her mother also protected the patient from the painful recognition that her mother's morality did not extend beyond her own self-orbit. Brigitte became her mother's selfobject insofar as she contributed to her mother's security operations and well-being.

Confessions thereby enable patients to reevaluate their own and others' perspectives on morality. For patients who are predominantly self-blaming, confession initiates a process in which the complex dynamics of *all* the actors who played a role in the secret are explored.

The working-through process, in such instances, sometimes results in a morality tilt in the opposite direction. Parents or siblings now may be seen as the villains who are judged responsible for the patient's present plight. As the patient continues to explore and more fully understand the complexities of the dynamics between the self and other significant objects, this abrupt shift from self-blame to other-blame in time gives way to a more moderate position in which understanding and greater acceptance are substituted for recriminations and blame.

Another variant of cognitive reappraisal takes place in confessions in which the patient's moral perceptions of self are altered. The consciously straitlaced or perfectionist patient who rediscovers his or her childhood "indiscretions" may initially reevaluate the self in a negative, esteem-diminishing manner. I have observed this confessional outcome particularly among patients who are wedded to an image of perfection or goodness that is shattered by any secret that blemishes this illusory self-image. The emergence of secrets forces such patients to uncover and recover hidden aspects of self that expand their notions of morality to produce a more balanced and less inflated or deflated self-image.

Thus following confessions of such incidents as theft, cheating, or lying, perfectionistic or narcissistic patients might initially shift their "all-good" image of self to one characterized by disillusionment and negativity. The working through of such confessions again involves a cognitive reappraisal in which the patient's moral sensibility is altered in the direction of greater self-acceptance. While the secret might have initially prompted the patient to reevaluate the self as bad or imperfect, the continual examination of such material in the empathic therapeutic milieu promotes a more diversified view of a self less encumbered by impossible moral expectations.

ADULT CONFESSIONS

Expanding Object Relations

As the individual's object world expands, the number of persons involved in secrets, as well as the number of potential confessors, dramatically increases. Whereas childhood confessions generally concern parental objects, adult confessions move from a primarily individual or familial focus to include wider societal institutionalized objects. A case in point is the patient who confesses homosexuality in psychotherapy, but shies away from revealing the sexual orientation to family, friends, employers, and the larger community. I recall one homosexual patient who wished to become a minister in a conservative parish, and so had to contend with a fundamental secret that concerned not only his immediate objects, but also the religious institution and the community of parishioners.

Since the consequences of such adult confessions can emanate from many more objects, adult confessions are often more risky. The homosexual patient who weighed confessing outside of therapy risked the loss of support of his conservative family, abandonment by certain friends, and occupational and social ostracism by the community in which he lived. Thus many adult confessions of this nature (e.g., membership in a deviant subgroup or social movement, alcoholism, abortion) involve potential social, political, or economic consequences within an extended object relational framework.

Further, along with the extended object parameters, adult confessions also encompass a broader thematic and emotional range than those of childhood. The adult patient, who now can assume multiple perspectives, is able to participate in collective family secrets far beyond the cognitive developmental range of the young child, who is captive within his or her own perspective.

In a previous paper (Hymer, 1982), I wrote, "Collective family secrets often become hotbeds of dormant volcanic confessions. Patients frequently take responsibility for the preservation of the family's 'good name'; illegitimacy, mental illness, and intrafamilial violence are seen by some patients as more stigmatizing events than individually committed acts. While the patient may have assumed no direct role in the 'scandal,' he or she feels the guilt or shame via association with the 'sins of the fathers'" (p. 134).

Collective confessions—those involving the patient's collusion in a dyadic or group secret—are generally perceived by patients as fraught with great risk. The patient's need to uphold prevailing societal stereotypes and obey the implicit familial rules, particularly the myth of the family romance, results in the erosion of a cherished belief system for the patient who confesses to a family scandal.

Marsha, a 27-year-old systems analyst, was a patient whose secret remained unacknowledged throughout childhood and was recognized as a full-fledged familial secret only as an adult. Marsha persisted in the brooding conviction that she was doomed to fail in her job and in her relationships with men. A bright, articulate, and attractive woman who received positive feedback from authority figures and peers alike, Marsha continued undaunted in her *idée fixe* of impending failure.

Marsha described her role in her family as that of the "bright star" admired by her parents and younger siblings. During one session I asked her to draw a picture of her family. A fourth sibling appeared who was positioned strikingly close to Marsha, with the other siblings separated by a respectable distance.

When I asked Marsha about this person, she seemed bemused at her oversight in not having previously mentioned him. Although Dirk was her older brother, in her fantasy she had superseded him in the family. To maintain the image of the family romance, Marsha tried to obliterate her brother, who had been diagnosed as schizophrenic. Yet, from the nature of her drawing, it was evident that Marsha identified with her brother's "failure" and "craziness."

When Marsha's parents tried to conceal the seriousness of her brother's condition from the siblings, Marsha outwardly went along with the family romance, while unconsciously identifying with her brother's failure. Her drawing served as an inadvertent nonverbal confession that provided an important breakthrough in unraveling the secret of Marsha's obsession with failure. Through exploration of the family system set in motion by her confessional drawing, Marsha was able to gain incremental insights into how massive denial was entered into by the entire family as a way of protecting the family name at the expense of reality and the emotional development of the individual members.

Another patient, Lana, a 29-year-old homemaker, originally sought therapy as a victim of assault. After being attacked by two teenage boys, she was unable to travel by herself and she developed startle reactions that occurred several times a day.

Lana readily revealed her current secret in order to gain relief and information about how to deal with her symptoms, as well as further confessions that had to be made to lawyers, doctors, and the court. What was more difficult for Lana to acknowledge was the familial violence pervading her childhood that cognitively reemerged following her victimization.

Whenever I would ask Lana about her family, she would either divert the conversation to the present crime or describe her parents in vague, amorphous terms. What finally prompted the patient to break the familial code of silence was the rage she experienced when her mother, five days after the attack, minimized the incident by saying, "You should be over it by now."

Lana angrily exclaimed, "My mother's motto has always been: 'the family is sacred. Never let anyone know the family secrets.' I remember when my mother broke a plate over my head and threw a knife at me. My grandmother saw what happened, but was told to keep her mouth shut, since she should be grateful that she was allowed to live with us. Since no one ever acknowledged my mother's violent nature, I grew up feeling isolated and alienated." In Lana's family not only was the violence concealed from the outside world, but the members also colluded with each other to disavow or ignore the mother's outbursts, which were attributed to "that time of month" or "a temper."

The strength of the affects and symptoms brought about by the crime prompted Lana to confess the current victimization, which unwittingly brought to the surface the hidden maternal crimes that no one dared acknowledge. The adult secret, involving a much broader range of institutionalized objects, evoked the even more painful childhood secrets in which the patient was the ongoing victim of a sadistic mother.

Select Content Distinctions

While all adult confessions contain childhood correlates, their content embodies distinct features. I have already mentioned a number of adult confessions (e.g., homosexuality, deviant subgroup or social movement membership, addiction, and abortion) that have an impact on a much more extensive object relational network than do childhood confessions.

A broad adult confessional category concerns disclosures falling under the rubric of illegal acts and *sub rosa* activities. They include prostitution, drug trafficking, large-scale theft, gambling, and sometimes even intent to kill followed by murder, as evidenced by the Tarasoff case. Again, recent court rulings in California and several other states favoring the community's welfare over therapeutic confidentiality imply that both therapists and patients must be much more wary about indiscriminate confessions that may place them in single or double jeopardy. The community here becomes a silent, yet powerful, object that intrudes itself into the therapeutic relationship, which heretofore had been considered inviolable.

Adult confessions often are a self-reflective product of age and experience. Such confessions may take the form of self-abnegation or reproach—a cognitive state pervading Saint Augustine's *Confessions* that is commonplace in adult confessions, while relatively absent from children's revelations. Note the self-loathing in this excerpt from Antonin Artaud's letter to Doctor Allendy in 1927: "There is something rotten in me. In my mental process there is a sort of basic evil which hinders me from enjoying what destiny offers me" (quoted in Khan, 1974, p. 304).

We can sense equally vitriolic self-recrimination in Kierkegaard's 1839 *Journals*: "The whole of existence is poisoned in my sight, particularly myself...no man can console me, only God in

Heaven and he will not have mercy upon me" (quoted in Weigert, 1960, 11, 275, p. 521).

Extreme loneliness, futility, and self-abnegation run through Kierkegaard's self-reflections. Confessions in which patients reflect on their lives often are accompanied by more intense emotions than are confessions concerned with discrete events or acts. Such self-reflective discourse takes the form of a confession precisely because these patients as adults found themselves too occupied with external events to come to terms with the secret nature of their inner lives.

In these instances therapy sometimes becomes the sole means of self-reflection in an action-oriented life-style that prevents many patients from acknowledging whether their lives have indeed taken a course that is in harmony with their inner desires and thoughts. Confessions that involve such sweeping life issues often shock patients who have remained unaware of such fundamental material for a good deal of their lives.

For some, self-reflection and resultant remorse occur relatively early in life. In Emerson's 1822 journal, he writes, "In twelve days I shall be nineteen years old; which I count a miserable thing. Has any other educated person lived so many years and lost so many days?" (1965, p. 38). In an even earlier (1820) self-purging journal entry, Emerson confesses, "I find myself often idle, vagrant, stupid, and hollow. This is somewhat appalling and if I do not discipline myself with diligent care I shall suffer severely from remorse and the sense of inferiority hereafter. All around me are industrious and will be great, I am indolent and shall be insignificant" (1965, p. 37).

The temporal dimension assumes far greater significance in adult confessions. The passage of time carries in its wake opportunities for greater remorse at deeds not accomplished and lives not meaningfully lived. Such ongoing issues sometimes take on the aura of confessions for the first time in therapy when the patient realizes that secrets involve not only discrete events, but also broader quality-of-life concerns, such as accomplishing goals and leading a meaningful existence. It is these latter secrets emerging during psychotherapy that provide the greatest impetus for the patient to reexamine the direction that his or her life has taken in order to reconnect with primordial desires and goals that have been subsumed by parental/societal currents.

Adult secrets involve self-image and self-esteem issues to a far greater extent than do childhood secrets. Adults deliberately hide secrets that threaten to alter their image, and this resistance may manifest itself in therapy, as well. One patient who prided herself on her thrift came into my office with a nicely wrapped package. It was only months later that she shamefacedly confessed that the package contained a piece of diamond jewelry that she had bought when she was depressed.

Another patient, Paul, a 33-year-old successful businessman, finally confessed after three years that he feared that his penis was too small. The patient remarked that he never would have told me this humiliating fact, but felt obliged to, now that he was experiencing marital problems. The patient's waning self-esteem became symbolically centered on his penis. Paul felt constrained from revealing this secret before because his penis size was not congruent with his mental stature and career. Patients like Paul, who are so invested in maintaining a grandiose self-image, fear that confession will reveal a disparity that will ruin this constructed image.

Confessions that eventually do emerge often involve tremendous discontinuities between the outer self and the self-as-experienced. Highly accomplished patients may confess to feeling like impostors, attributing their success to luck or unforeseen factors. The secret self, estranged from the trappings of external achievement, is experienced by many such patients as lacking in confidence, stupid, unworthy, or even a failure.

Existential Factors

Many adult secrets pertain more to states of being than to concrete events. I have already mentioned patients who internally experience themselves as impostors or as deficient in some manner in tandem with their externally successful *mitwelt* social relationships. Patients who reflectively look back on their lives discover existential secrets that envelop their entire being, rather than more circumscribed childhood secrets. The child who engages in petty theft as a peer group maneuver is not likely to label himself or herself as a thief in adulthood, if such childhood behavior is abandoned. In these confessions the adult self is not likely to have incorporated the concept of thief as a permanent aspect of the patient's being.

The case of Gerald illustrates how a confession involving drugs may be seen as a state of being that becomes the patient's major, and eventually only, ongoing confession. Gerald, a 32-year-old designer, became heavily involved in a weekend drug-filled marathon in which he progressed from marijuana and cocaine to a dangerous mixture of drugs, including LSD, amyl nitrate, and a

number of amphetamines. While he initially discussed the motiva-
tion for his drug patterns in terms of a need to escape, have fun, be
paid attention to, and be admired, he would show little affect whenever he would tell me about his preoccupation with drugs, nor did
he make any effort to desist from or diminish drug usage.

During one session Gerald suddenly adopted a very serious
demeanor and pondered out loud, "I wonder what these drugs can
do to me?" I quietly said, "I wonder." Gerald became silent and then
burst into tears. "These drugs can kill me. Sometimes I think I want
to die. Why am I really taking these drugs? To escape from myself. I
loath myself. And the drugs aren't working to change that."

When his hidden, "loathsome" self emerged in affective and
cognitive technicolor, the patient realized that he was faced with the
difficult decision of further delving into this hidden aspect of self or
continuing to exist on the precarious, frenzied edge of life. Patients
who shy away from continuing to remain in contact with and
exploring all aspects of self, may find themselves in a situation parallel to that experienced by Henry James' protagonist, ironically
named Marcher, in *The Beast in the Jungle* (1903/1962). He spends
his life in readiness for a surprise, but nothing happens. By chance
Marcher meets May Bartram, whom he has not seen for ten years,
and she reminds him of the secret that he had revealed to her and
no one else.

Bartram summarizes the secret: "You said you had had from
your earliest time, as the deepest thing within you, the sense of
being kept for something rare and strange, possibly prodigious and
terrible, that was sooner or later to happen to you...and that would
perhaps overwhelm you" (p. 411). Marcher represents the grim
spectacle of the alienated, uninvolved self passively waiting for
something to fill the void. In Marcher's words, "It isn't anything I'm
to *do*, to achieve in the world... It is rather something...to wait for"
(p. 412).

May Bartram dies and the truth is revealed to him. "The fate he
had been marked for he had met with a vengeance—...he had been
that man of his time, *the* man, to whom nothing on earth was to
have happened" (p. 449). Marcher's passive uninvolvement was
revealed to him too late.

My patient, Gerald, actively became involved in drugs in order
to fill the void that plagued his existence. Not unlike Marcher, Gerald was waiting for the drugs to work their magic and change his
life. Through the therapeutic interchange, Gerald came to the startling realization—not too late—that drugs as a way of life enslaved
rather than liberated him. The drug-induced illusions of omnipo-

tence, charisma, and fearlessness provided only a fleeting state of well-being that unsuccessfully masked Gerald's loathsome and recriminatory self.

Cognitive Factors

The greater cognitive complexity and awareness ushered in by adult development allow the adult patient to recognize a greater quantity and quality of issues as secrets. Many secrets are only recognized as such at a more advanced age. The child with homosexual propensities may only fully acknowledge this sexual orientation and deem it a secret in adult life. The feeling that one is an impostor or that one's life is meaningless requires a broadening of experience along with self-reflection that only cognitively ripens into a secret later in life.

More confessional possibilities accrue with greater comprehension and facilitation with language. As we move from concrete to abstract thought, we not only broaden the potential range of secrets, but also have more sophisticated defenses available to disavow secrets.

The move toward abstract thought and greater phenomenological awareness is evidenced, for example, in confessions pertaining to patients' reassessment of their parents' influence on them. In a remarkable letter to his father, Kafka confesses, "You have been too strong for me.... Sometimes, I imagine the map of the world spread out and you stretched diagonally across it. And I feel as if I could consider living in only those regions that are not covered by you" (quoted by Broyard, 1982, p. 47). This confession reveals not only a cognitive mastery of a painful childhood continuum, but also the greater emotional range of adult confessions.

Many adult confessions concern power and ambition. A Hungarian patient confessed to me that during the war the only free item was sex. The patient continued, "Sex was the only thing you didn't need a coupon for, and that's what got me through the war." Another patient pleaded poverty for years and paid me a correspondingly low fee. Only after receiving a large inheritance that made her feel financially secure did she confess that she had a sizable bank account hidden away these many years. Without delving into the dynamic and transferential implications of these cases, suffice it to say that each patient's confession encapsulated the greater cognitive resourcefulness and power manipulations utilized by adult patients embroiled in adult secrets.

Contemporary secrets encompass far greater cognitive complexity, along with a broadened range of emotional possibilities and subject matter. The fact that adult secrets may involve actual repercussions or may pertain to the very core of the patient's being explains why patients are often more forthcoming with childhood secrets.

7

When Confessions Fail—Betrayal

Who among us has not experienced the sting of betrayal? Betrayal not only provides the subject matter for tragedy and melodrama, but also touches each of our lives. Yet, despite its ubiquity, scant psychoanalytic attention has been devoted to betrayal. One of the few direct references to betrayal was made by Freud (1905a) who wrote, "No mortal can keep a secret. If his lips are silent, he chatters with his fingertips; betrayal oozes out of him at every pore" (pp. 77–78).

Confession is not always salutary for patients. Their disillusionment with parental objects and other significant figures who betrayed them in the past may be revived in the transference. Moreover, analysts who have incompletely worked through their own feelings of betrayal may find themselves in the grips of negative countertransference with certain patients.

The *Oxford English Dictionary* (1971) offers three basic definitions of "to betray":

1. To be or prove false to; to disappoint the hopes or expectations of.
2. To mislead; seduce; deceive.
3. To disclose; to show incidentally.

Patients frequently allude to experiences of betrayal throughout the life cycle. The word betray derives from the Latin *tradere*—to deliver or hand over, in the sense that Judas betrayed Christ. Emily Dickinson (Coffin, 1862/1969) writes, "Except thyself may be/Thine Enemy—/Captivity is Consciousness—/So's Liberty" (p. 408). While most of us are abundantly aware of how we remain prisoners of our childhood, Dickinson exhorts us to become cognizant of our ability to free ourselves from the more oppressive shackles of our past.

Such deliverance from betrayal is not, and cannot be, provided by the idealized "analyst/rescuer." It is rather the initiative-taking patient, in concert with the examining, empathic analyst, who is able to undertake the challenging task of unraveling the web of betrayal into which the patient has fallen prey over a lifetime.

Certain secrets, though we may have knowledge of them, are not ours to confess. When Tantalus, the mythological king, revealed the secrets of the gods to his fellow mortals, punishment was swift and severe. As he stood under a fruit tree, up to his chin in water, the fruit and water retreated whenever he tried to satisfy his hunger or thirst. The gods of antiquity were equally merciless on Prometheus, who divulged to mortals the gods' secret of how to make fire. He was bound to a rock, and his liver unremittingly pecked at by birds of prey. In Dante's *Purgatorio*, the detested captain of the exiled Neri faction was dragged to Hell at the tail of a horse, his body shredded and hideously disfigured. This was Dante's punishment for one he saw as a traitor.

Betrayal was viewed as the ultimate infamy by the ancients. Punishment meted out to the traitor was regarded as harsh, but just. With our patients betrayal at the hands of parents is more subtle and less easily discerned (Miller, 1983). Parental betrayal is often denied or repressed by the child. Indeed, parental stratagems may be too sophisticated to be processed and evaluated by the young child.

Conversely, the child may confess parental secrets to outsiders. From an early age, the child learns that he or she is not an autonomous being, but a creature bound by loyalties and alliances. These bonds multiply as friends, lovers, spouses, children, and business associates come into our lives and make their claims on us.

As with the traitors of mythology, history, and literature, the stigma against betrayal in everyday life is strong—so strong that we have developed laws to rescue our traditional confessors from the dilemma of knowing to much. Husbands and wives are exempt from testifying against each other, while codes of confidentiality, for the most part, protect the special status of doctors, lawyers, and clergy.

Many patients have encountered betrayal in the form of blackmail, duplicity, or other stratagems at the hands of such high-risk confessors as parents, friends, or lovers. From a developmental perspective, the primary caretaker (generally the mother), in her desperate attempt to control her children, views efforts toward separation as betrayal to be extirpated. The child dares not become aware that he or she feels betrayed for fear that the connection to mother will be severed.

Betrayal impedes the development of trust as a necessary foundation for the confessional experience. Since betrayal not infrequently involves disclosure that has resulted in disappointment, deception, and disillusionment, patients who have experienced these adverse effects are reticent to confess. Awareness of the roots of betrayal, and of the resultant resistances manifested in psychotherapy, enables the analyst to deal with this phenomenon as an influence that interferes with both the development of intimate relationships and the pursuit of individualized aspirations in which the true self is empowered to thrive and prosper.

THE ROOTS OF BETRAYAL

Since many of our patients remain unaware of the existence of treachery on the part of parents who manipulated or deceived children "for their own good" (Miller, 1983), it is important that analysts begin to understand the historical antecedents of betrayal. The parents that Miller so ably depicts in *Prisoners of Childhood* (1981) and *For Your Own Good* (1983) view their child's efforts to separate from them physically and/or psychologically as a betrayal to be countered by withdrawal of love or other forms of psychological warfare. In passing through childhood as the parents' compliant child-automaton at the expense of the true self, the child dares not become aware that he or she feels betrayed.

Betrayal may be experienced at different stages of the life cycle by both members of the mother—child pair. The mother all too often feels betrayed by the "willful child" who persists in being himself or herself despite threats of reprisal. Maggie Tulliver, George Eliot's (1860/1965) child heroine, continues to be a nonconformist (e.g., cuts her hair in a "nonladylike" manner and briefly runs away to join the gypsies) in a family that is strictly rural Victorian. Maggie finds her contemporary equivalent in Rita Mae Brown's (1973) Molly Bolt—a gutsy southern girl who acknowledges her lesbianism and becomes a film student despite the provincialism that pervaded her childhood.

Both heroines decide to be their true selves despite everything. Such heroines capture our imagination and win our approbation precisely because they refuse to betray themselves (that is, to be disloyal to who they are) in order to maintain a tenuous relationship with parents they cannot respect. In lieu of adopting the "schizophrenic solution" of escaping parental tyranny by withdrawing into the fragmented self, such individuals were able, early on, to develop a cohesive sense of self in that both had "good enough fathering" to partially offset maternal deprivation.

The 11-year-old Molly's strong sense of self becomes apparent in her interchange with her not-so-bright cousin, Leroy. Leroy begins, "You say you're gonna be a doctor or something great. Then you say you ain't gettin' married. You have to do some of the things everybody does or people don't like you." Molly retorts, "I don't care whether they like me or not. Everybody's stupid, that's what I think. I care if I like me, that's what I truly care about" (1973, p. 36).

Molly, in part, is able to be self-affirming in that she has a source of support in her father, Carl. After Molly has locked her mother in the cellar, Carl defends her. "Carrie, the child's high spirited and she's smart, you got to remember that. That kid's quicker than all of us put together. She started reading all by herself when she was three with no help from any of us. You got to treat her with some respect for her brains. She's a good girl, just full of life and the devil, that's all" (p. 39).

Carl is here mentioning the one pedagogical principle that Miller (1983) advocates: the need to respect the child. While patients come to experience the resentment, rage, and sadness inherent in never being allowed to express the full range of thoughts and emotions intrinsic to the true self, heroines such as Molly and Maggie were able to avoid being betrayed by reaping the benefits of a second chance at being mirrored and being able to idealize their fathers (Kohut, 1977).

Many patients are unable or unwilling to recognize parental betrayal in childhood. Miller (1983) explains, "Since training in many cultures begins in infancy during the initial symbiotic relationship between mother and child, this early conditioning makes it virtually impossible for the child to discover what is actually happening to him. The child's dependence on his or her parents' love also makes it impossible in later years to recognize these traumatizations which often remain hidden behind the early idealization of the parents for the rest of the child's life" (p. 4).

The child who is prematurely thrust out of the nirvana of good-enough mothering may subsequently experience betrayal in the stark realization that he or she can no longer trust mother to be there on command solely for him or her. From the child's perspective, the widowed mother who suddenly acquires a lover or husband is betraying the sacred constancy of the mother-child bond. Betrayal here becomes linked to feelings of separation and abandonment.

Many subsequent betrayals assume the complexity of three or more persons who, in general, are affectively tied to each other. A frequent familial example of betrayal concerns mother reporting the child's misdeeds to father, who proceeds to punish the child. The child thereby comes to feel that mother is father's ally and not the child's. Mother may thus be experienced as betraying the child's expectations of her as supportive and understanding rather than retaliatory and persecuting (Klein, 1975).

Another illustration of interfamilial betrayal concerns siblings who report each other's wrongdoings to their parents in order to curry parental favor. Siblings betray each other by disclosing each other's indiscretions to powerful parents with whom they can identify and from whom they can gain approval. Unfortunately children discover that such stratagems are shortlived as each, in turn, falls victim to disclosure of his or her misdeeds, thereby giving the other siblings temporary leverage. Only in retrospect are siblings able to discern that their parents were the ultimate victors in being able to wield control through the constant round of betrayals perpetrated by siblings upon each other.

FUNDAMENTAL THEMES IN BETRAYAL

Control

One of the key elements in betrayal is the power to disclose or reveal. In Pinter's *Betrayal* (1978), Emma, the wife, who is having an affair with her husband's best friend, Jerry, is clearly the character with the most power, since she is the one with the most knowledge. Emma, for example, reveals her infidelity to Robert, her husband, four years before she tells Jerry about that confession. Thus Jerry lives under the assumption during those years that they are deceiving Robert and that the friendship between the two men is unaffected.

Rich (1979) writes, "Lying is done with words, and also with silence" (p. 186). In *Betrayal* each character knows how to manipulate the others by timing the disclosure of secrets or deceiving each other with the silence of withheld information.

In a similar vein, narcissistic parents attempt to maintain control of all information concerning relationships through deception and other manipulations. In order to maintain total control over children, such parents often attempt to keep siblings away from each other. Each child can thereby give his or her undivided attention to the parent.

In such familial matrices, the narcissistic mother often functions as the hub of the wheel, with all sibling spokes directly connected to her. She dares not allow affective relationships between siblings, since she views such cross-currents as disloyalty to her expectations that others be there unconditionally for her. In *Betrayal*, all the characters fear the severed connection with each other, but for narcissistic mothers, to be involved in relationships with others is to be disloyal to these mothers' needs to be the center of each person's universe.

Many patients view such controlling parents as vulnerable, and so maintain the *idée fixe* that their parents need to be shielded at all costs. Ruth is a 26-year-old copy writer whose mother operated on the principle of "divide and conquer." After her parents were divorced, her mother made her feel guilty if she spent any time with her father or spoke fondly of him. All three siblings grew up believing they disliked each other, only to find as adults, living apart from their mother, that they were beginning to discover and like each other for the first time. The mother's need to exert absolute control by having all information filtered through her, made each sibling realize, with sadness and regret, that their mother had sabotaged virtually all of their childhood relationships.

This patient was now debating whether to reveal to her mother that the patient's aunt (her mother's fraternal twin) was coming to visit the patient, since the two had been estranged for years. Ruth felt the need to protect her mother from the knowledge that she wanted to have a relationship with her aunt, because she believed that her mother was "not strong enough" to accept this fact.

Ruth came to realize that she had the right to both relationships and was not going to feel guilty for allegedly betraying her mother. She told her mother and was amazed to discover that while her mother did seem hurt, and attempted to dupe her into reconsidering, Ruth was able, for the first time, to resist this maternal maneuver in order to be true to her "true self" (Winnicott, 1975). A situation was thereby established in which familial relationships began to shift in the direction of choice, openness, and mutuality in lieu of control. As the siblings no longer cooperated with their mother's need to have exclusive relationships with each one, the mother, through her own analysis, was able to recognize her desperate need to control the world along with her readiness to see betrayal in anyone who wished to undertake an intimate relationship with someone other than herself.

Tanya, a 28-year-old businesswoman, received a birthday card from her mother, who added the following greeting: "For a dear daughter/With warm memories." Inside the card her mother continued, "Sweetheart—I don't know why, but my memories of you when you were a baby and a little girl are so dear and vivid."

The stunned patient offered her own apt interpretive translation of her mother's sentiments: "What she's really saying is that is when she could control me and make sure I loved her, since I was afraid not to, and didn't have any options."

The last sentence read, "I treasure some of my recollections and, without sounding maudlin, I love you for being one of the most terrific things I've done." This self-congratulatory ending not only epitomized this mother's omnivorous need always to hold the limelight—even on her daughter's birthday—but also betrayed, through the inclusion of the word "thing," her view of her daughter as a plaything, or even an inanimate object, there for her mother's enjoyment.

Such children often shy away from seeing how they were betrayed by mothers who, in their need to deceive in order to maintain absolute control, engage in all types of subterfuge. Rich (1979) comments, "The liar lives in fear of losing control. She cannot even desire a relationship without manipulation, since to be vulnerable to another person means for her the loss of control" (p. 187). For these patients the paramount need for engagement with such mothers allows these mothers an almost unlimited latitude for guises that ensure that their children remain extensions of themselves, and that they remain unaware that they were being betrayed.

Victimization: Self-Destructive and Other-Destructive Confessions

When we think of betrayal as disclosure of information, the notorious image of Judas Iscariot often comes to mind. Judas delivered Jesus up to his enemies secretly, by craft, in exchange for money. The secret Judas betrayed was the meeting place in Gethsemane, with the sign of betrayal to identify Christ ironically being a kiss.

In the biblical tale of Samson and Delilah, Samson's infatuation with Delilah proved to be his undoing. Here we find a double betrayal: Samson betrays himself in revealing that the secret of his strength lies in his hair; Delilah proves to be disloyal by collaborating with the Philistines to extract from Samson the secret of his strength.

The Bible presents betrayal to convey lessons in morality. Judas is ultimately remorseful and commits suicide. The archetypal villain repents. The victim (Christ) becomes the conqueror, and the betrayer becomes the guilt-ridden victim of his own actions. In the story of Samson and Delilah, Samson is presented as a sinner with overbearing hubris and sexual desire. As such he falls victim to his own lust and resultant vulnerabilities.

In instances of parent—child betrayal, the villains and heroes are usually not so clear cut. Often neither parent nor child is aware of the web of duplicity and complicity woven by parents who demand total attention and children who desperately comply in order not to be condemned for perceived slights that are magnified into major acts of disloyalty. Such parents continue to collect injustices over the years, so that children regularly fall victim to blackmail, dismissal, withdrawal of love, or other forms of condemnation.

Extratherapeutic confessions may result in the destruction rather than redemption of relationships. Many married couples implicitly or explicitly collude with each other to conceal their affairs. Should either partner decide to confess "for the good of the marriage," the unconscious need to destroy the partner and union is simultaneously satisfied.

In Shaw's *Mrs. Warren's Profession* (1894/1919), Mrs. Warren first confesses to her daughter, Vivie, her rise out of poverty through prostitution. It is Mrs. Warren's two subsequent confessions that embitter Vivie. Vivie finds out that she and Frank (the rector's son) are brother and sister, thereby abruptly ending their romance. The final coup that cements the destruction of the mother—daughter relationship is Mrs. Warren's disclosure that she is still a madam with "hotels" in various spots in Europe.

Vivie is unable to reconcile and integrate past transgressions with present happenings. Not only does she feel a victim of deception, but she also finds her hopes and dreams dashed in the wake of learning the truth about her mother's "secret life," which destroys her illusions of maternalism, respectability, and conventionality.

Simmel (1950), advising against indiscriminate disclosure, comments, "An ideal sphere lies around every human being...this sphere cannot be penetrated, unless the personality value of the individual is thereby destroyed" (p. 321). Every person is entitled to an area of privacy. Too much self-disclosure in marriage, suggests Simmel, can exacerbate marital difficulties.

Similarly, patients who indiscriminately bare all to the analyst during the first few sessions are often prime candidates for premature termination, fearing either that they have betrayed another's trust or that the analyst, with whom trust has not yet been sufficiently established, will betray them. I have already alluded, in previous chapters, to the therapeutic desirability of the analyst's setting limits on "overconfession" by borderline and schizophrenic patients during the earliest phases of therapy.

Patients who unswervingly trust others are especially prone to betrayal. Often prey to their own self-deception, they are more likely to be victims in others' schemes of deception.

Shakespeare's tragedies *Othello* and *Hamlet* force us to acknowledge how the protagonists' accumulation of distrust and self-deception ultimately results in self-destruction and other-destruction in the aftermath of the rage evoked by feeling betrayed. Othello's childlike naiveté enables Iago to enjoy Othello's blind trust. Iago's false show of loyalty enables him to betray Othello by falsely confessing to him and succeeding in the destruction of the innocent Desdemona, followed by Othello's suicide.

Hamlet expresses his rage in being "played upon" by Guildenstern. "Why, look you now, how unworthy a thing you make me! You would play upon me; you would seem to know my stops; you would pluck out the heart of my mystery;...do you think I am easier to be played on than a pipe? Call me what instrument you will, though you can fret me, you cannot play upon me" (111, ii, 371–379). Hamlet is enraged at the manipulations of those who seek to destroy him. His awareness of impending betrayal momentarily helps put him in charge of his life.

In Chapter 5 I described the patient, Jim, whose later bondage masturbatory fantasies related to his having tied up a six-year-old girl when he was an adolescent. Jim became victimized by his mother's betrayal of his indiscretion to relatives and neighbors. So great were the guilt and shame engendered in the public disclosure of a private aspect of Jim's sexuality that he was unwilling to trust himself with any form of interpersonal sex until he was 30 years old. Such betrayal in the form of public humiliation magnifies the significance of the incident in such a way that the patient not only is victimized by the betrayer, but also engages in self-victimization in the form of loss of self-esteem and an impoverished self-image.

Abandonment

Patients who have been psychologically or physically abandoned in childhood often come to rely on things, rather than people, to counteract massive feelings of betrayal by parents who failed to live up to their children's expectations of object constancy. Searles (1979b) has emphasized the adaptive, nonpathological aspects of communion and union with the nonhuman environment. "The theme that...expresses the deepest and the most comprehensive meaning of any human being's identity struggle...consists in his effort...to maintain, and further develop, meaningful relatedness with those also vast areas of the objectively nonhuman world which can contribute affirmatively to his own internal human world—can "help" him...to find consolation, strength, absorption-in-life and, above all, a meaning in existence through the knowing that he is at once uniquely individual and indissolubly part of the universe" (pp. 46–47).

For Michael, a 27-year-old engineer, things had served as transitional objects with which to pass the time and help him through the urban loneliness that was his lot as an only child in mid-Manhattan who was not allowed to play in the streets. His toys were his constant, faithful companions, which, unlike people, could not betray him. One of Michael's earliest memories concerned the playful activity of mixing colored water in test tubes that his father, who had died when the patient was seven years old, had given him. Test tubes came to represent his deceased father, and to provide an actual link to one of the few instances in which his father's smile of approbation permanently touched the young child.

This same patient became enraged when he perceived that things abandoned him. When his new shirt that was only two months old started to unravel, Michael angrily exclaimed, "I felt betrayed and let down. I put my faith in things, since people are so fickle. Now it seems that things can be fickle too." I commented: "It hurts when things let you down, since you expect them to be constant." To which Michael immediately replied, "Yes, I take good care of them, and expect them to do the same by me."

While Michael's statements might appear to reflect his animistic view of a world in which things express intentionality (Piaget, 1923/1977), over time it became clear that things represented an extension of the patient's self, with which he could identify and which he could control. Michael periodically stated, "I see things as a radiation of self—who I am and what I am. That's why I feel so betrayed when things break down or fall apart."

For Michael things not only served as selfobject extensions, but also harkened back to his deceased father who came alive when Michael engaged in chemical experiments or played with his model trains and camera equipment. Commerce with things strengthened Michael's sense of self along with his identification with his deceased father.

With patients like Michael, it is important that the therapist not "correct" the patient's perception, but garner as much material as possible in order to understand the underlying meaning of "thing betrayal" in the context of the patient's life history. It is equally useful for the therapist to monitor any negative countertransferential reactions that may emerge in which the patient is seen as foolish or childish. Such feelings are particularly dangerous when they induce the therapist to educate and advise the patient rather than to explore the meaning of betrayal within the context of the current transference as well as historical relationships. In Michael's case such explorations revealed that Michael's relationship to things, far from being a pathological manifestation of animism and psychotic identification, underscored his hidden identification with his beloved, deceased father.

For many patients who underwent parental losses in their childhood or adolescence, "thing constancy" comes to replace the betrayal experienced in the form of ultimate disillusionment through unforeseen parental death. Especially for the very young child whose expectations encompass parental omnipotence, and even immortality, death is the ultimate betrayal. Yet these feelings often remain outside of awareness, partly because the child is not given the opportunity to process the death with empathic adults or is not developmentally ready to conceptualize death (Stolorow & Lachmann, 1980), but also because the child may feel responsible for the death and thus believe that he or she has no right to such sinister feelings. Since the child's perceived disloyalty (in thought or action) makes him or her feel, in part, culpable for the parental abandonment, he or she dares not become aware of the betrayal that has been experienced.

Greg was a 29-year-old attorney who had experienced the double trauma, between the ages of 15 and 16, of losing both his father and mother to sudden illnesses. Over the past few years, Greg had adopted the avocation of buying and selling antiques with a fervent passion. He remarked on several occasions, "I love the look and feel of these things in my hand. The ones I really love I can keep forever."

When Greg's girlfriends upbraided him for his emphasis on "surfacy" pastimes, he was both disappointed and bemused by these reactions. What emerged several years after the onset of therapy was that Greg did cherish things over people, since he viewed things as immortal and therefore totally reliable and controllable. Thing constancy was substituted for object constancy. Greg tearfully related, "People die on you, and leave you when you most need them. My antiques will always be with me."

The False Self and the Selfobject

Betrayal often takes place in the context of the narcissistic parent who disappoints the child's expectations. Miller (1981) writes, "Later, these children not only become mothers (confidantes, comforters, advisors, supporters) of their own mothers, but also take over the responsibility for their siblings and eventually develop a special sensitivity to unconscious signals manifesting the needs of others" (p. 8).

In Chapter 4 I introduced Margie who, as an unusually precocious nine-year-old, was forced to take over all household responsibilities following her mother's coma and convalescence that extended over years. While Margie cheerfully performed these duties (Miller's "the parent is always right" pedagogical tenet), during therapy she began to show resentment over her lost years of childhood devoted to the "Cinderella ideal" extolled by her parents. Not only had this patient begun to experience betrayal through the belated realization of parental deceit and manipulation, but also in the acknowledgement of her lost childhood. Margie wistfully noted, "I was a mother to my mother and still play that role. I never knew better until now, and was always made to believe that this was my due. Even now, I wish that I would be the child and my mother could be like a real mother."

Pinter's aforementioned *Betrayal* is the story of three people: a woman, her husband, and her husband's best friend, with whom she has had an affair. Over the course of seven years, the original betrayal—the woman of her husband, the man of his best friend— begets others, so that deceit and betrayal enter into other relationships, including that of the lovers themselves.

Underlying this rather simple theme is a wealth of psychological issues revolving around the fear of autonomy and the erection of the compliant false self to escape the loss of the other. The three characters will deceive each other and play the roles they believe the other expects so as not to be rejected. Like some of our patients who are willing to do or be anything in the service of becoming their parent's selfobject, Pinter's characters are willing to betray each other and be betrayed in order to circumvent the difficulties that arise with the emergence of the autonomous self.

Since our patients, like Pinter's characters, are often unwilling to accept the coexistence of the dual-track system of consciousness (Grotstein, 1981)–that is, our need simultaneously to seek connectedness and independence–too often they find themselves locked into deceptive situations in which the false self is ascendent in order to remain tied to the object at all costs. Jerry, the lover, for example, at several points discusses his inability to exist separately from Emma. Jerry's attempt to capture Emma suggests a desire not for relation but for completion.

Our patients, like the trio in *Betrayal*, adopted the only solution that they thought was available to them in childhood to contend with parental betrayal. Since, from such parents' perspectives, betrayal involved independence of will and activities, such children developed a compliant false self to fit the parental need for selfobject relationships. The cycle was thereby established, maintained, and perpetuated into subsequent generations (should such children not become aware of these patterns of betrayal in adulthood): namely, the child dares not be his or her true self and become aware of parental betrayal; and the parent dares not allow the child to develop an individual existence for fear of loss of control, entitlement, attention, and love.

BETRAYAL IN THERAPY

Both patient and analyst can experience actual and/or transferential/countertransferential betrayal. Some brief examples are offered to illustrate these different aspects of betrayal.

Analysts may, in fact, engage in sex with their patients, break the rule of confidentiality, and so on. Such primal betrayal not infrequently is experienced by the patient as a double blow, in that the analyst not only may deny the veridicality of the event, but also accuse the patient of hysterical transference distortions (Freeman & Roy, 1976).

The analyst's actual betrayal of a patient escalates the patient's distrust, in that the institution of psychotherapy not only tends to elicit transferential feelings of trust, but, in addition, involves an actual verbal or written contract and basic frame (Langs, 1978) that is designed to guarantee safety and trust. When the analyst acts "out of character" by making sexual advances or asking the patient for favors such as advice on stock transactions, the patient again feels used and abused and ultimately disillusioned by an object who allegedly was different from the betrayers in the patient's past.

The analyst may likewise experience actual instances of betrayal. Many analysts have had patients who attempted to defraud them of money or who substantially misrepresented their income so as to be charged lower fees. Still other patients "borrow" books or other artifacts from the analyst's office without permission or intent to return them.

Actual instances of betrayal in the patient–analyst dyad also overlap with transferential–countertransferential betrayal. Both analyst and patient may, at times, see in the other the parade of traitors who manipulated and deceived them. Since the earliest instances of betrayal at the hands of parents most often remain unacknowledged (Miller, 1983), the reevocation of feelings of betrayal in therapy can provide intense reactions that range from bitterness to despair as one or both members reexperience the earlier trauma of betrayal.

Transferential–countertransferential betrayal, on the other hand, need not be contaminated by actual misdeeds on the part of patient or analyst. A common example of transferential betrayal presents itself in the context of the analyst being perceived as the narcissistic mother who is robbing the patient of the right to be his or her true self. Such patients might fear that the analyst no longer will like them, or might even take revenge on them, if they express anger. Betrayal here takes the form of fears that the analyst will not live up to the patient's expectations of the "good mother" ideal and prove to be disloyal or manipulative.

Analysts who experience their patients as ingrates who take them for granted and do not appreciate them often countertransferentially feel themselves in the grasp of the rapacious parent whose impossibly high expectations for the child involved the notion the "everything is not enough." The "analyst/child" with such a history of impossible parental expectations, who has not fully worked through such issues in his or her own analysis, is destined for more than his or her share of perceived betrayal by patients.

A second common countertransferential perception of betrayal is felt when the patient terminates prematurely, or, in extreme situations, at all. The analyst, in such instances, often experiences betrayal in all three of its meanings: the patient is perceived as disappointing the analyst's expectations of a completed, successful analysis; the patient is deceiving himself or herself and the analyst; and, finally, the patient may inadvertently disclose some of the analyst's shortcomings to others, if termination does not take place on a mutually agreeable note.

Miller (1983) cites the methods employed in "poisonous pedagogy" to suppress vital spontaneity in the child: "laying traps, lying, duplicity, subterfuge, manipulation, 'scare' tactics, withdrawal of love, isolation, distrust, humiliating and disgracing the child, scorn, ridicule, and coercion even to the point of torture" (p. 59). Many patients who were thus manipulated and whipped into compliance remain unaware of being betrayed and hold fast to the image of the saintly parent. A 60-year-old patient who had enshrined the memory of his deceased mother one day revealed the method that his mother used to "cure" him of his fear of the dark. She locked him in a dark room and the terrified nine-year-old boy forced his hand through the window in order to escape. This same patient also suffered from childhood psoriasis, yet refused to acknowledge the coercion that was perpetrated upon him.

Many such patients who have repeatedly experienced childhood betrayal deny and split off even glaring parental defects in order to preserve the image of the idealized parent. For some patients so extreme is the splitting mechanism that when they begin to experience positive feelings toward the analyst, they become uneasy. These patients' parents exerted such omnipotent control over their children that alternative affective attachments were often frowned upon or censured. As such, these patients come to experience positive transference manifestations as parental abandonment. Should these patients "slip" and report negative parental attributes to the analyst, they may view these confessions as disloyalty to be met with by real or fantasized reprisals.

Many patients, moreover, often retrospectively legitimize the form of parental betrayal to which they fell victim. The reader may recall from Chapter 6 the patient Brigitte, whose father was a philanderer who rarely came home but did manage to get her mother pregnant on one of his visits. When Brigitte was ten, her mother dressed her in maternity clothes and sent her on errands. Everyone would make comments, such as "that poor child."

While Brigitte was empathetic to her mother's needs, and was able to rationalize this bizarre maternal manipulation, she at first was unable to empathize with the little girl who was subjected to public humiliation. For a long time, Brigitte could not experience the rage, pain, and sadness that went along with the realization that her mother had betrayed her on all three counts:

1. "Being false to." Her mother had misrepresented and manipulated the mother–child relationship.

2. "Deception." Her mother had knowingly and willfully deceived all public contacts by shifting the shame of her pregnancy onto her daughter.

3. "Disclosure." This mother manipulated her daughter into making a "false confession" of a spurious secret.

These examples, in particular, illustrate some of the basic tenets of poisonous pedagogy outlined by Miller (1983): "Adults are the masters (not the servants) of the dependent child. They determine in godlike fashion what is right and what is wrong.... The parent must always be shielded.... All this must happen at a very early age, so the child 'won't notice' and therefore will not be able to expose the adults" (p. 59).

While in some theoretical schema narcissistic patients are assumed to adopt the characteristic narcissistic transference configurations of mirroring and idealization (Kohut, 1971, 1984), patients who are betrayed by narcissistic parents initially may strongly resist any kind of positive transference reaction, as the formation of attachments and the development of trust are unconsciously associated with parental betrayal. The analyst simply functions as an "ear" to take in, passively, the contents of the patient's discourse. In this early phase of treatment, if the analyst appears too enthusiastic, or even supportive, the patient may become even more defensive or may terminate prematurely, since such outward gestures may be transferentially viewed as ruses to enable the patient to be betrayed again.

Since denial and splitting often operate as primary defenses during this early phase so that the patient can uphold the myth of the family romance and unblemished childhood, it is important for the analyst to be aware of countertransferential feelings, including frustration and impatience, that can inadvertently lead to confronting the patient in order to uncover the darker side of the patient's past. Should the analyst find himself or herself dealing with the patient in this manner, splitting can become intensified as the analyst is now viewed as the malevolent betrayer who is disloyal to the patient's conception of the past. The patient's parents may thus become even more entrenched as idealized figures.

Alternatively, the analyst who remains unobtrusive and yet receptive to whatever the patient has to offer is likely to keep such patients in treatment as they move into another phase in therapy. Since distrust is a fundamental element in betrayal, the analyst may now find himself or herself frequently being tested by the patient to see whether the analyst lives up to the expectations of "good parent" that have, in part, transferentially gelled.

Patients may, for example, deliberately miss sessions without calling or hand over bad checks to see whether the analyst will abandon them. Another form that testing might assume is the patient's identification with his or her own betraying parents by, for example, falsifying his or her income in an attempt to dupe the analyst into setting a low fee. While such patients expect the analyst to discover the deceit and retaliate against them, at this stage they also secretly hope that the analyst will accept them regardless of these external circumstances.

The analyst who proves that he or she can set limits and interpret such behavior, yet also remain constant in his or her loyalty to the patient throughout this testing period, can now monitor the gradual changes in the relationship with the patient. In some instances the patient for the first time feels that he or she has permission to enter into a relationship in which the patient can develop autonomy without fear of repercussions. With the gradual emergence of the true self, the patient no longer feels the need to remain bound to anyone again in a selfobject capacity out of fear of betrayal.

8
Preoedipal and Oedipal Confessions

Freud (1924, 1931) rendered the Oedipus complex the central secret of the child's existence. Nevertheless oedipal secrets cannot be divorced from their preoedipal precursors. Just as Oedipus' abandonment by his father and mother molded his subsequent triangular conflict, recent revisions and amplifications of Freudian theory (notably, Chasseguet-Smirgel, 1976; G. Blanck, 1984) assign major importance to the role of the omnipotent preoedipal mother and early object relations respectively. Preoedipal secrets, often strongly resistant to retrieval and/or verbal discourse, nonetheless are crucial for analyst and patient to understand in order to work through the "complete Oedipus complex" (G. Blanck, 1984).

Freud's first mention of the Oedipus complex appears in the Fliess correspondence on October 15, 1897 (Freud, 1887–1902). Once Freud was able to acknowledge his own Oedipus complex, he was able to contend clinically with the centrality of oedipal issues in his patients' lives. "Everything I experience with patients I find here," Freud confesses (quoted in Bernstein, 1976, p. 404).

With the oedipal issue sharply in focus, analysts and patients together could now decode the meaning of triangular relationships. Moreover, Freud, in *The Ego and the Id* (1923), argues that both positive and negative aspects must be taken into account in order completely to come to terms with the Oedipus complex. "In my opinion, it is advisable, in general, and quite especially where neurotics are concerned, to assume the existence of the complete Oedipus complex...the result is a series with the normal positive Oedipus complex at one end and the inverted negative one at the other, while its intermediate members exhibit the complete form with one or other of its two components preponderating" (pp. 33–34).

This broadening of the Oedipus complex enabled patient and analyst to explore multilayered secrets emanating from preoedipal origins through the oedipal period without having to resort to reductionistic formulations. Saint Augustine, for example, was extremely attached to his mother and reproached his father for his excessive sexuality, as well as for not being Christian. From a simplified oedipal perspective, one can here discern the kernel of the positive Oedipus complex (that is, maternal love and paternal rivalry).

If we now take into account the multiple facets of the oedipal drama, however, we see that the Oedipus complex is not neatly resolved by identification with paternal values—even if we assume God to be Augustine's surrogate father. Augustine renounces his common-law wife and illegitimate son in substituting a religious for a conjugal existence.

Yet even a cursory reading of his *Confessions* offers the reader clues to the secret sexualized passion Augustine lavished on God, the father, toward whom he demonstrated both a passive submission and active ardor. In short, at different periods in his life, Augustine demonstrated *both* positive and negative Oedipus complexes, with the latter only becoming manifest in a veiled, theological form that somewhat neutralized his confessional longing for union with God.

The etymological link between secrets and secretions underscores preoedipal roots in which the child deals with anal or urethral secrets as shameful or valuable assets. From a psychosexual perspective, both Gross (1951) and Hoyt (1978) viewed patients as being ambivalent about retaining or expelling their secrets. The connection between secrets and sexuality has likewise been made (Greenson, 1967; Meares, 1976). In the nineteenth century, "secret" in slang referred to the vagina or copulation, and secretions also refer to sexual emissions.

Theoretical, developmental research and clinical formulations have greatly facilitated the task of retrieving both self-contained preoedipal secrets and oedipal secrets that influence the shape that the oedipal conflict assumes, and the timing of its onset. It is to these preoedipal facets that we now turn.

PREOEDIPAL SECRETS

Theoretical Contributions

While Gross and Hoyt alluded to the instinctual and ego psychological underpinnings of preoedipal secrets, Klein (1975) introduced an object relations approach that made intentionality an integral aspect of even the very young child's cognitive repertoire. The archaic mother was not simply an outlet for drive discharge, but also became a part object, and then whole object, for the baby's aggressive and sexual fantasies.

Heimann (1952), in summarizing Klein's oedipal formulations, noted that boys and girls oscillate between homosexual and heterosexual positions and between libidinal and destructive aims. While these views essentially concur with Freud's (1923) theory, that they are transferred to the first year of life blurs some of the essential distinctions presented by a developmental line set in motion by preoedipal conditions that influence the later onset of the Oedipus complex. In my clinical work, I have found that it is important not to condense preoedipal and oedipal periods, since the secrets of these periods are distinct, yet often continuous, and involve dyadic and triadic concerns respectively.

The following example illustrates how a patient's secret can assume radically different meanings from preoedipal and oedipal perspectives. Simone, a 37-year-old banker, confessed that she felt that she was afflicted with the same heart disease as her mother, who had just died. While separation issues are clearly involved in all deaths, two major positions are set forth as possible explanations for the patient's perceptions:

> 1. On an oedipal level, perhaps the patient secretly longed for her mother's death. Guilt, and the unconscious need to be punished (Reik, 1959), resulted in a reaction formation in which the fantasized acquisition of her mother's disease concealed her malevolent wish for permanent separation.
>
> 2. On a preoedipal level, the patient may have never securely passed through the stages of separation-individuation, so

that this crisis forced her to retreat to the earlier symbiotic phase to reestablish a lost oneness with mother.

While other intermediate possibilities exist, the therapist who is empathically and interpretively attuned to the patient's developmental needs is better able to cull the essence of the preoedipal or oedipal secret from the transference situation, which, in turn, can spark genetic material from the corresponding historical time period. Simone's early history revealed that she was the second child of a mother who, at Simone's birth, not only had to take care of the older child, but also worked in the family store. Simone's earliest memories, dating back to one and half years of age, included her development of hypochondriachal symptoms to get her mother's attention. An early yearning for her mother's mirroring and undivided attention, set in motion by her mother's physical absence and overburdened home life, made it difficult for Simone to spend time by herself, having never built up Winnicott's (1958/1965) capacity to be alone consonant with the mother's encouraging preoedipal presence.

It became clear from Simone's associations and amplifications of preoedipal interpretations that the "secret" of her over-identification with her mother, following her mother's death, primarily involved difficulties with the preoedipal mother in Mahler's (1968) practicing subphase of separation-individuation, rather than a triangular conflict with both parents. Lacking an adequate mirroring frame of reference, the patient was hindered from making a smooth transition from a symbiotic to a more autonomous mode of existence.

To the drive, ego psychology, and object relations approaches to preoedipal secrets, one can add the self psychology perspective. Both Piaget (1923/1977) and Kohut (1971, 1977, 1984) emphasized the primacy of self and selfobject relations in preoedipal life. Since the preoedipal child's morality is based on the possibility of detection by external authorities (see Chapter 6), the young child or the patient rooted in preoedipal problems is likely to confess if he or she believes in the inevitability of getting caught by the parent or therapist. Confessions may be forthcoming in the latter instance if the therapist is perceived as reading the patient's mind via magical thinking or primitive guilt that is projected onto the therapist (Klein, 1975). *Mutatis mutandis*, patients harboring preoedipal secrets may also confess to the therapist when he or she is transferentially seen as a positive mirroring or idealized selfobject to lend cohesion to the nonautonomous self, or as a safe container (Bion,

1977) into which the patient can deposit secret, sometimes toxic, contents (Spotnitz, 1976) via projective identification.

Preoedipal Cues

Blum (1977) points out that Freud's first reconstruction involved the psychological meaning of the birth and death of his younger brother, Julius. Such reconstructions of early experience are garnered from dreams and screen memories. Noting the Wolf Man's sexual overstimulation when he viewed the primal scene at 18 months of age, Blum goes on to say, "Preoedipal disorder can be noted in the patient's relation to the analyst: the transference, the therapeutic alliance, the attunement to reality, and the quality of object relations" (p. 781).

Still, we can humbly ask: Can therapy ever succeed in sorting out the vagaries of preoedipal secrets from subsequent repetitions and distortions? While the objective veridicality of our earliest experiences can rarely be ascertained, the origin of early secrets can be developmentally approximated, both from the transference and from extratherapeutic object relations, as well as from the actual content of the material and the patient's manner of coping with the material, then and now.

Trauma and Emotional Deficits

The preoedipal child responds to trauma and deficits by disillusionment in mother (Brunswick, 1940; Jacobson, 1964), beginning with weaning as the first major interference between mother and child, and including a host of later developments, such as toilet training, birth of siblings, and mother's prohibition of masturbation. While these developments sever the symbiotic tie, they also propel the child into readiness for the separation mode of existence that disengages him or her from mother's perspective and facilitates the development of independent thoughts and initiatives.

Once the child has attained a measure of individuality, he or she is better able to differentiate his or her perceptions from those of parents. In analysis preoedipal secrets emanating from the period just prior to separation-individuation proper are thereby easier to retrieve than those from earlier, less differentiated times.

Confessions concerning emotional deficits and trauma, such as parental death, childhood illnesses, and violence (Pine, 1984; Spitz, 1965), can often be developmentally pinpointed and corroborated by others. At times even the earliest preoedipal incidents can come to the fore through parents' spontaneous comments or responses to patients' specific questions. While the veridicality of some of this information may be questioned, a number of validating witnesses can sometimes confirm this material that is now revived in the transference.

In this regard Christy, a 28-year-old auditor, who would berate me and threaten to leave therapy whenever a session was marked by feelings of closeness following confession, agreed with me that being dependent upon a mother who valued self-sufficiency in herself and others had been disappointing. Christy alternated between yearning for closeness and retreating into self-sufficiency to prevent inevitable disappointment. Christy's mother unwittingly confessed an early traumatic incident, not viewed as such by the self-absorbed woman, who simply thought that Christy would be fascinated by her mother's unconventional behavior.

Christy's mother informed her that since she loved the beach more than taking care of babies, she had thought of an ingenious plan whereby she would keep baby Christy in a pen with a bottle propped a few feet away from her. At home she would always use the propped bottle, since she was not the kind of mother who enjoyed physical contact.

The astonished patient burst out crying, to her mother's consternation. Through her mother's confession, Christy began to realize how she was forced out of symbiosis and into premature self-sufficiency so early in life. Her mother's confession was confirmed by her father and her grandparents.

The photograph can become another source of validation for preoedipal secrets. Christy began to pore through family albums and found picture after picture of herself with her propped bottle, surrounded by her many toys, with her mother nowhere in sight.

Thus it is the parent's confession that often serves as the pivotal trigger in eliciting parallel genetic secrets from the patient. The additional sources (that is, other relatives and family photographs) not only strengthen the genetic links, but also stimulate the patient to recall related material and work it through in the current, more benign, preoedipal analytic dyad.

Christy's case illustrates that preoedipal secrets can be garnered *both* from multiple historical sources (e.g., parents, relatives, and photographs) and from multiple current sources (e.g., the transference and current object relationships, the patient's dreams, and her memories stimulated by her mother's original confession). Confession of the secret begins a process of disempowering the preoedipal mother and reempowering the patient. Just as the patient comes to realize that the analyst is different from her mother, she also, in time, concludes that she no longer has to maintain a defensive self-sufficiency in order to survive.

The preoedipal world is, at times, one of helplessness, dependency, and passivity. If the mother is "good enough," this experience simply becomes a necessary prelude to the emergence of separation and the new tripartite oedipal relationship. Alternatively, should the mother be deliberately withholding or demonic, patients may never develop defenses or skills needed to withstand future trauma, nor be able to extricate themselves from the fantasized omnipotence of the preoedipal mother.

In previous chapters I discussed the desirability of the analyst's limiting the traumatic, panic-inducing confessional outpourings of borderline and schizophrenic patients. There are times, however, when such preoedipal confessions actually facilitate therapeutic progress. Judy, a 41-year-old schizophrenic patient, anxiously confessed that she should have been killed or committed suicide at three months of age. When I inquired what had happened then, Judy disclosed, "My mother told me that she had to stop breast feeding me because she could not use one breast and that was the breast I wanted." She continued, "Why am I talking such nonsense? Sometimes I think I don't know anything."

To which I replied, "Sometimes I think you know too much." Judy continued, "You're right. I see too much. I need protection from myself."

Judy's confession, in which she was terrified at the possibility of losing "the good breast," is mirrored in her current comment that she needs protection from herself. Khan's (1974) notion of the protective shield underscores Judy's need for the preoedipal mother's/ analyst's protection from her own toxic introjects. The analyst's fantasized good breast serves as a buffer between the dangers of the external environment and the internal object world.

Many authority-related secrets stem from preoedipal trauma rather than oedipal conflict. Lou, a 26-year-old patient, confessed that he wanted to scream whenever he was in a theater or school auditorium. While he was aware of hating authority figures, especially teachers, and remembered oedipal material pertaining to his rivalry with his father, Lou felt that something had happened even earlier that had irrevocably affected his life. One day, at a family gathering for his new niece, his mother said, "She's so cute, while you were such a handful as a colic baby."

Lou turned pale at the term "colic baby" and started to shake. The "return of the repressed," triggered by the association to the term colic baby, produced the traumatic memory that Lou had kept secret from himself for all these years. At one year of age, Lou recalled being held down by his mother and brother while tubes were put up his nose to drain the mucus. The helplessness and rage experienced toward his parents and doctors were subsequently displaced onto other authority figures, resulting in symptoms in which the preoedipal secret was, in part, concealed and revealed.

Security-related secrets frequently attest to the continuing effects of preoedipal deficits. In this regard the role of the preoedipal father has been overlooked or minimized (Spieler, 1984).

After four years of therapy in which the patient Ron had shared with me a number of confessions fraught with guilt or shame, I was surprised to discover that one entire segment of his early life had remained a secret. Ron confessed, with some trepidation, that now that he had moved in with a woman, it was difficult to hide some of the behavior that he had evinced in the privacy of his own apartment. After many attempted starts and protestations of what I would think of "such childish behavior," Ron confessed that his girlfriend came home early one day and found him rocking back and forth in bed. Ron continued, "I only do this when I'm alone. It's comforting and makes me feel better."

Exploration of Ron's early life revealed that his borderline mother was in and out of hospitals from the time he was born until he was ten. For the first three years, he slept in the same bed as his father, who allowed the little boy to snuggle up to him. This early preoedipal fathering embued the patient with a feeling of warmth and security that abruptly terminated at age three when the father became critical and told him that now that he was a big boy he would have to sleep by himself. Having been rejected by both mother and father, Ron retreated into a position of self-stimulation to offset the pain of object loss.

For patients like Ron who experienced traumatizing preoedipal events, one can well wonder how they were able to survive, and even thrive, in later life. A number of historical factors play a role in patients' successful coping with preoedipal secrets involving parental failings. Many patients report retrospectively that even at two years of age, they had an active fantasy life in which they would conjure up playmates and benign others who loved, or even adored, them. Such fantasies would tide them through many a traumatizing experience. One patient confessed that whenever her mother locked her in the bathroom after a fight, she would read comic books that she had hidden in the hamper and would play make believe to pass the time. Such confessions convey the idea that precocious cognitive development and ego adaptiveness can partially offset the severe consequences that could accrue to the children of sadistic or self-absorbed parents.

Further, early trauma involving parental abandonment and rejection was adaptively coped with by some patients by "adopting" friends' families or becoming the favorite of an aunt or uncle. The depletion of narcissistic supplies was thus, in part, counterbalanced by the mirroring obtained by extraparental objects who became alternative sources of gratification.

Not all patients are fortunate enough to have developed high-level ego adaptations to cope with trauma. Carlos, a very handsome 22-year-old model, initially came to see me because he wanted to have plastic surgery on his nose for the third time and the surgeon suggested he seek psychological help. This patient, who had "star quality" features, including his nose, stated that he also wanted to have his teeth capped, his cheeks chiseled, and so on. The narcissistic features of these wishes obfuscated a deeper, preoedipal secret centered on the patient as a young child being told by his father that Puerto Ricans were inferior and that Carlos was "a nothing, like his father."

Carlos confessed that he would look in the mirror at least 25 times a day. This behavior, which began when the patient was two, involved Carlos' desperate need to validate externally a sorely fragmented self that sought mirroring from older men in homosexual relationships, in conjunction with the proof that he was still there that Carlos could derive only from the mirror itself.

Sam, a 27-year-old graduate student, was another patient whose security-related problems derived from preoedipal deficits. He began one session by saying, "Do you mind if I turn the lights on?" (The room was still well-lit by external sunlight.) "It's funny, but as a kid, I used to be just the opposite about lights. I would remember coming home from school when I was very young and closing the thick drapes and just loving being in the dark. Both my parents worked, and I am sure they were never aware of my penchant for remaining in the dark." Sam then grew very quiet and blushingly added, "I never told this to anyone before, but while I was in the dark, I was also constipated, and I loved the feeling."

I interposed, "The lonely little Sam needed to hold something in for himself. You were able to retain something for yourself and have some control, while being in the dark would simultaneously allow you to reexperience a womblike security with a mother who could not leave you."

Sam began to weep softly, and then spoke. "I know why I like the lights on here. Because while with you I am not afraid to see the light and open myself to you. In telling you how I feel, I don't feel that I'm losing a part of myself, but rather am gaining more of myself."

Sam had acquired enough security in the transference to risk the double exposure emanating from both the contents of the confession and literally being in the light. As a preoedipal child, Sam held on to his bowel contents both to control himself and to stave off the emptiness emanating from the evacuation of inner contents. The establishment of a safe and secure analytic relationship enabled Sam to risk confessing as a way to share his inner contents with a selfobject that was seen as enriching rather than depleting his self contents.

In Proust's massive ode to recollection, *The Remembrance of Things Past* (1913–1927/1981), he recalls the satisfaction derived from his mother's kiss before he went to bed, along with the pain at the brevity of the kiss and the realization that immediately afterward she would leave and descend the stairs. Proust links this early memory of the peace experienced by his mother's presence at bedtime with the peace from his eroticism with Albertine.

Such early bedtime memories often form the subject matter of patients' confessions. Jordan, a 43-year-old architect, bitterly confessed that sometimes he wanted to kill his wife for not wanting to have sex with him every night. Although he was able to see the logic in his wife's wish, Jordan nonetheless had felt an overwhelming sexual need since his marriage 20 years before. In Jordan's words, "I need sex for relief. It is hard to fall asleep without it."

As we continued to examine Jordan's wish, it became clear that the patient hoped to reestablish the preoedipal bliss he had experienced with his mother, who loved babies and young children, but who took a job when the patient was four and became heavily involved in her career. Jordan remembers his mother saying, "Babies are so cute but later, when they get minds of their own, they become unbearable."

The security engendered in sexual union with his wife temporarily blotted out his doubts and anxieties, and enabled Jordan to be soothed into sleep. In his interpretation of Mrs. R., Laing (1962) similarly notes, "As it was, her sexual life and phantasies were efforts, not primarily to gain satisfaction, but to seek first ontological security. In love-making an illusion of this security was achieved, and on the basis of this illusion gratification was possible" (p. 64). Jordan was one such patient who, above all, craved continual return to the preoedipal security that was wrenched away from him by his mother's abrupt transition. Jordan was thus not given sufficient developmental leeway to move into separation-individuation proper secure in the knowledge that his mother would still be there to support and encourage his growth into full autonomy.

Behavorial Cues

Behavorial cues, such as eye gaze, oral cravings (e.g., patients asking me whether I have anything for them to eat), going to the bathroom immediately before or after a session, and nonverbal sounds, such as sighing, also provide gateways to the patient's preoedipal secrets. Each of these presents a dynamic signal of a potential preoedipal secret to be decoded by the transferentially revivified preoedipal mother–infant dyad aided by the patient's subsequent strengthened cognitive functions, especially language, memory, and reasoning.

I will focus primarily on one preoedipal cue—the gaze—whose multiple nuances and object relational significance facilitate the emergence of preoedipal secrets.[1] The patient's gaze can underscore either alienated reflection (Merleau-Ponty, 1962; Sartre, 1971) or selfobject affirmation (Winnicott, 1965; Kohut, 1971). The mother, or analyst, who frequently looks away or who ruthlessly glares at the baby or patient, may be perceived as demonic (Elkin, 1972) or poisonous (Klein, 1975). In either instance the child is likely to withdraw defensively and fear direct visual contact or internalize the toxic introject that may be sporadically expelled via visual hallucinations (Bion, 1967).

The look is endowed with object relational significance, with the object not only being the looked upon, but frequently also a number of additional significant objects *in absentia*. The analyst can often tease out the preoedipal or oedipal origins of secrets through visual cues. Patients may shy away from revealing some family secret lest they betray the family member whose presence is felt to be in the room. One female patient confessed that just as she was getting extremely sexually aroused, she perceived snapshots of her mother and father looking disapprovingly at her. In this instance the omniscient, omnipotent parental eyes of childhood become endowed with magical power and retributional potential— fantasized ocular attributes that subsequently reappeared in the transference.

[1]Portions of this section are extracted from my paper "The Multidimensional Significance of the Look," *Psychoanalytic Psychology* 3:149–157 (1986).

The aggressive element in the look is indicated in commonplace phrases, such as the evil eye, daggers shooting from the eyes, dirty looks, and so on. In all instances the look can be regarded as more than a simple instinctual discharge. It becomes an important communicative focus to uncover and explore secrets within the current dyadic object relational context. One patient, for example, developed a recurring eye problem in which she was literally "seeing red"—a symptom that symbolically communicated the extent of her anger and sadness as a result of her father's abandonment of the family when she was two. Having never explored or integrated this early trauma into her life, she was able to signal nonverbally to the analyst her need to revive this early secret that was subsequently further brought to light and elaborated upon via verbal associations and dreams.

Lampl-de Groot (1946) also lists behavior in the analytic hour, along with acting out, as criteria in the recognition of preoedipal material. It was Mack-Brunswick (1940) who clearly delineated the dyadic nature of the earliest mother—child attachment discernible in the transference.

In the process of cataloguing and studying the secrets of both my own and my colleagues' patients, I have noticed that whereas preoedipal secrets primarily concern the mother, a certain segment of these earliest secrets also pertains to the preoedipal father. Nevertheless, because the child in our culture still generally relies more on the mother as primary caretaker and love object, the tendency to disavow, repress, or rationalize parents' early betrayal of the child (see Chapter 7) makes confession, coinciding with this dependency-oriented preoedipal period, fraught with resistances. Preoedipal secrets may be difficult to retrieve not only because of temporal distance, but also because of the lack of cognitive and emotional differentiation necessary to select and synthesize secrets that often become lost forever through the child's tie, as a nondifferentiated selfobject, to the mother's or father's perspective.

Freud (1937) refers to the earliest period in which something forgotten returns as "something that the child has seen or heard at a time when he could hardly speak and that now forces its way into consciousness...." (pp. 266–267). Our earliest histories do tend to repeat themselves, but our reconstructions take on new meaning in the light of subsequent variations that take effect as the therapeutic relationship deepens and the patient's interpretive and integrative capacities facilitate the retrieval of preoedipal secrets. Burgess (1983) comments, in an analogous vein, about the recapitulation in music: "When, in the recapitulation of a movement in sonata form, the exposition is made to return, this is not a reproduction of the past, since its content, though heard already, is radically changed by what has happened between its first and second statements" (p. 47).

Since "experience is remolding us every moment" (James, 1890, p. 234), we can never be certain that the patient has extracted the pure ore of preoedipal secrets; however, the aforementioned behavorial and transferential cues facilitate the emergence of preoedipal secrets distilled and inevitably transformed in the face of later developments. Perhaps "we can never go home again," (Wolfe, 1940), but we can approximate a recapitulation to those primal secrets that cogently reappear in endless variations in dreams and screen memories, behaviorally, transferentially, and in extratherapeutic relationships. As these preoedipal themes repeatedly insert themselves into the patient's existence, enough material thereby incrementally presents itself to enable the patient to put preverbal experiences into words.

The analyst plays a pivotal role in facilitating the emergence of preoedipal secrets. Pine (1984) emphasizes the analyst's knowledge of the importance of the gaze and awareness of other nonverbal interactions between mother and child so that the analyst can "speak to the patient in a language closer to his or her early experience" (p. 22). The analyst's nonverbal receptivity, attunedness, and mirroring provide the soil for the patient's reevocation of a time and frame in which preverbal or early verbal secrets can grow until they are ready to reach conscious awareness.

Preoedipal Precursors of Oedipal Issues

Analysts have increasingly begun to acknowledge the overlap, convergences, and continuities between preoedipal and oedipal experience (Lampl-de Groot, 1952; Schafer, 1974; Chasseguet-Smirgel, 1976; G. Blanck, 1984). Freud (1931) also pointed to the need to understand the girl's preoedipal period to gain a fuller understanding of female development.

The dichotomy between preoedipal and oedipal development has traditionally consigned the preponderance of paternal influence to the oedipal period, while research on the preoedipal period has primarily addressed the mother's early influence. Perhaps one of the better kept secrets has been the enduring and substantial influence of the preoedipal father on subsequent development (Abelin, 1975; Lamb, 1980; Spieler, 1984).

I have already cited clinical material attesting to the crucial role that the preoedipal father can play in the traumatization of the child. Kohut's (1971) bipolar self concept, in turn, emphasizes the beneficent functions that the preoedipal father can assume as an alternative source for mirroring and idealization to counteract the mother's empathic failure. Abelin (1975) has described the preoedipal father's role in encouraging exploratory behavior, thus fostering differentiation and individuation. Finally, Lamb (1980) found that infants become attached to both parents preoedipally and under certain circumstances show preference for their fathers.

In short, data exist that demonstrate that the father is recognized and internalized preoedipally, contributing to the child's entry into the oedipal phase (Spieler, 1984), while paternal absence or rejection contributes to disturbed oedipal and subsequent heterosexual relations.

The case of Ethel illustrates the vital role played by the preoedipal father in the formation and subsequent elaboration of a secret. Ethel, a 28-year-old intern, began one session by saying, "It is embarrassing to confess that I have this obsession over so many years, but I know I have to do something about it before it drives me crazy. Eight years ago, when I was 20, I was helping my friend Tim build his house while his girlfriend was away. He had laid down the foundation and had the wood frame inside. It was my job to tighten all the bolts around the frame."

"After more of the house was erected, I had the horrible conviction that I had failed to tighten all of the bolts correctly, so that something awful would happen to Tim and the house. I felt terrible guilt about not telling Tim, and yet something stopped me. I had always loved Tim, and wished that we could live together in the house, and felt morbidly guilty about this thought."

Ethel, who had had a stiflingly close relationship with her father, remarked after many months of painstaking exploration, "If the house collapsed, Tim would be crushed. Sometimes I think I really hate him. No—what am I saying? Yes—and my father too. I can't believe I'm saying this. And yet I love Tim and my father. But Tim chose Jane when he could have had me."

Over the course of the year, following Ethel's confession, we were able to unravel further the oedipal and preoedipal separation issues that constricted this patient's existence through her obsessions. The patient's unconscious wish (and conscious fear) to destroy the house's foundation (thereby symbolically ridding herself of her father and surrogate father, Tim) also contained the hope of beginning anew, away from the stifling confinement of her father's love and demands. Her subsequent oversolicitousness with both the house and her work in general represented her attempts to control her hostile impulses (in accordance with traditional structural formulations), but also to conceal from herself a new, fledgling identity apart from the overwhelming demands of her father's brand of love.

While the oedipally based triangular rivalry with Jane existed as an important element in Ethel's obsession, it became increasingly clear from her associations revolving around her preoedipal father's smothering love and demands for total attention, as well as from related material borne out by dreams and screen memories, that Ethel's primary separation problems concerned her relationship with the preoedipal father. Having never separated from the preoedipal father, Ethel's hostile and sexual feelings were intensified in the oedipal period in which her fierce, unresolved attachment to the preoedipal father was further complicated by the addition of hostility now directed at both mother and father. Ethel despised her mother for not protecting her from her father's overbearing need for control, and because of her burgeoning feelings of sexual rivalry.

While the preoedipal mother's influence is generally recognized as a symbiotic force to be overcome in the turning toward father in the oedipal period (Chasseguet-Smirgel, 1976), Ethel's secret, manifested through her obsession, concerned her smoldering rage over her preoedipal selfobject relationship with a father who would not tolerate separation. She was thereby initially stymied in her efforts to resolve the challenges of the oedipal period predicated on a semblance of release from preoedipal selfobject enmeshment.

Both Schafer (1973) and Chasseguet-Smirgel (1976) underscore the preoedipal mother's power over the child's sense of worth and, indeed, over the child's very life—a power that renders her a potentially castrating figure, as well. Chasseguet-Smirgel's theory of phallic monism, in particular, emphasizes the child's wish to break away from the omnipotent mother, which results in the projection of her power onto the father and his penis. She views penis envy in both sexes as a triumph in overcoming symbiosis with the archaic mother. Exploration and understanding of the pivotal role played by both parents preoedipally and oedipally enable patient and analyst to tease out those preoedipal and oedipal cues that become the stuff of secrets and, finally, confession.

OEDIPAL SECRETS

The Quest for Identification and Autonomy

In Sophocles' trilogy Opedipus never got the chance to identify with his father, and instead adopted the stance of infantile omnipotence. It is only after Oedipus blinds himself, following Teiresias' confession of his tragic secret, that he is able to be redeemed and transformed by surrendering his illusory omnipotence in identifying with Theseus—a loving, paternal surrogate. To this end Searles (1959) maintains that acceptance of the oedipal solution is effected *not* by identifying with the forbidding, rival parent, but through the discovery that the beloved parent responds to the child as a worthwhile, lovable being. This situation enables identification as well as separation-individuation, since the child is secure in the parent's love.

Oedipal secrets are not always of the patient's making. At times patients comport themselves in such a way as to comply with a parent's secret, which is internalized and then acted upon in myriad ways. While the secret goes unspoken due to the unconscious collusive pact of silence, the development of trust, the formation of the therapeutic alliance, and the gradual development of selective identifications facilitate the emergence of such secrets.

Carol, a 33-year-old accountant, alternated between very rigid and proper behavior (with accompanying obsessional symptoms and bruxism) and clownish antics. "I act silly, dress bizarrely, and take center stage." These alternations stemmed from identification with her father, who either rigidly adhered to societal standards or did unconventional comic routines.

Carol eschewed taking the middle course, since she identified such an approach with her mother "who is superrational and has no creativity." She felt a strong bond with her father, and both father and daughter viewed the patient's mother as being essentially different from them. While one can discern aspects of an oedipal triumph, identification with her father began in the preoedipal period when he would entertain and win the little girl's heart with his antics and magnetic presence. The seeds of the ego ideal had been sown by the patient's preoedipal identification with her father (Lampl-de Groot, 1952).

The secret that emerged in due time was that Carol was convinced that her father had wanted a son. The patient complied with his unspoken secret request by:

1. Remaining sexually amorphous—continuing to dress and comport herself as an androgynous adolescent.
2. Entering the male-dominated accounting profession.
3. Engaging in daredevil hobbies, such as hang gliding and rock climbing.

Carol and her father colluded in this unverbalized secret. Carol's wish both to please her father and to be like him culminated in her adherence to her father's secret wish that enhanced the preoedipal idealized bond. An amorphous, incomplete oedipal situation was thereby created at the expense of separation-individuation.

During the course of therapy, Carol started to identify selectively with me (e.g., changed her hairstyle and started to wear dresses as well as pants). She sought a better paying job (thereby showing partial identification with her mother's business acumen), while continuing to engage in clowning routines with her father.

Since resolution of the oedipal dilemma involves both identification with (Schafer, 1960) and detachment from (Freud, 1905b) parental authority, Carol continued to identify selectively with me, as well as with aspects of her mother. Concomitantly with these new identifications, she experienced a resurgence of her repressed femininity and sexuality, and began to experience her own personhood.

While oedipal secrets have tended to be weighted in the direction of children's feelings toward parents, some of the most resistant, affect-laden secrets concern parents' counteridentifications with children (Searles, 1959; Rangell, 1955).

Parents' erotic or rivalrous feelings toward offspring are considered especially dangerous secrets to reveal, since legal and moral sanctions against incest and child abuse carry far-reaching repercussions. Patients are less reticent to confess analogous, veiled secrets involving, for example, a father's hatred for his daughter's boyfriends or a mother's flirtation with her new son-in-law.

Oedipal secrets can resurface at various points during the life cycle. Freud (1905b) mentions the resurgence of the oedipal struggle at puberty when the adolescent must detach from parental authority. Others have described the revival of oedipal conflicts in early adulthood, parenthood, and even old age (Rangell, 1955; Blos, 1962; Loewald, 1978/1980; Blanck, 1984). Parents and grandparents resolve these conflicts by vicarious identification with the lives of their children and grandchildren (Rangell, 1955).

Such counteridentifications, however, are often initially ensconced in resistance, since to confess libidinal or aggressive investment in one's children is generally considered by parents (and society at large) to be more morally reprehensible than children's complementary feelings toward parents. The notion that "children don't know better" along with the Rousseauesque romance of "childhood naiveté" generally render childhood oedipal secrets easier to confess than parental oedipal feelings directed at children.

Atkins (1970) points out that Oedipus was the abandoned victim of the filicidal impulses of both parents. Incest and child abuse are common, yet vehemently guarded secrets that are often more likely to emerge through apprehension of bruises by school authorities or legal complaints than in the therapist's office.

I have found that such confessions, when they do surface in therapy, are most likely to be made by patients who were victims of child abuse and wish to break the vicious cycle by acknowledging and working through their secret, terrifying childhoods. Further, patients who are parents and sense incipient tendencies in themselves to repeat their childhood secrets of abuse may confess these urges to prevent the intergenerational continuation of their own abuse-ridden histories.

It is only through the process of working through such confessions that patients can disidentify with the internalized abusive parent in order to develop a sufficiently autonomous self to become their own fathers (Brown, 1959). In developing the capacity to become a self-parenting individual, such patients not only radically alter the self in the process of disidentification, but also learn to substitute self-reflection for impulsive behavior.

Incest

Oedipus' unwitting incest is one of the two major secrets (patricide is the other) that dooms his existence. Incest often involves a triangular relationship in which overt denial by the nonparticipating member helps create and maintain the secret. Rist (1979) cites data showing that once the secret has been discovered by an extrafamilial person, incest almost invariably ceases.

The covert crossing of generational boundaries puts the patient/incest victim in a double-bind situation, in which a message of sexual parity is transmitted to the unequal child/partner. The child who is threatened or bribed to hide the secret often internalizes a "blame the victim" attitude, thereby augmenting guilt and shame, especially if the child is at all aroused by the forbidden venture. Thus only recently, with the emergence of victim advocacy, assistance, and support groups (Hymer, 1984b), have incest victims and victimizers risked confessing these deeds in order to redeem themselves. In so doing these patients attempt to understand and curtail the incestuous cycle in an effort to establish renewed family relations devoid of intergenerational sexual or aggressive behavior.

The recent controversy provoked by Masson's (1984) alleged debunking of Freud's concept of fantasized infantile seduction seems to be essentially a red herring. The burgeoning literature on incest, as well as clinical confessions attests to the alarming number of incest victims. These facts, however, do not preclude the coexistence of a substantial number of patients whose incestuous fantasies figure prominently in their genetic histories elucidated through the transference. Further, as Lewis (1984) points out in her review of Masson's book, while Freud remained aware that actual seduction was traumatic, "what he did *not* accept was that it was such a frequent source of historical symptoms" (p. 351).

A few brief examples suffice to illustrate the prevalence of the situation in which *fantasized* childhood incestuous relations predominate. Several patients have disclosed that my having sex with them would actually facilitate therapy, "since I would get to know them so much better." The therapist's intervention is important, both for the continuation of therapy and to offset a potential narcissistic blow stemming from rejection. I have found that such confessions are best worked through in the context of the patient seeing the parallels between the therapeutic and the parent–child relationship.

I asked one such patient, "What do you think of a parent who sleeps with a child?" He replied, "That's disgusting and exploitative." I added, "Just as the good parent respects rather than exploits the child, the good therapist does the same." While such interchanges have not always put an end to these resistances, and once backfired in a patient who was actually stimulated by the question, in most of my patients who made sexual suggestions further investigation revealed childhoods replete with fantasized rather than acted-upon incestuous longing.

Some middle-aged women patients confess to fantasies involving having affairs with young boys, while others have acted out their fantasies. Male patients, alternatively, are, for the most part, less reticent about confessing, often with bravado, about their exploits with young girls. All such confessions connote ways of acting out forbidden, incestuous fantasies.

That the external social atmosphere has become more accepting of December–May romances still leaves to therapy the task of decoding these confessions to arrive at the fantisized or actualized incestuous roots of these subsequent relationships. Since incestuous secrets have an intrinsic fascination for many, it is important that the therapist not be seduced away from understanding and interpreting the meaning of such activities for the patient, or engage in counterresistance in which patient and therapist collude with each other to conceal the dynamic issues by focusing solely on *zeitgeist* sociological changes in male and female roles.

Patricide, Matricide, and Filicide

Patricide is the second great secret that was kept from Oedipus, either due to the gods' machinations or owing to his unconscious denial in order to preserve his own self-interest by hiding the damaging secret from himself (Schneck, 1974). Steiner (1985) likewise points out that there is evidence in Sophocles' text to suggest that certainly Teiresias, but also Creon, and even Jocasta, suspected that it was Oedipus who had killed Laius and had married his own mother. Steiner continues, "One can argue further that each of the participants in the drama, for their own reasons, turn a blind eye to this knowledge..." (p. 164). Oedipus, like many patients, who both know and do not know the information contained in interpretations of secrets, disavowed or denied the facts.

While patricidal and matricidal impulses are pervasive, the actual deed is a rarity. Conversely, in ancient Greece, deformed children were routinely left atop mountains to die, and until recently, the Murray Islanders killed the excess of whatever gender endangered the sexual balance. Thus although matricide and patricide have always been viewed as the most heinous of crimes, filicide has been an organized form of population control in some societies.

Perhaps one of the most famous literary examples of patricidal wishes and the ensuing guilt and confession involves the psychological changes undergone by Ivan Karamazov following the murder of his father in *The Brothers Karamazov* (Dostoevsky, 1881/1957). Ivan, the most rational and intellectual of the three brothers, struggles to repress his own wishes regarding his father's death. Having never concealed his hatred toward his father and, on several occasions, having hinted that he wished his father dead, evidence arises that perhaps Smerdyakov (the real murderer) committed the crime under the influence of Ivan's ideas.

Smerdyakov confesses to Ivan that he killed Ivan's father but says that he did so in accordance with Ivan's expressed desire, and thus Ivan was the real murderer and Smerdyakov was Ivan's instrument. Following this confession, Ivan returns home and experiences his first hallucinations. Guilt leads to a need for punishment (Reik, 1959, Loewald, 1978/1980) and Ivan punishes himself for his patricidal wishes by plunging into madness.

Ivan confesses his guilt at the trial. But, like many neurotic patients, Ivan's *wish* makes him unbearably guilty. The mental equation of the wish with the deed facilitates both obsessional thinking and confession to assuage the guilt and gain relief. Through his confession Ivan struggles to acknowledge the truth that has remained buried for so long (that is, that his true values are Christian).

Ivan's confession holds out for him the possibilities of relief and redemption from madness and guilt, culminating in a renewed existence in which he is freed from the chimera of a world order predicated on atheism. Loewald (1978/1980) writes, "Without the guilty deed of patricide, there is no autonomous self" (p. 393). The superego, in this instance, represents both guilt and atonement for usurping parental authority.

Like Ivan, many patients' secret patricidal wishes are revealed through obsessions or somatic symptoms, such as the derealization experienced by Freud (1936) when he journeyed to the Acropolis and guiltily confessed to himself that he had surpassed his father. Yet it is precisely the acknowledgement and working through of patricidal and matricidal wishes that enables patients to experience the guilt and redemption integral to the establishment of an individuated existence.

Narcissistic Aspects of Oedipal Confessions

A rather common confession by male patients is that they believe their penis to be too small. Such a confession is a cogent illustration of the deleterious effects of a lack of appreciative mirroring during the oedipal period. However, although it is impossible for the analyst to validate whether the patient's apprehensions contain an element of reality, we can say, in most instances, that such confessions relate to a poor body image and uncohesive self tied to parental understimulation (lack of mirroring) or overstimulation (seductive rejection) during the oedipal phase.

Kohut (1977) has pointed out that the oedipal period need not be characterized by trauma and conflict. He views empathic failure on the part of narcissistically disturbed parents as contributing to oedipal pathology. Conversely, should parents experience pride in the oedipal child's burgeoning affectionate and sexual desires as well as self-confident, competitive feelings, the child can pass through this period with a minimum of trauma and with intact self-esteem.

To return to those patients who worry that their penises are too small, many of their family histories reveal parents who belittled or criticized their children indiscriminately. Being minimized often results in a corresponding deflation of the normally valued genitals, which thus are also devalued.

Even for patients with parents who did not demonstrate narcissistic pathology, the visual comparison of the oedipal boy's genitals with those of the father results in the realization that he cannot possibly satisfy mother, and that he is small and weak in comparison with father. Nevertheless, whether or not the little boy internalizes and represses genital inferiority as a secret depends upon parental reactions to the child's budding sexuality and aggressivity. If the parents appreciate the child's sexual curiosity and benign exhibitionism, the child's awareness of genital differences with father will result in identification and pride in his own developmental achievements. Alternatively, should the forbidding, critical parental superego predominate in the face of lack of parental empathy, the little boy is left with feelings of unworthiness and inferiority that may become centered on his allegedly small penis—a secret which, when confessed in psychotherapy, is generally invested with a high degree of shameful affect.

The sort of narcissistic problem that distorts the successful resolution of oedipal experience was disclosed by Rousseau in his *Confessions* (1781/1977). Rousseau confessed that, lacking the courage to make sexual advances, he exhibited himself to women who were drawing water from a well in such a way that he was viewed as ridiculous rather than seductive. Ridicule by these women resulted in low self-esteem and a legacy of sexual misgivings that pervaded his later life.

Sexual overstimulation or understimulation during the oedipal period profoundly affects the child's sense of self. Rose, a 27-year-old supervisor, disclosed, "My mother couldn't wait for the evening to change into her low-cut dresses and show off her cleavage." While her mother openly taunted the little girl for being a prude, her seductive father told her to lower the sleeves of her dress so that she would look sexier. "When I asked him what sexy meant, he said it's what happens when men whistle at you." Rose went on, "Even then, I felt like a powerless object for men's needs and desires. That same year, when I refused to play doctor in the shed, Jed stuck his penis through a hole in the shed and urinated, barely missing me."

Rose recalled that at age five she did act somewhat flirtatiously with her father, only to retreat in order not to seem provocative like her mother or risk the hurt of not getting the same reactions that her mother received. Since neither parent responded in an empathic manner to Rose's conflictive, emergent sexual feelings, she chose to withdraw rather than continue to risk paternal teasing and maternal competitiveness. Rose's mother's self-absorption would not allow her to see the need to tone down her provocative sexuality temporarily in an effort to mirror and encourage her daughter's sexuality.

Rothstein (1979) depicts contradictory and confusing oedipal situations alternating between gratification and disappointment. Mother's overvaluation of her son, for example, can render her sleeping with another man a more intensely felt narcissistic injury. Cases are cited in which mothers use sons as narcissistic objects to humilate fathers. Only tenuous oedipal victories are thereby gained, however, since castration fears due to father's retaliation and mother's devouring him if he does not live up to her narcissistic expectations still loom large.

Finally, I am reminded of a case that underscores the narcissistic elements contributing to the waxing and waning of oedipal conflicts (Loewald, 1978/1980). Darlene, a 26-year-old artist, confessed, in tears, that she had had an affair after only one year of marriage, and was frightened that her husband might find out and also that she might be tempted to have an affair again.

When the patient's oedipal history was explored in detail, the dominant theme that emerged was that she felt the need to be larger than life in order to gain attention, since she perceived both of her parents as not paying attention to her in the way she craved. Her overworked father would rarely spend time with her, and her self-absorbed mother was constantly involved in self-improvement projects that drastically cut into the time she spent with Darlene.

The man she married did shower her with a great deal of attention, but she became despondent and sought extramarital mirroring when her husband's business temporarily increased in volume, thus requiring more of his time. Feeling abandoned, she sought revenge against her husband and parents by indulging in an affair.

The confluence of narcissistic and oedipal elements also became manifest in her fantasies, initially disclosed with reticence and shame. "My favorite fantasies involve ten men with gigantic erections viewing me around a table. Each one of them is dying to ravish me, but none of them can get near me." Exploration of this fantasy again revealed the emergence of the narcissistic need to awe men who appreciatively mirror her in unison like a Greek chorus, in a manner that makes her larger than life. This fantasy offset the oedipal trauma of insufficient mirroring, as well as enacted revenge on the oedipal father who was rarely present.

PREOEDIPAL AND OEDIPAL CONFESSIONS: FURTHER THOUGHTS

This chapter examines divergences as well as continuities between preoedipal and oedipal secrets. The thesis is presented that preoedipal experience often shapes the development and repression of oedipal secrets.

The prototype of all subsequent confessions resides in the preoedipal parent–child relationship. Should the preoedipal mother or father exaggerate the moral severity of a misdeed or otherwise traumatize the child, this early event may set the stage for later feelings of guilt or unworthiness. Since the good parent does not "trade confessions" with the child, the child does not risk disillusionment from the parent, who can remain an opaque idealized figure. The idealized image of the early parental imago is subsequently transferred onto the benign analytic superego.

For Freud children's secrets from parents, later unraveled during analysis, centered on the oedipal conflict. Because of the unacceptable nature of the secret and the lack of confessional outlet, the complex underwent repression until an acceptable substitute analytic channel of expression became available in adult life.

Although the importance of the oedipal confession remains incontrovertible, the developmental vicissitudes of the self likewise play a crucial role in preoedipal and oedipal secrets. Whether or not the parents empathize with the oedipal child's developmental achievements dictates, in large measure, the revelation of one's burgeoning sexuality, assertiveness, and self-mastery or the repression of secrets born out of feelings of shame, guilt, or inferiority.

9

The Role of Confessions in the Consolidation of Self

Confessions can be viewed as a multilayered reflection of self. Secrets buried in the deepest layers of the unconscious were the jewels that pioneering psychoanalysts sought to mine. Regarding the earliest memory, Freud (1917c) wrote, "Indeed, it usually happens that the very recollection to which the patient gives precedence, that he relates first, with which he introduces his confession, proves to be the most important, the very one that holds the key to his mental life" (p. 147).

Later theorists (Winnicott, 1971; Kohut, 1984) noted that patients repress not only memories, but also significant aspects of the self. Winnicott's (1965, 1971) submerged true self connotes not only repression of the content of specific secrets, but also repression of an entire segment of the patient's being at variance with parental expectations. Kohut's (1977, 1984) repressed grandiose self can be conceptualized as a hidden aspect of self that has never been given the opportunity to develop at the phase-appropriate period.

Other confessions are tied to the conscious layer of self. Khan (1974) views the patient's pervasive defense regarding self-experience

174

as "staying dissociated and hidden, not repressed" (p. 294). Sartre's (1971) concept of bad faith pertains to the inauthentic self that consciously navigates through life in this manner. In Buber's (1937) I–thou relationship, an authentic mode of being becomes possible through a conscious effort of will.

The decision to confess or withhold is a reflection of the child's (or patient's) attempt to maintain a stable level of self-esteem. Because the child may be castigated for confessing, he or she may choose to conceal such information in the future. The naughtiness of the deed becomes secondary to the perceived folly of getting caught. Alternatively, for some children the relief that comes with the perceived self-justified punishment (Reik, 1959) outweighs the moral anxiety emanating from the continuation of the secret.

Each secret contains an aspect of our self-image. Secrets that remain hidden grow in importance or bizarreness, having never had the chance to be tested in the interpersonal realm. The longer the true self remains repressed, and the greater the split between the true and false self, the more the eruption of such hidden aspects of self is likely to be perceived as psychotic (Laing, 1960).

Confessions can often confer closure and continuity on the patient's ruptured self. A Zen story tells of a pilgrim who mounted his horse and crossed mountains and rivers to seek a famous wise man in order to ask him how to find true enlightenment. After months of searching, the seeker located the teacher in a cave. The teacher listened to the question and said nothing. The pilgrim waited. Finally, after hours of silence, the wise man looked at the horse on which the pilgrim had arrived, and asked the pilgrim why he was not looking for a horse instead of enlightenment. The pilgrim responded that obviously he already had a horse. The wise man smiled, and retreated to his cave.

Like the pilgrim, the patient, in confessing, comes gradually to rediscover the essence of the true self. Yet this discovery rarely, if ever, involves a one-trial insightful learning experience. The patient who takes the first step—*risk*—immediately makes a major advance in peeling away the layers of the false self. The relief that is afforded, however, can itself become resistance if the patient becomes lackadaisical in undertaking the final working-through process involved in *redemption/renewal*. The patient reparatively redeems the self by coming to terms with the meaning of the secret as it pertains to the larger scope of the self. It is only in integrating the confession into the patient's self structure, rather than absolving the self through attempting to excise the secret, that confession truly contributes to self-consolidation.

The very resistances that block confession attest to the reigning strength of the secret. The secret is often viewed by patients as a source of self-empowerment in an all-too-powerful parental world. Paradoxically, confession can become a source of power as well, which frees, redeems, and transforms the confessant. The patient who risks confessing wrests power from those fantasized or real oppressors who would demean the patient's self-integrity. Confession thereby redeems the self from the burdensome secret and from the confines of internal and external objects hitherto endowed with awesome power.

THE DRAMATURGICAL PERSPECTIVE

Confession produces a shift in the representational world (Sandler & Rosenblatt, 1962). Whereas a representation is seen as having "a more or less enduring existence as an organization or schema constructed out of a multitude of impressions" (p. 133), confession changes this drama as the analyst becomes a leading player.

Sandler and Rosenblatt compare the representational world to a stage. Characters represent the child and the objects in his or her life. The confession per se becomes a miniature drama, with the self as hero (narcissistic confessions) or villain (guilt-ridden confessions) or victim/victimizer (shameful confessions). This drama remains static, however, without an audience. The analyst, as both audience and participant observer, helps the patient retrieve disavowed aspects of self, and delineate these aspects via the working-through process.

The patient becomes a character in his or her own internal play, repeating old roles (Sandler & Rosenblatt, 1962). Confession helps free the patient from the tyranny of these patterns by cutting through the cycle of repetition. In confessing the patient severs the unconscious or conscious collusive pact of silence with internalized objects and allies the self with the analyst, who becomes a new pivotal object in the patient's cast of characters.

Redemption of the self from the powerful objects of the past is a principal part of the confessional experience. Having described the nonverbal confessional modalities (see Chapter 10 for a detailed discussion), I wish to mention another dramatic instance involving a creative effort inextricably tied to the severing of archaic bonds connected to the creator's secret self.

In a verbal confirmation of a nonverbal confession, Picasso elaborated upon how African sculpture forced him to probe the depths of his innermost self. "When I went to the Musée de L'homme...the masks were not just sculptures....They were magical objects...intercessors against everything—against unknown, threatening spirits....They were weapons—to keep people from being ruled by spirits, to help free themselves...."*Les Desmoiselles*" must have come to me that day, not because of the forms, but because it was my first canvas of exorcism!" (quoted by Flamm, 1984, p. 53).

Flamm hypothesizes that *"Les Desmoiselles"* was a personal exorcism relating to Picasso's conflicting attitudes toward women—a confessional posture that has also, at times, been attributed to de Kooning's "women's series" of paintings, in which women are portrayed as terrifying, teeth-baring witches.

In *"Les Desmoiselles"* the terrifying face at the lower right—associated in Africa with malignant spirits and in Western culture possibly with the terrifying Medusa's head (Freud, 1922b) or with the omnipotent, dreaded preoedipal mother (Chasseguet-Smirgel, 1976)—becomes a confessional fetish to protect the creator from omnipotent forces.

Such nonverbal confessions transform the powerful, unseen object into an iconic representation that is now exorcized on canvas. The dreaded becomes less dreaded once it becomes known and substantial through confession. The secular exorcism afforded through art or therapy redeems the self by initiating a process of projection in which malevolent objects are expelled. The very act of articulating a secret in psychotherapy realigns the patient with the new analytic object, who provides continuity and constancy after the patient begins to free the self from such internalized objects.

In contrast to Sandler and Rosenblatt's (1962) representational world, the Goffmanian (1955, 1959) world is one of anonymous roles in which ritualized social interactions allow the actors to "save face" by avoiding honest self-disclosure through impression management. Goffman (1955) elaborates, "Whatever his position in society, the person insulates himself by blindness, half-truths, illusions and rationalizations" (p. 230).

In Goffman's dramaturgical perspective, our lives are divided into "backstage" and "out front" activities. Most of us are so preoccupied with maintaining a favorable persona that we may, like O'Neill's Hickey, actually convince ourselves that our compliant false self is our core identity. Bearing in mind that in Goffman's purview all the world really is a stage, it is not surprising that the many roles that each player plays bolster the false self at the expense of authenticity. Should patients define themselves in terms of their versatility in donning various roles, this chameleonlike behavior strengthens the resistance to the unmasking of the true self.

REDISCOVERING THE TRUE SELF

The ancient Egyptians held that when those who had died encountered their judges in the underworld, they made lengthy confessions of the crimes they had not committed, but omitted their actual sins. In this way they could protect the malevolent contents of their true selves and so remain less vulnerable in the afterlife.

The patient's need to protect the true self produces a series of defenses and subterfuges, which, prior to psychotherapy, may have served the patient well in everyday social interactions. Although drawn to revealing the true self, the patient is reticent to confess to the analyst, who is seen as both a new, benign object and an old, transferential object who demands compliance at the expense of the true self.

The true self/false self dichotomy does not always do justice to the complexities of human interaction. In *Confessions of a Mask* (1958), Mishima reveals how such facile dichotomies may obscure, rather than elucidate, the various layers of self. Mishima, like Tolstoy's Ivan Ilyich (1886/1975), reveals his true self, only to be viewed by others as a poseur. "And in this house it was tacitly required that I act like a boy. The reluctant masquerade had begun. At about this time I was beginning to understand vaguely the mechanism of the fact that what people regarded as a pose on my part was actually an expression of my need to assert my true nature, and it was precisely what people regarded as my true self that was a masquerade" (p. 27).

Winnicott's (1971) true self—alive, spontaneous, and creative—emerges out of the good-enough mother's adaptation to the infant's needs. The mother who is unwilling to support the infant's omnipotence forces the infant instead to comply with her gesture. The false self is thereby created.

Each confession brings the patient closer to the realization and affirmation of the true self. Yet, since the false self has often served patients well in many aspects of living, one can well ask what motivates patients gradually to let go of the false self facade via confession. Many patients come to realize that a major discrepancy exists between role-related achievement and success in personal relationships. For those patients who become aware that intimacy cannot be attained by "being on" 24 hours a day, the therapeutic relationship provides an opportunity to wrestle with the possibilities of intimacy without risking abandonment and disillusionment.

Confession, in this context, becomes one way gradually to shed the pretenses of the false self and risk bringing the true self "out of cold storage" (Winnicott, 1954/1975). Further, confession need not involve a return to primal regressive states (Winnicott, 1954; Balint, 1979), but may proceed from the surface to greater depths as patients take incremental risks in slowly bringing the true self to light.

Patients who are pervasively dissatisfied with the perceived meaninglessness of their lives become less reticent in revealing the true self. Recent findings on the "impostor phenomenon" (Clance, 1985) attest to the discrepancies that many externally successful "model" patients experience between the social self, as judged by societal criteria, and the inner self, judged by many of these patients to be disappointing or worthless. To confess that one experiences oneself as an impostor becomes a major avenue for such patients to begin to come to terms with true self/false self discrepancies.

For some patients the true self may be so buried by the false self that the belated emergence of the true self may be experienced as akin to a breakdown. A very distraught, 27-year-old, highly accomplished patient came into my office beset with fears that she was falling apart. She had decided that her dealings with overly competitive executives in a high-powered industry had corrupted her and that going to graduate school was what she really wanted to do. Because she had grown up in a family that put a premium on status and money, this patient perceived her "identity crisis" (Erikson, 1959, 1962) as synonymous with a breakdown rather than as a breakthrough in which the true self began to emerge. Having developed a sophisticated false-self defensive system, the shock of acknowledging what she wanted was, at first, perceived as catastrophic.

Finally, the analytic process itself fosters the emergence of the true self. The safety, confidentiality, and constancy of the analytic setting, along with the alliance and transferential relationship established, enable most patients to risk revealing at least select aspects of the true self.

With regard to the false self and interpersonal relationships, Buber (1965) discusses the essential problem of "being and seeming." "The widespread tendency to live from the recurrent impression one makes instead of the steadiness of one's being...originates in man's dependence upon one another. It is no light thing to be confirmed in one's being by others, and seeming deceptively offers itself as a help in this. To yield to seeming is man's essential cowardice, to resist it is his essential courage....One must at times pay dearly for life lived from the being; but it is never too dear" (p. 78).

Resistance to authenticity often relates to the patient's dread of self-discovery or self-revelation to the analyst. Bugenthal comments, "Resistance is the name that we give to the general defensive wall the patient puts between himself and the threats that he finds linked to being authentic. Resistance is [simply] antiauthenticity" (quoted in Fisher, 1982, p. 117).

A wall of secrets, moreover, results in both self- and other-alienation. Confession bridges the gap and lays the groundwork for intimacy, if the analyst is perceived as enough of an ally that sharing secrets in lieu of withdrawing becomes the preferred mode of existence.

The therapeutic task of helping patients recognize their yearnings for love and care, as well as their anger at those early objects who failed to provide them, is an especially challenging goal with narcissistic patients. Bromberg (1983) writes, "For narcissistic patients, living becomes a process of controlling the environment and other people from behind a mask" (p. 361). He goes on to describe the narcissistic patient's only initial hope of success in treatment as the ability "to perform for the analyst and be rewarded by 'cure'" (p. 368).

Should the analyst unconsciously wish such a patient to perform like a traditional neurotic patient and attempt to hack away at the patient's resistances, the patient may perceive the analyst as the narcissistically invested parent or persecutory figure. The patient then may retreat even further into false self-compliance or resort to idealization to protect the analyst from the sadistic, hate-filled, and retaliatory wishes housed in the true self.

Confession helps erode the false self facade as well as to alter the shape that the self has hitherto assumed. If authenticity includes "the capacity to assess and accept what is real in both the external and inner world, regardless of the narcissistic injury involved" (Nemiroff & Colarusso, 1980, p. 114), then confession that couches the self in a nonsocially acceptable cast is a major step toward enabling the patient to risk narcissistic injury. In so doing the process of consolidating an authentic self freed from the burden of parental compliance is accelerated.

For those confessions ushered in by the emergence of the grandiose self, working through of such material, in time, transforms the grandiose self into a self that may still be regarded as special, albeit not unique and perfect. The analyst's noncensorious acceptance of confessions mirrors to the patient an affirmative attitude that encourages the patient to be authentic, despite the initial narcissistic injury incurred in unmasking the false self.

Let us again focus on Sartre (see Chapter 4), who, as a model child, developed multiple means to bolster the false self. Sartre (1966) writes of himself, "Consider the following: alone in the midst of grownups, I was a miniature adult and read books written for adults. That already sounds false since, at the same time, I remained a child....The fact remains that my hunting and exploration were part of the family play-acting, that the grownups were delighted by it, and that I knew it" (pp. 43–44). By the age of nine, Sartre had developed showman-like routines, had started to write, and made comments well beyond his years. Atwood (1983) describes Sartre's sense of inauthenticity as "an experience of his own conduct as always involving pretense and imposture" (p. 143). In the foregoing quote, Sartre confesses to the erection of a false self to win adult approbation, and reveals an early yearning for continuous narcissistic supplies from the collective other (later translated into universal readership).

The emergence of truth and selective abandonment of collusive secrets tied to archaic objects enables patients temporarily to withstand narcissistic injuries in the light of self-transformation. To this end Cassimatis (1985) notes, "Self-esteem, existentially speaking, is largely a function of authenticity or truth. And truth must be an individual, not a collective, truth" (p. 71).

Confession provides a means for the patient to be authentic with another, and hence self-authentic as well. One cannot be false in confession, unless one is disclosing a false confession to buttress the false self. Through risking authenticity, self-esteem is temporarily elevated. Yet the patient may again start to feel demoralized, since, by confessing, he or she is revoking the pattern of displaying the false self that was hitherto mirrored by the analyst.

The transferential equation of the analyst with the archaic parents demanding compliance at the cost of the true self initially accounts for a major source of resistance. As the therapeutic alliance unfolds, and the patient comes to see the analyst as a new object who is there for the patient, the new alignment allows the patient to take greater risks in order to attain authenticity.

UNIFICATION OF THE DIVIDED SELF

Confessions facilitate the restoration of the divided self. Saint Augustine (398 A.D./1961) provides a vivid example of the discordant self. "So these two wills, one old, one new, one carnal, the other spiritual, were in conflict and between them they tore my soul apart" (p. 164). When Saint Augustine confessed to his sins of sexual lust and nonbelief in God, he achieved redemption through his faith in God. In so doing he achieved self-integration. William James' eighth lecture, in his *Varieties of Religious Experience* (1902/1963), alludes to the divided self and the process of its unification through secular or nonsecular means. "But to find religion is only one out of many ways of reaching unity; and the process of remedying inner incompleteness and reducing inner discord is a general psychological process, which may take place with any sort of mental material, and need not necessarily assume the religious form" (p. 175). Whereas Saint Augustine resolved his conflict by renouncing the carnal aspect of self, confession in psychotherapy is concerned with the acknowledgement and assimilation of split-off aspects of self in order to achieve self-consolidation.

In the previous section, I discussed the major split between the true and false self. Laing (1960) transposes this split to the existential plane in describing the basic division between the inner self and the body and world in schizophrenia. The schizophrenic's inner true self is often experienced as futile or murdered, though the body and false self live on. In *I Never Promised You a Rose Garden* (1964), a series of confessions takes place in which an analyst's willingness to enter into her schizophrenic patient's world enables the patient to risk revealing the splits between her constructed inner world of characters and her deadened outer world. This patient, Hannah Green, first acknowledges the transformation in her split-off bodily self when she burns herself with a cigarette and actually feels the pain.

The analyst must be especially careful not to convey the impression that positive feelings toward the patient are contingent upon confessions being forthcoming. The unconscious communication of such messages results in the transferential repetition of the split between the external false self and the inner self, which now includes the analyst in the parade of objects to be hated, envied, and vilified. For schizophrenic patients, in particular, voluntary confessions are most likely to take place in the accepting stillness of the analytic environment. In this environment the patient can gradually come to experience the analyst as an affirming, soothing object who is different from the demanding parental objects who expected compliance at the cost of individuation.

Cary, a 29-year-old schizophrenic patient, would constantly ask me if I were real. Eventually Cary revealed the meaning of her secret linguistic code. For Cary, her family and most people in the world were "real"; that is, phony, conventional, and hostile. To be "unreal" was to be an ally in Cary's inner world and help her come to terms with how to remain unreal (Laing's preservation of the inner self) and still exist in the real world of the false self.

Cary wanted me to be unreal and allow her to disclose her inner self to me without being destroyed. While Cary was initially reticent to express anything but her compliant false self to me, as she gradually came to perceive me as unreal through my non-intrusive, silent affirmation of her, she began to risk small secrets. These confessions pertaining to her feelings of annoyance at her entire family's treatment of her as invisible slowly expanded as the analyst, as "unreal self container," was seen as capable of absorbing more "unacceptable" secrets of the inner self.

We consciously and unconsciously acquire a number of ingenious means to compartmentalize the self. While splitting can facilitate adaptive cognitive functions in which attention and discrimination are enhanced, splitting can also defensively foster schizoid withdrawal and other mechanisms that contribute to resistance to confession. Again I turn to Godwin (1983), who writes about the benefits of confessing to one's diary in fostering self-discovery. "I have found so many sides of myself in the diaries of others. I would like it if I someday reflect future readers to themselves, provide them with examples, warnings, courage, amusement even. In these unedited glimpses of the self in others, of others in the self, is another proof of our ongoing survival, another of the covenants eternity makes with the day-to-day" (p. 29). Patients who are adept at "confessing all" to their diaries, however, may split the secret self into a part that is safe to reveal to the analyst and another more forbidden or dangerous part disclosed to the diary.

Splitting takes place both within the self and between the self and external and internal objects. Freud and Breuer's (1895) studies in hysteria concerned forms of macroscopic splitting (Grotstein, 1981) marked by dissociation and repression. Breuer, in discussing the case of Anna O., noted two distinct states of consciousness involving two selves—a real one and an evil one that forced her to behave badly. What was reparative in these pioneering patients' confessions was not simply the articulation of forbidden material, but also the transferential relationship established with the analyst/father confessor that offered new possibilities for relating and respite from their all-consuming relationships with their fathers.

It was Melanie Klein (1975) who carefully delineated both the defensive and adaptive functions of splitting. Reparation represents a means with which to heal the splits within and between the self and objects. Confession offers two specific reparative functions (*Oxford English Dictionary*, 1971) bearing on the patient's self[1]:

> 1. "The restoration or renewal of a thing or part." As patients reparatively integrate repressed memories and/or the grandiose self via confession, they come to experience themselves in a renewed way as a whole object better able to regulate self-esteem.
> 2. "The restoration of a person." Once patients develop the capacity to maintain a more or less stable self and object representation, they may then be able reparatively to adapt to higher order transformations involved in creativity.

With regard to the second point, I previously wrote about how the transformational nature of self-reparation is often evident from the shifts in a patient's choice of literature (Hymer, 1983). Mr. P., a 33-year-old insurance salesman, during a depressive cycle, confessed how much he identified with Grygor Samsa, the character who turned into a cockroach in Kafka's *Metamorphosis*. Mr. P. revealed, "I, too, sometimes think I'd be better off in the world as a cockroach." During a hypomanic phase in which Mr. P. became the best salesman in the office, he brought in Napoleon Hill's *How To Grow Rich*. Mr. P. exuberantly commented on how he was no longer reading "depressing, morbid stuff," but had instead decided to focus his attention on "books that allow me to use my talents creatively. I might as well discover how to make my first million faster." Mr. P.'s shifts in literary preferences reflected his rapid oscillations in self-esteem as he passed from the depressive to the manic cycle.

With psychopharmacological interventions and further therapy, Mr. P.'s self-image stabilized. At this juncture he was able to utilize his more stabilized self creatively in his work. Having revealed the splits pertaining to his grandiosity and sense of worthlessness through his identifications with literary characters, Mr. P., in time, was able to modify these extremes to attain a better regulated, adaptive self.

Through the relative safety afforded by Mr. P.'s confessions in which projective identification onto literary characters protected the self from undergoing direct scrutiny by the analyst, Mr. P. estab-

---

[1] Refer to my paper "The Therapeutic Function of Art in Self-Reparation" for specific examples, including the case of Mr. P., of how art contributes to the reparation of splits in the self.

lished a split between the grandiose self and idealized selfobject and the deflated self and debased selfobject (Lichtenberg, 1975). We can also make a case, as does Eisnitz (1980), for viewing Mr. P.'s identifications as splits within the self representation—the multiple conscious and unconscious mental images and roles the self assumes.

Grotstein (1981) mentions a form of dissociation of selves he terms demoniacal posssession marked by "the belief that they (the patients) had, at one time or another in childhood and later, disavowed themselves in order to become invisible, so as not to confront some crucial experience. They believed that their self-forfeiture or disavowal had been achieved via a pact with the Devil" (p. 67).

I came across a similiar scenario when Arline, a 34-year-old hair stylist, blushingly revealed a particularly vivid dream in which she was totally passive and accepting as her boss injected a fungus into her back as she lay on her stomach. Her associations included the feeling that she was an experimental subject for Dr. Mengele, but that this was the price she had to pay for the security of a father figure. Since Arline had started to introduce such terms as evil and sin into her vocabulary, I asked her what evil meant. She replied, "Evil is the total surrender of self to another—the forfeiture of a separate identity." The fungus in the dream referred to the patient's view of the self as being condemned and spoiled.

Grotstein (1981) sees treatment as beginning with the therapist's awareness that he or she is dealing with separate selves that have different agendas and motivations. For Fairbairn (1954) the essential task of psychotherapy is to unite the splits.

Still, especially with psychotic patients, splits of objects and the self into minute fragments run counter to unification, as they attack links in communication and conceptualization (Bion, 1953/1967). Bion enjoins patients to empathize with split-off aspects of the self from which they withdrew—a process facilitated by the analyst's empathically entering into the patient's world in lieu of attempting immediately to decode the patient's labyrinthine confessions. The more the analyst attempts to objectify and evaluate such communications, the more the analyst is perceived as a bad object split off from the true self's world view.

In my tripartite description of the confessional process, the *risk* inherent in confession concerns the patient's acknowledgement of a split or multiple splits in the self. The analytic task is to help the patient own the split. The second step, *relief*, is afforded by the patient's learning to empathize with split-off parts of the self—a process that can be facilitated by the Gestalt "empty chair" technique (Perls et al., 1951), in which the patient becomes the split and has a dialogue with the conflictive aspects of self. In so doing the patient finds relief both by unburdening aspects of the split-off, secret self to the accepting analyst and by becoming familiar with these splits by literally "giving them a voice."

To reiterate, it is important to realize that the greater the strength of internalized objects, the more the patient's perceived betrayal of these alliances may initially exacerbate self-criticism. If the patient succeeds in working through the confession in lieu of retreating and realigning the self with powerful internalized objects, *redemption* can ensue.

Finally, unification of the splits shapes the self in a new way as links to the new analytic object encourage the patient to risk further consolidating the self. By integrating disavowed aspects of self into a renewed self system, the patient's wishes, aspirations, ambitions, and creativity can grow both from the unification of the split-off segments of self and from those conscious aspects of self (especially Freud's observing ego and Schafer's self-as-agent[2]) that become manifest and strengthened through the therapeutic alliance.

ESTEEM ENHANCEMENT

Bakan (1954) cites people's awareness of their own shortcomings as the major reason for keeping secrets. The maintenance and enhancement of self-esteem are a prime motivator in both hiding and revealing secrets.

In narcissistic confessions (see Chapter 4), a perceived defect may be transformed into an asset as the grandiose self emerges. A secret that may have been viewed by parents or others as the subject of derision or criticism is reprocessed as meaningful or special in the analytic environment. A patient whose father constantly derided her for accepting writing assignments for which she was not paid revealed how worthless she felt after these paternal tirades. Lengthy discussions in therapy centering on her love of writing and positive feedback received from teachers resulted in the patient's perception of the analyst as different from her father, who grew impatient whenever the patient tried to get him to understand her persistence. The patient's self-esteem was heightened as her worthless self was slowly transformed into a competent self, as a result of external mirroring and of the acceptance of her first magazine arti-

---

[2] See the section on esteem enhancement for a further discussion of this concept.

cle for publication, which enhanced her feelings of self-competence from within.

One of the major sources of self-esteem mentioned by Freud (1914a) was the fulfilment of the ego ideal. For the young Sartre (1966), writing became such a self-extension that not only furnished him with an identity, but also resulted in self-redemption through the sense of accomplishment. "I was born of writing….By writing I was existing, I was escaping from the grown-ups, but I existed only in order to write, and if I said 'I,' that meant 'I who wrote.' In any case, I knew joy" (p. 95).

Lampl-de Groot (1962), like Freud, also saw living up to ego ideals as a major source of self-esteem, yet for narcissistic disorders, the inability to regulate and maintain self-esteem (Kohut, 1971) often produces discrepancies between what Jacobson (1964) refers to as self representations and the wishful concept of the self.

The narcissistic patient's unusually severe, perfectionistic self-expectations may exacerbate the split between the patient's disappointed image of self and wished-for self. Thus, any confession that underscores perceived defects meets with resistance. It is only when the analyst as selfobject is seen as a safe container that confessions enable the patient to reevaluate the self in a way that brings the self-as-experienced and idealized self into closer harmony.

The analyst, as selfobject, becomes a receptive self extension rather than a separate evaluative object for the patient's confession. The analytic climate in which the patient's self is not subject to the esteem-diminishing criticism provided by parental objects enables the patient to risk confession without risking diminution in self-esteem. The analyst, as selfobject, also facilitates the emergence of the grandiose self in which idealized self and object images heighten self-esteem.

White (1963) has convincingly demonstrated that a patient's sense of worth derives not only from external mirroring, but also from an internal sense of competence. Confession can enhance the patient's sense of effectiveness. Many patients who have achieved success and recognition in their careers are hesitant to risk sharing their inner selves. The act of confessing thus becomes a momentous developmental step in the direction of enhancing intimate relatedness.

For patients who risk confessing, the self-as-agent function (Schafer, 1968) is strengthened; that is, the self as knower and doer. Confession becomes an active process in which the patient emits, processes, and evaluates information to gain further self-understanding and self-acceptance through interaction with the analyst. Joining forces with the analyst augments rather than depletes the patient's self-integrity.

Feelings of competence, following confession, derive from the following:

1. For patients at primarily preoedipal developmental levels, the ability to verbalize inner contents in itself is an esteem-enhancing activity. Indeed, for patients at any level who are able to retrieve and articulate secrets emanating from primordial experience, meeting such a cognitive challenge tends to heighten feelings of competence. Confession not only exercises the ego's expanding linguistic ability, but also helps order thought and self and object discrimination (Lichtenberg, 1975).

2. The ability to trust another sufficiently to share one's inner secrets is an achievement for those patients who, voluntarily or involuntarily, shut themselves off from others. The move from *eigenwelt* (inner world) to *mitwelt* shared experience signals an incipient openness and trust that results in a stronger sense of relatedness set in motion by confession.

3. Risking confession without ensuing catastrophe sets the stage for further confessions that are perhaps even riskier and more elaborate in their ramifications. With each ensuing confession, the patient develops increasing competence in utilizing a number of ego capacities successfully, most notably memory, articulation, synthesis, interpretation, and integration.

The sense of efficacy thereby garnered is, of course, complemented and supplemented by mirroring from others and esteem-enhancing play activities, which are later translated into the analytic domain (Winnicott, 1971). (See Chapter 6 for a discussion of the nature of play activities in confession.)

SELF-COHESION

The self that has a strong measure of internal constancy (Blum, 1982b) and that is cohesive and continuous (Lichtenberg, 1980; Kohut, 1984) is better able to risk confession, since fragmentation or annihilation is unlikely to ensue following self-disclosure. Confession may at first, however, produce temporary disequilibrium as the patient experiences a shift in the balance of self-experience, marked by the emergence of the secret self.

For patients with a cohesive self, however, such shifts are adaptive and reversible. A patient who confesses a long-suppressed secret may initially perceive the self as "being on the line," yet simultaneously experience the self as being strong enough to risk the fantasized consequences.

The cohesive self is increasingly experienced as an active agent in directing the fulfillment of conscious and unconscious goals. The act of confession sets in motion the completion of an incomplete self experience. The analyst helps the patient sift through the meaning and implications of the secret to arrive at diverse goals. Goals can vary from the nonspecific unburdening of a secret to attain relief to macrolevel self-transformation in which confession helps break the grip of the archaic mother (Lichtenstein, 1964; Chasseguet-Smirgel, 1976), whose pervasive influence recedes as the patient–analyst bond is strengthened.

The analyst who acknowledges and empathizes with the patient's secret self facilitates parallel processes in the patient, who discovers a new ally to help secure release from the powerful hold of the archaic parent. Since such early traumas generally occur before the dawn of self-awareness, the patient may only be able to rediscover the primordial true self through benign regression in which the trauma can be reexperienced and subsequently worked through in the safety of the analytic environment. The patient's alliance with the good-enough analyst/mother, along with the development of a cohesive self, encourages the patient to weaken the primacy of the preoedipal mother without fearing self-disintegration.

A clinical instance of the nature of confessions in self-consolidation is exemplified in a vignette I term "the two handwritings of Mr. J." Mr. J. was a 29-year-old physician who confessed that, beginning in the sixth grade, he would meticulously recopy all his notes, since he could not allow cross-outs or other mistakes.

"At that time, the teacher treated a slovenly fat slob in the class as if he were a future Pulitzer prize winner. This same boy had terrible penmanship and would read his essays from crumpled pieces of paper."

I remarked, "Perhaps your way of standing out and receiving recognition was through meticulous penmanship." Mr. J. went on, "Yes, people would comment. It's a form of discipline that continued for years. Even in medical school, I would spend hours recopying my notes. This gave me discipline and a sense of purpose."

Mr. J. subsequently adopted his girlfriend's style of handwriting, which was large and bold. "It was easy, especially when you live with someone and see her writing everyday. Now I have two handwritings."

I asked, "May I see them?" Mr. J. began to write—a form of confession that was to yield unexpectedly fruitful results in the process of self-consolidation. The first handwriting, representative of his selfobject identification with his girlfriend, resembled his description of her handwriting—light, large, bold, and free-flowing.

Mr. J. was then able to effect a remarkable switch as his handwriting prior to the relationship emerged—a tight, heavy, shaky, small script in which some of the letters resembled the writing of a palsied, elderly person. The contrast in self perspectives evinced by the written confessional products attested to the patient's shifting levels of self-esteem: firm versus shaky, expansive versus restrictive.

Since each person's handwriting represents a unique instance of eye-hand-brain coordination, that Mr. J. was effortlessly able to acquire and assimilate another's handwriting in part attested to deficits in the development of a cohesive self. His eagerness to merge with his friend by acquiring her handwriting, along with many of her traits, revealed extreme discontinuities between his accomplished occupational attainments and a sense of personal identity cut short by a hypercritical, emotionally unavailable mother and a household of sisters who would tease and embarrass their younger brother.

The patient's second chance at self-redemption through paternal idealization (Kohut, 1977) was aborted, as his father was rarely present, and when at home, would withdraw into reclusive television viewing at the young boy's expense. Mr. J. experienced his father as kind, but "namby-pamby and ineffectual, never providing me with any direction in life or taking a firm stand against a household of witches—I mean women."

The lack of maternal mirroring and paternal devaluation left Mr. J. bereft of sources of self-affirmation and idealization. He subsequently sought to consolidate the self by entering into relationships with women who enabled him to merge with them and selectively borrow aspects of these objects to assimilate into his nascent self.

Since our unique signatures are an aspect of our identity that renders us different from all others, the relative ease with which Mr. J. assimilated his girlfriend's handwriting demonstrated a fluidity of boundaries in which he desperately sought to shore up his shaky self through identification with an idealized object.

Mr. J.'s verbal elaborations confirmed that his shift in handwritings also paralleled a disparagement and renunciation of his former identity as reflected in the compulsive, rigid pattern his handwriting had assumed. His wish to merge with, and thereby emerge victorious from his relationship with a successful, self-confident woman was condensed in the handwritten disclosure.

The analytic process involving the patient's achievement of self-consolidation was greatly facilitated by this disclosure. Both oscillations in self-esteem and loose self-boundaries underscored by these handwritings contributed to the patient's understanding and articulation of formerly unexpressed verbal genetic material pertaining to deficits in self-development.

SELF-DECEPTION

Patients utilize a number of defense mechanisms to keep secrets from the self and the analyst, thus resulting in self-deception. Goleman (1985) cites neurophysiological evidence and social psychological studies to buttress his central thesis that the brain protects itself against anxiety by refocusing attention and creating a blind spot marked by self-deception.

Defense mechanisms or any other attention-deflecting mechanism can block confession. The self-deception thereby created not only enables aspects of the self to remain hidden, but also allows an illusory self-esteem to be maintained at the expense of reality.

An unforgettable example of the dangers wrought by the centrality of self-deception as a life theme is evidence by Willy Loman in Miller's *Death of a Salesman* (1957). After Willy's death, his oldest son, Biff, remarks, "He never knew who he was" (p. 221). Biff is one of the few characters who does not collude with Willy in his self-deception, knowing that his father's grandiose schemes and simplistic notions of being liked as the key to success are far from the grim reality of their lives. Willy's lonely funeral underscores the falseness of his self-perceptions. He had lived his life unable to reveal who he was to himself. Boasts of future prosperity were face savers that neither he, nor anyone else, eventually believed.

Since Willy's identity was focused solely on what he did, failure at sales constituted psychological self-annihilation. Miller, in his introduction, states about Willy, "He can prove his existence only by bestowing power on his posterity, a power derived from the sale of his last asset, himself, for the price of his insurance policy" (p. 34). Ironically, physical annihilation through suicide is seen by Willy as his opportunity to redeem himself by enabling the family to be solvent. If Willy had had the opportunity to unburden himself and scrutinize the self in such a way as to gain self-acceptance concurrently with the diminution of unrealizable grandiosity a less tragic scenario might have ensued.

Patients who enter therapy find themselves in the paradoxical situation of both wanting to change and wanting to remain the same. Since change in the direction of self-revelation is often painful, many patients initially hold on to their resistances even more tenaciously in the battle to maintain cherished illusions for a while longer.

The conscious decision to risk confession or the spontaneous emergence of confessions during free association signals a turning point in therapy. Confessions help diminish the distortions caused by self-deception. The act of verbalization itself lessens the patient's adherence to the myopic secret self committed to self-deception.

Schafer (1973) sees self-deception as faulty self-observation. "By resisting, the analysand somehow continues to keep many truths from himself or herself" (p. 270). And since the revelation of truth was the prized goal for at least the first 75 years of psychoanalysis, self-deception was viewed as a key obstacle to be removed in order for treatment to progress.

With the advent of resistance analysis (Reich, 1972; Spotnitz, 1976), resistance became a powerful signifier that simultaneously illuminated and obscured the undisclosed. The act of resistance helps bare the secret. The discerning analyst–patient team that embarks upon understanding the origins, meaning, and essence of resistance gets closer to the secret in the process.

In Shakespeare's *Othello*, we see a variety of defenses coalescing and culminating in the malignancy of self-deception. Othello allows his own perceptions of Desdemona's goodness to be transformed by Iago's machinations. From the first scene, Iago reveals himself as a creature of deception, "I am not what I am" (I.i.65).

In the final bedchamber scene in which he kills Desdemona, Othello has fallen prey to Iago's demonism. Othello bids Desdemona confess her sin of loving Cassio. Juxtapositions of true and false confessions underscore the tragedy of self-deception. Desdemona's confession of innocence is received with scorn; Iago's false confession of Desdemona's infidelity based on circumstantial evidence is believed. Confession, in Iago's hands, becomes a weapon of treachery and deception, rather than an unfolding of the true self.

Self-deception generally occurs in an atmosphere of dimmed awareness in which anxiety is assuaged by the withdrawal of attention. I have found it useful phenomenologically to conceptualize a fourfold schema to understand the interactions of the patient's and analyst's varying levels of awareness in the resistance to and emergence of secrets.

Secrets

1. Self aware (suppression). . . . . Analyst unaware
2. Self unaware (self-deception). . . . . Analyst aware
3. Self unaware (self-deception). . . . . Analyst unaware
4. Self aware (confession). . . . . Analyst aware

Self Aware—Analyst Unaware

Patients tend consciously to suppress secrets during the initial stages of therapy in which face-saving subterfuges are still held onto in order to preserve the status quo level of self-esteem. Before the firm establishment of the therapeutic alliance and the development of trust in the analyst, the patient tends to adopt a defensive posture. The analyst, in turn, has few contextual cues about the meaning and fit of material in the larger context of the patient's life, and so awaits the deepening of the analytic relationship and process. A frequent example of the patient's suppression of material to control an unfamiliar situation, as well as to protect the vulnerable self, involves the patient who confesses, after several months of therapy, the "real reason" for entering therapy.

Secrets such as virginity, homosexuality, prostitution, and drug problems are suppressed, as less threatening secrets are offered in their stead. The patient, nevertheless, often productively uses the intervening time to become acclimatized to the therapeutic process and to enter into the therapeutic alliance, in which sufficient trust is accrued to enable the patient to risk revealing the major secret.

Self Unaware—Analyst Aware

In this first example of self-deception, the patient's defensive structure protects him or her from anxiety and assaults on the self-image at the expense of both truth and self-consolidation through enhanced awareness. The analyst, in this combination, may become aware of the patient's self-deception through projective identification; that is, the patient unconsciously deposits disavowed aspects of self into the analyst, who may silently and empathically process or interpretively feed back this information to the patient, if the patient is deemed ready to assimilate and work through this material in the transference.

The analyst may also become aware of secrets before the patient does, by attending to the patient's free associations and the resistances the patient may initially experience, but not evaluate, in the absence of the observing ego. The analyst may, initially, assume this function for the patient, who may be so swept away by the affects connected with free associations that he or she relies on the analyst to facilitate the integration of disavowed aspects of self.

Self Unaware–Analyst Unaware

This level constitutes the deepest layered secret or series of secrets. Transferential and countertransferential catastrophic, traumatizing material can result in an unconscious *folie à deux* in which patient and analyst collude with each other in mutual deception.

A colleague related his "dis-ease" regarding his sense that one of his patients was torturing or otherwise abusing her child. The patient, who appeared to be a gentle and thoughtful person, nonetheless continually mentioned dreams marked by violence and triumphant scorn of her victims. While the analyst dutifully dealt with the transferential aspects of the patient's desire to kill the analyst/ father, he avoided analyzing the real dangers pertaining to her hatred of her child. This analyst, who had incompletely dealt with his animosity toward his own children, could not become aware of his patient's and his own "unacceptable" parental feelings.

The patient's child, discovered by a neighbor with severe bruises, was rushed to the hospital. The analyst has since reentered analysis.

Self Aware–Analyst Aware

Confession facilitates the furtherance of self-awareness when the empathic acknowledgement of disavowed aspects of self results in the working through of material and the elicitation of further confessions that enable the patient to own and integrate the secret self into a consolidated self-structure. For example, the habitually, "nice, good-natured" patient, through confession, adds hostility, envy, and hatred as selectively acceptable affects in an expanded self-image.

Conversely, the indiscriminate celebration of confession by patient and analyst can itself constitute a resistance, if the patient unconsciously views disclosure as a way of gaining relief without working through this material in the context of larger life themes.

The therapist who seeks dramatic disclosures to fulfill voyeuristic or narcissistic strivings unconsciously colludes with the patient by reinforcing confessional outpourings without giving weight to less dramatic, everyday material that also contributes to the composite picture of the patient's self.

The patient who complies with the analyst's unconscious thrill at the evocation of unusual confessions erects a new variant of the false self in which he or she becomes more intent on pleasing the analyst than on coming to terms with the more gradual process of consolidating such material into an integrated self-image. The analyst, in turn, who "lives" for patients' confessions is engaging in an equally harmful form of self-deception in which the illusion is maintained that lasting change is inherent in catharsis rather than in the working-through process eventuating in a gradually transformed self-structure.

Confession that does not serve resistance stretches the boundaries of awareness in both patient and analyst. The addition of secret aspects of the self affords the patient a unique opportunity to risk cognitively and affectively assimilating such material in the secure, encouraging presence of the analyst.

10
The Nature of the Object in Confessions

The confession, by its very nature, is tied to objects. Social animals from the time of our intrauterine existence, even the most solitary among us seeks to confess, if only to journals and diaries. Confession is always an interpersonal phenomenon in which the nature of the object is crucial for a satisfactory outcome. The entire panoply of these manifold objects becomes part of the analytic experience, both as internalized presences and as transferential products that become linked to the person of the analyst.

Freud (1922a) recognized the importance of object relations in his decision to dispense with hypnosis. "It was true that the disappearance of the symptoms went hand-in-hand with catharsis, but total success turned out to be totally dependent upon the patient's relation to the physician...if that relation was disturbed, all the symptoms reappeared, just as though they had never been cleared up" (p. 237). Integral to Freud's own self-analysis, and hence the establishment of psychoanalysis, was his relationship with Fliess. Bernstein (1976) notes Freud's propensity to form idealized transferences with several of his mentors, including: Brücke ('the greatest authority I ever met'), Meynert ('in whose footsteps I follow with such veneration')" (p. 166). Still, it was predominantly through his relationship with Fliess that Freud came to realize the importance of the other in the discovery of the secret self.

Jourard's (1964) writings on self-disclosure revolve around the premise that we can only know ourselves by disclosing ourselves to another. Authentic self-disclosure becomes a major criterion for growth and health. Heidegger's "being-in-the-world" always involves the world one shares with others—the *mitwelt*. Moreover, one can never not be with objects. Even the most severely withdrawn schizoid patient occupies an inner world peopled with bad objects (Fairbarn, 1954; Guntrip, 1969) or split self-object-affect units (Kernberg, 1976, 1979) that dominate his or her waking and sleeping thought. When such patients can risk gradual disengagement from these objects, concurrent with the strengthening of the therapeutic bond, confession becomes possible.

In short, with all manner of patients, the decision whether or not to confess depends not only upon the patient's level of self-development and ego strength, but also upon the patient's relationship with current and past objects, internal and external, as well. The patient encounters, in addition to the analyst, a host of significant others whose enduring presences continue to exert an influence on the analytic outcome, especially in the realm of disclosure or resistance. Thus the patient who opts for concealment may be protecting, consciously or unconsciously, not only the self, but also parental or sibling objects whose collective presence operates to undermine confession.

In our culture many patients who feel cut off from objects seek the analyst as an alternative object, yet simultaneously resist disclosure. Fears revolving around betraying a family secret or destroying an object by "ruthless" (Winnicott, 1975) evacuation of prized contents into the analyst are two common object-related resistances. The patient, in the midst of a sea of objects, utilizes confession selectively to separate from and also to become attached to objects.

Grotstein (1981) has emphasized the dual-track system of consciousness predicated upon the complementary tracks of separation from objects and intersubjective empathic reliance on objects or selfobjects (Kohut, 1984) throughout life. Confession underscores the dilemma undergone by patients who find themselves pitted against past and present objects in a drama in which release from oppressive past objects or selfobjects simultaneously connotes attachment to the analytic object.

In instances of projective identification, the confession, placed in the analyst for safekeeping or mirroring, aligns the analyst with the patient *against* past objects. Conversely, should the analyst be seen as the container of malevolent, split-off contents of self and objects, the analyst becomes allied *with* past objects against the patient. Under what circumstances the dialectic becomes resolvable is a major therapeutic issue in confession.

While confessions have always existed as part of the human condition, it was Freud's great contribution to systematize a form of discourse in which confession to the analyst enables catharsis coupled with insight to free the patient from restrictive self and object relations. The analyst became the conduit in the elicitation of confession, as well as the verifier and interpreter of the patient's disclosures.

In the case of Elizabeth von R., Freud and Breuer (1895) described the analyst's role in facilitating confession. "The interest shown in her by the physician, the understanding of her which he allows her to feel and the hopes of recovery he holds out to her—all these will decide the patient to yield up her secret" (p. 179). Freud here implies that the analyst's active receptivity is a potent factor in the emergence of confession. The analyst is viewed as a pivotal object whose functions include a great deal more than that implied by the metaphor of the dispassionate surgeon.

Freud (1895) goes even further in extolling the active, educative functions of the analyst in enhancing the working-through process. "One works to the best of one's power, as an elucidator..., as a teacher..., as a father confessor who gives absolution, as it were, by a continuance of his sympathy and respect after the confession has been made" (pp.327–328).

In his papers "On Narcissism" (1914a) and "Mourning and Melancholia" (1917a), Freud subsequently discovered that objects could be reckoned with in their own right. With the full-blown emergence of object relations theory, both internal and external objects were recognized as forces that might block confession in addition to or in contradistinction to drive derivatives (Mitchell, 1984).

Confessions outside psychotherapy have always played a part in justice, education, medicine, and family relationships. Such confessions were designed to protect the state, clan, or group against the individual confessant—a notion eloquently expounded by Dostoevsky's Grand Inquisitor—whereas confession in psychotherapy radically reverses this process in potentially freeing the patient from the hold of powerful objects.

Foucault (1980) states, "Confession frees, but power reduces one to silence; truth does not belong to the order of power, but shares an original affinity with freedom..." (p. 60). To the extent that the patient is in the grips of a transferential dilemma in which the powerful analyst/parent is perceived as attempting to extract a confession, confession is seen as too risky an experience. Truth, in instances of perceived power, often becomes subordinated to expedient secrecy.

When the analyst is perceived as aligned with the patient, confession then may be seen as a tool to wrest power away from the historical object and empower the patient. Freud and Foucault's truth-bestowing and interpretive functions for confessions are placed in an object relational perspective by Meissner (1976), who states, "We have come to recognize that an interpretation must take place in the context of and as an impression of an object relationship" (p. 132). With the advent of object relations theories (Greenberg & Mitchell, 1983), confession as a means of establishing or enhancing relatedness superseded, or existed in tandem with, the truth-gaining aspect of confession.

MAJOR FUNCTIONS OF THE OBJECT

The relative neglect of countertransferential issues until the 1950s resulted in a deemphasis of the contribution of the analytic object to the confessional process. Freud (1925b) himself began to emphasize the object-related social context in which confessions emerged: "The personal emotional relation between doctor and patient was after all stronger than the whole cathartic process..." (p. 27).

The confession dramatizes the struggle between dependency on and separation from the object. The child's/patient's relationship with the object thereby becomes a prime consideration in whether or not to confess. How the object is viewed or utilized is dependent upon the patient's level of self-development and genetic history with objects.

If the child experiences massive disillusionment in the maternal object, the child correspondingly fails to develop the requisite amount of narcissistic supplies. An unattuned object along with constitutional deficits can result in a fixation at Mahler's (1968) symbiotic stage.[1]

In such instances during psychotherapy, confessions that are forthcoming in the silent stillness of the holding analytic environ-

[1] Major segments of this section are extracted from my paper "The Therapeutic Nature of Confessions," *Journal of Contemporary Psychotherapy* 13:129–143 (Fall/Winter 1982).

ment allow the patient tentatively to develop a relationship to self devoid of extraneous verbal "noise" from a separate analytic object. During the first six months of Sherry's analysis, this 43-year-old schizophrenic woman would show strong reactions to any questions from me that would break the silence. She would start and say, "It's noisy in here. The noise makes my brains feel like scrambled eggs." In an atmosphere of complete silence, Sherry came to be able to verbalize confessions "to the infinite horizon" and thereby slowly to formulate a less fragmented self-identity uncontaminated by the noisy voices that plagued her both from within and without.

The analyst who seeks to elicit genetic confessional material must first take into account the patient's level of self-development, since many confessions or secrets are concerned with the maintenance of a congruent self-image in the absence of the perception of an individuated object. In such instances the analyst can best elicit a confession by serving as a silent ally of the patient's self via the patient's merger with the selfobject (Kohut, 1971).

Because the child develops a sense of self and object in an interrelated context (Lichtenberg, 1979), therapeutic flexibility is required so that the analyst can become a fine-tuned, attuned object relating to and reflecting the patient's developing self. For patients at the level of emergent grandiosity, the analyst who mirrors the patient's grandiosity enables confession to serve as a vehicle to enhance the patient's self-esteem. In the capacity of an idealized object, the analyst enables some patients to realize fantasies of being saved through confession.

Since shameful or guilt-ridden confessions are contained and accepted, rather than utilized to hurt or demean the patient, the analyst becomes a nonthreatening, reflective extension of the patient's self that can be both controlled and benignly manipulated (Winnicott, 1968/1971) by the patient. (For a detailed analysis of the narcissistic aspects of confession, see Chapter 4.) Particularly when such patients view themselves as bound to persecutory figures or simply unredeemable parents, the idealized analyst offers the prospect of boundless narcissistic supplies and deliverance from past objects.

Patients who relate to the analyst as a need-gratifying object often are wont to confess in the presence of a mirroring analyst whose supportive, empathic responses confirm the patient's self-worth. With such patients a gentle, encouraging question is often sufficient to elicit a confession. A patient prefaced her hesitation in revealing her secret to me by stating seductively, "I've never told this to anyone before. I don't even know if I can tell you, because it's really shameful and sick."

I replied, "You can tell me whenever you feel ready and comfortable." The patient, smiling impishly, said, "I might as well tell you now, since I've already brought up the topic." In such instances patients at the need-gratifying level tend to respond to accepting, unintrusive statements from the analyst.

Patients who have attained an individuated self now experience a multitude of objects as separate entities. In tandem with the oedipal stage, in which both the self and the object can be seen as distinct, secrets revolving around bodily and sexual functions become more important. While still concerned with the maintenance of a favorable self-image, the child also wishes to preserve a bond with the object, who is now seen as separate from the self. As such the object is empowered with the ability to affirm or retaliate against the self; to empathize or criticize; to offer psychic stability or to abandon the self. The analytic object, therefore, is especially vital as a focal point in the reexperiencing or reevaluation of the incident years later.

In the positive transference, patients become particularly attached to the analyst, because they feel that the analyst has understood them in a way that they have never before been understood. Strachey's (1934) early contribution involving the patient's introjection of the analyst as a good object related to the analyst's not retaliating against or entering into the patient's neurotic vicious cycle. In accepting the patient's confession, the analyst becomes transformed from a strict parental superego to a benign and loving superego (Strachey, 1934; Schafer, 1960). Patients can thereby assimilate the analyst as a good object and become correspondingly less harsh on themselves.

Patients experiencing positive transference feelings often perceive the analyst as powerful, but nonjudgemental. Confessions become reparative to the extent that patients recreate a situation in which the benign and valued parent now accepts them unconditionally. In this scenario past object relationships are literally "recreated" rather than statically repeated. Parental and other significant objects are given the opportunity to be transformed and redeemed *in vivo* in the context of an ongoing therapeutic relationship.

Camus' protagonist in *The Fall* (1956) surmises, "Inasmuch as every judge some day ends up as a penitent, one had to travel the road in the opposite direction and practice the profession of penitent to be able to end up as a judge" (p. 138). Every mother has been a child and every therapist a confessant/patient. A patient's willingness to entrust confessions to the therapist involves the development of a bond of trust between them—and also the patient's knowledge that the therapist has been there. To the extent that the analyst is seen not only as a mirroring object reflecting the patient's self, but also as an intersubjective presence who has empathically lived a similar experience, the likelihood of confession increases.

The patient who projects toxic contents into the analyst is likely to perceive the analyst either as a safe receptacle who can process and return secret contents to facilitate self-integration or as a dangerous, predatory container that may be contaminated, and possibly destroyed, by the "ruthless" patient's confessional contents. In an alternate fantasy, the analyst is transformed into a persecutory object retaliating against the patient for dumping toxic confessional contents, metaphorically viewed by some of my patients as "toxic wastes," into the object.

For patients engaged in primitive idealization, the omnipotent analyst remains impervious to the toxic contents of their projective identifications, and, in fact, is able to transform these dangerous secret aspects into a benign form via neutralization (Hartmann, 1964) or reverie (Bion 1962/1967). That is to say, the analyst assists the patient in developing the ability to neutralize destructive rage or sexuality by the analyst's not being destroyed by the confession, and teaches the patient to reflect upon rather than act on unneutralized affects accompanying the confession.

When I informally interviewed several of my colleagues and they, in turn, questioned their former patients, there was surprising agreement about the therapist's major qualities that facilitate confession. The following words or phrases appeared most often in descriptions of the therapist:

    1. Nonjudgemental: The therapist would neither adopt a religious confessional posture in branding the confession sinful nor repeat the critical, evaluative stance of past significant objects.

    2. Safe and trustworthy: The patient was free to confess anything because the analyst could not betray him or her due to the rule of confidentiality.

    3. Soothing: The analyst could both contain the patient's confessions (Bion, 1977) and return them to the patient in a more palatable form to be dealt with further. The analyst is also seen as a soothing selfobject whose empathic presence contributes to catharsis and calmness following confession.

    4. Empathic: The analyst is able to hear the confession without interpreting it. This function is particularly important when schizophrenic, borderline or certain narcissistic patients

first offer tentative confessions. Since interpretations during the early stages of therapy may be seen as distancing devices that render the analyst distinct and alien or dangerous, a minimum of interpretation enhances the object bond and encourages the patient to continue to risk confessing without the fear of overt reactions, including interpretations, from the analyst.

5. Nonintrusive: Many schizophrenic patients regard even the most neutral question as interference, which causes them to withdraw further. I have mentioned that confessions are thus most likely to be evoked when the analyst blends with the environment and silently awaits the patient's confessions. For narcissistic patients the nonintrusive analyst is most likely to become a selfobject extension that allows mirroring and idealizing transference configurations that facilitate confession to develop. To confess, in such circumstances, is to articulate and share an aspect of self with another aspect of self embodied in the selfobject.

6. Understanding: Traditionally consigned to the analyst's interpretive function, the analyst's empathy likewise enters into acceptance as well as cognitive processing of the confession. Kohut and Kernberg both view empathy as integral to attuned interpretations. Interpretations thus facilitate the truth-gaining function of confessions and also strengthen the object relationship.

7. "Nonphony": Both patients and analysts repeatedly mentioned this phrase to connote that the analyst was genuinely concerned and interested in the confession, rather than simply doing a job by rote. The perception of the analyst as an authentic, caring object strengthened patients' conviction that the confession would be taken seriously and followed through to completion.

Confessions tie the patient to the analyst with the cement emanating from the true self as binder. To this end Jung (1933) comments, "For we are all in some way or other kept asunder by our secrets, and instead of seeking through confession to bridge the abyss that separates us from one another, we choose the easy byway of deceptive opinions and illusions" (p. 36).

Stolorow and Atwood (1979) relate the poignant story of Jung's secret wooden manikin representing a feared Jesuit priest that became both a transitional object and an object for grandiose identification. The authors comment, "The reassurance provided by his secret existence of grandeur and immortality came at the price of terrible feelings of alienation and estrangement from his family, his peers, indeed, from the whole of humanity" (p. 98). Jung (1945/1965) thirsted for an empathic object to relate to, but "nowhere did I find a point of contact; on the contrary, I sensed in others an estrangement, a distrust, an apprehension which robbed me of speech" (p. 63).

Jung's secret existence to protect the vulnerable self took place at the expense of the dismantling of the edifice of human relatedness. His secret manikin, in itself, became a personified object to which he related. Such surrogate relationships often provide an illusory satisfaction at best, since the object, via projective identification, can turn on the patient, or serves as a reminder to the patient of how lonely she or he really is. These secret objects are utilized by schizoid patients to separate from rather than to join with other people.

With regard to the psychodynamic functions of nonhuman objects, I am reminded of a former patient, Candy, a 27-year-old clerical worker, who had served time in jail for various misdemeanors. Candy was especially reticent about revealing the circumstances surrounding a number of tattoos that she sported. At one time she had been proud of these objects, which served as emblems of her "butch, macho image" (the patient's characteristic phrase to describe herself). However, she finally blurted out the story behind them, since her fear of the consequences of an impending operation to remove the most prominent tattoo outweighed her embarrassment.

Candy confessed, never raising her eyes from the ground, "I carved 'Sandra loves Candy' into my skin with a lead pencil sharpened against the concrete floor of the jail." The patient had tattooed herself to please her girlfriend, Sandra, a large, matriarchal-looking black woman, and when the patient finally ended the relationship, Sandra sadistically gloated, "Now I'm under your skin forever."

This patient began life by being violently separated from her mother, whose water broke on the way to the hospital. She continued to live with her mother—who denigrated her, engaged in sex in front of the child, and actually reported her daughter to the police for allegedly stealing her car. Through all of these traumas, Candy continued to yearn for any kind of relationship with her rejecting mother. "After all, she's the only mother I have." In Fairbairn's schema the rejecting object became the sought-after, exciting object.

Wrenched out of the at-one-ment of symbiosis, Candy's tattoo became the symbol of symbiosis with a loved, cherished maternal object. The fact that this girlfriend also renounced and taunted her, in conjunction with the establishment of a nascent, symbiotic tie with me, eventuated in Candy's decision to undergo surgery to remove the tattoo and simultaneously to start to separate from the bad maternal objects pervading her existence.

Grotstein's (1982) nutritive and stimulating functions of the object are especially important in confession. The "feeding analyst," who is perceived as giving, is more likely to get back confessions in a form of mutuality inherent in good mother–infant interactions elucidated by Winnicott. Yet such mutuality does not consist of identical functions, but of complementary tasks. In other words the good mother/analyst does not trade confessions with the child/patient to provide arbitrary gratification, seduction, or competition, but gives by attending to and showing concern to match the needs of the growing child/patient. In this fertile environment, the patient, in turn, is impelled to give to the object through confession, as an outgrowth of the complementary functions of the therapeutic dyad.

Grotstein (1982) cites the positive functions of the stimulating object, including "the capacity...to teach, to awaken, to evoke initiative in the infant so that the infant can discover its own self-stimulation along with self-regulation" (p. 67). The analyst who is seen as encouraging rather than exhorting helps teach the person to become a patient. Confession is a natural therapeutic outgrowth of becoming a patient. The patient does not learn to confess by listening to the analyst's confessions, but develops the courage and initiative to risk confessing by being with the receptive, interested analyst whose stance, rather than overt behavior, fosters confession.

Finally, the analyst's container function (Bion, 1977) enables confessions to be processed and understood by the patient in a new way. Rosenfeld (1983) notes that projective identification can serve as a defense against acknowledging disavowed aspects of the self by getting rid of them via expulsion into the analyst. Confession can thereby be facilitated if the patient perceives that undesirable secret contents are expelled, but not lost, since the analyst serves as the repository for these contents that may thus be controlled. If patients thus divest themselves of bad objects, they do not suffer the loss of total separation as they are still able to relate to these objects that are rendered less dangerous at a distance.

"THE PLAY'S THE THING"

Play in psychotherapy becomes a special form of communication in which confessions can emerge in an atmosphere of spontaneity and stimulation. Winnicott (1971) ascribed a creative, feeding function to the patient's and analyst's playing together in therapy. But play and games can also operate in the service of self-deception and inauthenticity to hinder confession (Goffman, 1959; Berne, 1964; Laing, 1970).

Before entering therapy, and even during the early stages, the patient may be so inured to inauthentic relating of the sort epitomized in Berne's *Games People Play* (1964) that self- and other-deception constitute the patient's primary mode of communication. Berne's "con games," in which others are manipulated and controlled, in Winnicott's world give way to guideless play in which intimacy and joy prevail. In risking confession patients have to pry themselves loose from Goffman's (1959) anonymous, game-filled world. The duality of experience inherent in Goffman's out-front (false self) and backstage (true self) schism becomes authentic self-revelation in confession.

Consider the following scenario in Laing's *Knots* (1970). "They are playing a game. If I show them I see they are, I shall break the rules and they will punish me. I must play their game, of not seeing I see the game."

Laing is here describing the dilemma of the person who decides to be inauthentic about his or her authenticity. Both the patient and therapist, at times, may find themselves stuck in one of Laing's knots.

Leonora, a 31-year-old schizophrenic patient, harbored a wealth of secrets she believed to be toxic enough to kill me, or, via *lex talionis*, to annihilate her. In the stillness of silent affirmation, she was slowly able to expel some of the less dangerously perceived secrets in measured doses to test me. Two years following the initial confessional testing period, Leonora tremblingly revealed that she sometimes wanted to kill me.

She went over to my toy chest, picked up a toy gun, and brought it to the couch. She then aimed it at various parts of the room and intoned, "Bang, bang, you're dead, Mother. Bang, bang, you're dead. Q. R. (her sister)." And finally, "Bang, bang, you're dead," pointing the gun at me. That I did not question, comment, or goad this patient in any way following her enacted confession enabled her to be the ruthless baby (Winnicott, 1975) who can destroy mother, but also can recreate mother, who remains unharmed.

The play element involved in the patient's use of a toy gun detoxified the full power of her rage. The medium of play enabled Leonora to convey the confessional communication and also to mute somewhat the aggressive drive derivatives. This patient was so relieved that I could serve as a container for her toxic confession and survive the onslaught of the confession that she felt increasingly freer to break the game plan of propriety and secrecy and continue gradually to reveal aspects of the true self.

The analyst who rigidly adheres to a limited treatment plan may find himself or herself locked into a game with rigid rules that benefit neither the patient nor the therapeutic relationship. The constraint that comes with adherence to an ego ideal of intransigent therapeutic standards prevents the therapist from adapting to the particular needs of each patient to facilitate the emergence and working through of confessions.

Confession, in short, is capable of cutting through or destroying games predicated on control and manipulation. Buber's (1937) famous dictum that "all real living is meeting" (p. 11) speaks to the authenticity experienced by many patients who confess in the therapeutic environment. Confession can represent a game-free communication that enhances intimacy and authenticity, unless the patient utilizes it as a game to bolster resistance.

The following are the major rules of the "game of confession"—a form of inauthentic self- and other-deception in the service of resistance.

1. Two or more players: patient and therapist (and/or group).

2. Goals:

a. To absolve the self without structural change enacted by working through of the material.

b. To absolve the self and continue to repeat the substance of the secret in the form of different variations on the same theme.

c. To offer the therapist a minor or false confession to protect the self from heightened vulnerability—"throw the dog a bone" strategy.

d. To relate, in group therapy, an even more dramatic, lurid, horrifying, or otherwise forbidden confession to triumph narcissistically over the other members—"can you top this?" strategy. Each confession here becomes a narcissistic nugget to win the fantasized sweepstake prize proffered for "best confession." The analyst would do well, in such circumstances, to analyze the resistance function served by this confessional group process.

In the game of confession, each goal is designed to protect the self and manipulate the analyst or group into colluding with the patient's conscious or unconscious aim of not passing certain limits in the exploration and resolution of the confession. While such games fulfill the risk and relief aspects of confession to a limited extent, redemption and renewal cannot come about in such a game-suffused environment. For Buber redemption connotes a return to relation that can come about only by way of authentic dialogical relating in a game-free environment.

One of Winnicott's great contributions to the understanding of what constitutes mental health was to add a play dimension to Freud's dual criteria of love and work. In Winnicott's conception of healthy play between patient and analyst, both move toward greater mutuality in an authentic atmosphere of joyful relatedness. Playing implies trust in the object and the capacity to be alone in someone's presence (Winnicott, 1958). The spontaneity of play enables the patient to discover the true self.

In *Playing and Reality* (1971), Winnicott states, "Playing facilitates growth and therefore health; playing leads into group relationships; playing can be a form of communication in psychotherapy; and, lastly, psychoanalysis has been developed as a highly specialized form of playing in the service of communication with oneself and others" (p. 41). Much, if not all, spontaneity on the part of the therapist becomes lost or disappears entirely when the therapist opts for strictly "playing by the rules" in lieu of engaging in Winnicottian creative playing. Such therapists show extreme counterresistance in helping the patient evolve from a state of not being able to play into a state of playful receptivity.

Greenacre (1959), in turn, has stressed the recreative aspects of play in adulthood. The patient who learns to play in therapy has found a medium by which to revive the past to achieve self-renewal. In the relaxed atmosphere of the analytic setting, the patient can flex his or her creative potential in fantasy and free association in the presence of the analyst/play companion. Confessions are likely to be forthcoming when the patient, in a state of relaxation, feels free confessionally to revive repressed memories or disavowed aspects of self and objects as a natural outgrowth of the play environment integral to the patient–therapist dyad.

Play allows the patient to search for and retrieve the lost object. Games such as hide-and-seek hold such a fascination for us because we know that the hidden object is not permanently lost and because the sought-after object is secure in the knowledge that he or she is not irrevocably hidden and out of sight. Thus the game of hide-and-seek strengthens the bonds of connectedness by ensuring that the lost object will be found.

In psychotherapy patients likewise search for lost objects through play with the analyst. With the analytic space becoming the "lost and found," the analyst, in turn, becomes the found object in two respects:

> 1. On a transferential level, the patient reenacts repressed secrets with parental objects that are retrieved and revivified in the patient's relationship with the analyst. The unfolding transference itself becomes a confessional revelation in which long-repressed interactions with archaic objects become manifest in the patient's current relations with the analyst. Disavowed aspects of objects likewise are disclosed through projective identification in which lost objects are found in the patient's perception and treatment of the analyst.
> 2. As a new object, the analyst's spontaneity and creativity encourage confession as one of the patient's contributions to creative expression. The analyst also enables the patient to risk dispensing with bad internalized objects by offering hope for a form of relatedness in which objects are redeemable and cast out of different molds from those of past objects.

One of the ways in which patients learn to play is by developing an interest in their dream world. The patient plays in dreams and the analyst/mother plays with the patient in analyzing dreams. Puns in several of my patients' dreams, in their literal capacity as plays on words, provided a nonthreatening, playful means for confessions to emerge in veiled form.

For example, one patient, whose dream experiences in the Metropolitan Museum of Art assumed an increasingly greater nightmarish quality, one day revealed with a start that her boyfriend's name was Art. Her relationship with him, which had been couched in a rosy shadow of self-deception, was somewhat disabused of its illusory quality in her "dream play." Another patient, who was never able to confess any of her hateful, envious, or angry feelings toward me, had a dream in which she was trapped in a concentration camp. From her associations it soon became apparent that concentration camp was a metaphor for the confining aspects of therapy, and more especially, for the suffocating aspects of her relationship with her mother and myself. My interpretation of the concentration camp as therapy evoked a delighted laugh of recognition from the patient, who was able to enter into the dream play with unselfconscious glee. As the dream was a safe, once-removed object, she was able to escape direct confessional confrontation with me.

Diamond's (1984) research on the brain's plasticity has convincingly demonstrated that even in the case of rats placed in an environment enriched with toys and playmates, the cortex begins to thicken after just a few days. The fact that neurological changes are evidenced in so short a time suggests the tremendous transformational potential of the brain following exposure to external, stimulating objects.

Diamond's research, which is now being applied to human populations, suggests that persons of all ages can experience a sense of renewal as a result of environmental stimulation. The analyst and patient who play together are engaged in transformational activities that pave the way for renewal. The confession itself constitutes an especially stimulating object exchange in which the patient, in an atmosphere of playful spontaneity, is better able to risk confession.

SELECT THEORETICAL FORMULATIONS REGARDING THE FUNCTIONS OF THE OBJECT IN CONFESSION

Mitchell (1984) points out that to view object relations theory as preconflictual in contradistinction to drive theory creates a false dichotomy. The coterminous nature of conflict and relatedness is embodied in the therapeutic process itself. To relate to the therapist is also to face the conflict of eventual separation. Indeed all patients and therapists are confronted with the paradox of embarking upon a relationship of sustained intimacy that ends in separation.

Klein

Once the patient has attained the depressive position, the object is seen as whole and the patient can experience ambivalence. That the patient has passed through the earlier paranoid-schizoid position implies that the predominant schizoid defenses of splitting, projective identification, denial, introjection, and idealization are relinquished, so that split-off bad aspects of the object can be reconciled with the good object.

The patient can thus view the object as better able to handle the patient's secret "bad" contents without being destroyed or retaliating. The analytic object is likewise not seen as so good and idealized that he or she would not be able to understand and empathize with the patient's secrets. The patient who is able to bring split-off envious parts of the self regarding the analyst and mother into awareness through confession can come to experience the analytic session as a happy feed (Klein, 1975). Acknowledgment and integration of split-off disavowed aspects of self and objects bring about feelings of gratitude directed at the whole object.

According to Klein the successfully analyzed patient sees objects more benignly in passing out of the paranoid-schizoid position. McGlashan and Miller (1980) extrapolate this concept to patients who show greater interest in a larger number of objects rather than being preoccupied with unrealistic private wishes and fantasies. Patients who replace excessive daydreaming, television watching, or sleeping with interactions with others fulfill this criterion of greater connectedness with external objects.

Confession initiates a move in the direction of inner to outer relatedness. What was once an excessive, private, inner preoccupation is now thrust into the domain of interpersonal relatedness as the patient risks sharing an aspect of the inner self with the analyst.

The expansion of the number and kinds of extrafamilial objects can be seen through the confessional lens, which encompasses more objects as analysis progresses. In extreme cases the analyst may be the first and only object on whom the patient bestows "exclusive rights" to the confession. For many patients, however, this push toward relatedness is a tentative step in the direction of generalizing such disclosures to extratherapeutic objects. Since the analyst is already transferentially invested with many of the qualities of extratherapeutic objects, a positive confessional experience in therapy sets the stage for a widening circle of objects in whom the patient feels comfortable confiding.

Searles and Fairbairn

Klein, Fairbairn, and Winnicott all maintain that the patient's full-blown experience of hatred, rage, and destructiveness consolidates object ties. The patient who blithely confesses the content of a long-concealed secret has certainly taken a risk in expressing and sharing an aspect of his or her inner self with another. But confession connotes more than the sometimes desiccated description of a historical happening. Confession is also a living, breathing experience that transpires in the presence of objects who evoke intense thoughts and feelings in the patient. Thus the analyst is interested not only in unearthing the historical residue of the confession, but also in tacitly encouraging the patient to express the forbidden emotions attached to the objects that enter into the confession.

Regarding the countertransferential import of jealousy as a frequently disavowed affect, Searles (1979) discovered that he was jealous of a patient's dialogue with hallucinatory objects who would direct his attention away from the analyst. My patient, Clara, engaged in conversations with God and Dram—her principal projections of internal objects. While I, at one time, was seen as the secret ally of the miscreant Dram, the patient began to see me as God's ally. "He tells me to listen to you, but Dram is strong and tells me not to eat, read, or do anything."

As I became predominantly a good object allied with God, Clara felt more comfortable in talking about Dram to the omnipotent, idealized, condensed analyst/God object. Dram, who at first was seen as an entirely invasive foreign object, became localized in the right side of the patient's brain. During one session Clara began to hold her head and shake, moaning, "Dram feels like he's part of me—not me, but yes, me too. I can't stand it anymore."

A nonpsychotic internal split is poignantly described by Updike (1985), who confesses how the first outbreak of psoriasis at age six influenced his subsequent relationships and creativity. "What was my creativity, my relentless need to *produce*, but a parody of my skin's embarrassing overproduction? Was not my thick literary skin...a superior version of my poor vulnerable own, and my shamelessness on the page a distraction from my real shame, my skin?" (pp. 55–56).

Updike's inner split creates the skin as an object in conflict with the rest of Updike's self. While Updike attributes a sexual aspect to his concern with his skin—"the moment of undressing, the supreme revelation and confiding," the desire for self-acceptance predominates. "Yet sexual contentment...never reconciled me to my skin or relaxed my wish to improve it, my war had to do with self-love, with finding myself acceptable, whether others did or not" (p. 55).

Searles (1979a) has also written about the internal object projected onto a nonhuman thing that becomes a third person in a jealousy-ridden triangular relationship; he cites the example of the patient who fantasized that the mother/analyst lavished care on the plants at his expense. The role of the nonhuman object in the elucidation of confession became manifest in a session in which my patient Rosanna, a 27-year-old laboratory technician, castigated me for my "ugly Hummel figurine"—a confession that enabled her to express her mounting feelings of rage at me, and also to disclose a complex series of relationships condensed in the one figurine. The nonhuman Hummel object contained three "forbidden" elements:

1. The figurine's link with Germany endowed it with persecutory qualities. Further exploration of what the object meant to Rosanna elicited the idea that I, too, would torment her by invading her. (This patient often perceived interpretations as invasions.) My purchase of the Hummel allied me with external enemies (the patient's assessment of Germans) and her own internal bad objects.

2. Rosanna, who was beginning to fear increased intimacy with me, was able to devalue me via my esthetic preferences, and thus establish more distance from me. The patient also chose to confess her feelings toward me directly through a third object that served to prevent indirectly verbal confrontation from taking place.

3. As a child Rosanna would accompany her father to museums and they would exclude her mother, who "does not understand and has no esthetic taste." The patient was thereby able to triumph over the internalized oedipal mother and transferential surrogate mother/analyst and to strengthen the bond with the oedipal father.

Guntrip (1969) relates how Fairbairn compared psychoanalysis to an exorcism in which the devils of our unconscious world are cast out. In Fairbairn's system these devils take the form of internal bad objects that must be abolished and substituted for relationships with real good objects in the external world.

Patients, however, often cling to their internalized bad objects—a defensive bond viewed by Fairbairn as a major form of resistance in which bad objects are considered better than no objects. Fairbairn (1943) elaborates, "The resistance can only really be overcome when the transference situation develops to a point at which the analyst has become such a good object to the patient that the latter is prepared to risk the release of bad objects from the unconscious" (p. 332). When the analyst comes to be viewed as a trusted, reliable good object, patients can begin to risk divesting themselves of their bad objects through confession.

From an object relations perspective, confessions not only involve the risk of revealing "forbidden" material, but also the fantasy of total object loss through the expulsion of internalized bad objects. In other words, for some patients confession carries the cataclysmic consequences of "throwing the baby out with the bath water." And just as bad habits are hard to break, such patients discover that bad objects are difficult to separate from.

Borderline and schizoid patients, in particular, cling to bad objects, since to disaffiliate oneself from bad internal objects is to be a "no-thing." For the patient who confesses experiences of being battered or of self-mutilation, the definition as a somebody is contingent upon relationships with bad objects who continue to hold sway in the patient's internal world. Such confessed self-destructive behaviors, in Fairbairn's view, are not indicative of the search for pleasure through pain or any other drive-derived theory, but disclose the need to establish and maintain relationships with objects who, no matter how abusive, still provide the patient with a vital human connection.

Mitchell (1984) views object relations theorists, such as Fairbairn and Guntrip, as subscribing to the view that the analyst offers himself or herself as a good object operating "outside the closed system of the patient's internalized object relations...the 'good object' must offer something real...which makes possible the leap out of the closed world of the patient's fantasized object ties" (p. 497). I have previously described (Hymer, 1984) the role of the friend as a good object offsetting the Danteesque horrors of Kernberg's (1975) description of the narcissistic patient's internal object world. "The intrapsychic world of these patients is populated only by their grandiose self, by devaluated, shadowy images of self and others, and by potential persecutors representing the nonintegrated, sadistic superego forerunners, as well as primitive, distorted object images onto whom intense oral sadism has been projected" (p. 282).

The other object relations approach described by Mitchell (1984) pertains to the analyst's providing missing relational experiences at the point of environmental failure. Both Winnicott and Balint advocate benign regression in which the analyst can help fill in the developmental need for object affiliation caused by the failure of fit between the child's needs and the mother's response. The analytic object thereby facilitates what Balint terms a "new beginning." In several previous chapters, I have outlined how the analyst as idealized or mirroring selfobject, in Kohut's (1984) schema, enables narcissistic structures to emerge, be played out, and be transformed into healthy narcissism. From a developmental deficit theoretical perspective, the patient's ability to merge with or experience control over the analyst facilitates confession. To confess in the presence of the empathic analyst without catastrophic consequences is to undergo a new experience with an object perceived as a "second self" (Cicero).

Balint, Modell, and Bion

Patients who confess or resist self-disclosure struggle with maintaining a balance between seeking the object and distancing from the object. Balint (1979) describes two types of object relationships: ochnophilia, in which patients intensely cling to objects for security; and philobatism, in which the inner world is clung to to ensure independence from dangerous external objects.

These clinical observations are in substantial accord with the developmental research findings of Ainsworth (Ainsworth, 1966; Ainsworth & Bell, 1970), who classified infants according to the bonds they formed with their mothers during the first two years of life. She observed that infants who experienced their mothers as available and responsible were the most secure. Insecure infants, in turn, either became clinging or withdrawn.

The back-and-forth movement between clinging and distancing, which is especially characteristic of borderline patients (Masterson, 1976) but is found in all categories of patients to varying degrees, becomes a special problem in confession. Patients who fear they have revealed too much, either because the analyst, via splitting, is now transformed into a persecutory, bad object or because they fear punishment meted out by internal objects for disloyalty, may retreat into a mode of self-sufficiency and/or an alliance with more familiar internal bad objects.

Modell (1975) elaborates upon the patient's narcissistic defense of blocking affects motivated by a fear of closeness to the analytic object. This defense is buttressed by the fantasy of grandiose self-sufficiency in which the illusion is maintained that the patient seeks nothing from the analyst. Confession is frequently accompanied by strong affect, as well as increased intimacy with the object, and so such patients strenuously resist confession.

Since these patients experience the need to defend the separateness of the self against the unempathic mother's intrusiveness (Kohut, 1971; A. Miller, 1983), the empathic analyst develops a patient receptivity in awaiting the gradual emergence of trust through the transferential establishment of the analyst as a self-object extension. This therapeutic configuration enables the patient to relate to a new good object who is willing to supply the patient with developmental experiences that facilitate the emergence of a cohesive self able and willing to risk confession.

For such patients the establishment of a degree of closeness with the analyst, facilitated by the passage of time and the development of narcissistic transference configurations, becomes a necessary precursor to risking confession. Norbert, a 34-year-old administrator, mentioned that he had been drawing in his summer home when his mother interrupted him and insisted on asking when he would start making improvements on the house.

Genetic reconstructions revealed various childhood incidents in which the patient's self-expression was thwarted by his mother's needs. What gave his recital of this recent incident a confessional cast was that the intrusion was disclosed with a good deal of affect and Norbert was aware of his rage at his mother's self-absorption.

The first year of therapy was spent primarily in unintrusive, receptive listening on my part. Norbert experienced this interlude as a period in which attention was paid to his needs in the absence of a hidden agenda in which he was forced to reenact the historical scenario in which he supported the maternal object's needs.

Norbert's original cocoonlike attitude (Modell, 1975) was evident in our first telephone interchange, during which he informed me that he would be coming to therapy only three or four times to clear up some problems.

Norbert's disclosure of his mother's interruption not only was articulated with considerably more affect than usual, but also was punctuated by the comment, "I could kill her!" The patient, taken aback by the vehemence of this disclosure, smiled, and then continued to verbalize, in more measured fashion, how angry he was at his mother.

This confession signaled a turning point in therapy in that Norbert was sufficiently able to separate from his mother and derive courage from the new analytic object relationship to acknowledge his anger toward his mother, and his hatred of her. The multiple instances of his mother's demands that he do her bidding had heretofore resulted in blind compliance, since the patient had unconsciously adopted his mother's view of the world as his own (A. Miller, 1981, 1983).

So as not to be sucked into my agenda, Norbert started therapy, from the first phone call, imbued with the narcissistic defense of self-sufficiency. In allowing him to take center stage and build up narcissistic structures by my becoming a transferential nonintrusive selfobject, Norbert was able to alter his perspective in slowly separating from his engulfment with his mother.

The analyst's reliable presence, as well as actual differences from the original intrusive object, facilitates a complementary shift from a selfobject relationship in which the patient is the mother's selfobject extension to one in which the patient occupies the foreground with the analyst as selfobject extension. This transition endows the patient with a new experience in which the object is there for his or her needs.

Bion (1953/1967) describes how the patient destroys closeness to the object by "attacks on linking" while simultaneously being able to redeem the link through the mother/analyst's reverie. The analyst's reverie contains and transforms the patient's projective identifications into a more satisfying, soothing form that enables the patient to reintroject the modified nonsensual aspect of the mother/analyst's love. With regard to confession, the analyst's thought (reverie) enables him or her to survive the explosive or malevolent confessional contents of projective identifications and to neutralize the confession so that the patient can digest, assimilate, and reintroject it in reconstructive rather than destructive fashion.

Bion's (1958/1967) conception of bizarre objects as multiple minute fragments refers to the psychotic patient's attempts to get rid not only of objects, but also of ego functions, such as attention and judgement, via attacks on linking. Such attacks can assume the form of efforts to destroy any semblance of connectedness between the analyst and patient. Yet these bizarre objects paradoxically constitute a primitive form of inadvertent confessional communication directed at the analyst, who, at times, becomes the receptacle for the objects.

The patient's bodily jerks, for example, can herald an involuntary confession of such a secret bizarre object. One patient, who always disclosed the presence of a bizarre object with an involuntary shoulder jerk, finally admitted that the "keeper of the key" was there, but that he prohibited her from discussing his nature with me. The demonic object (a fragment of the patient's disavowed self) was projected outward, followed by attacks on linking in which further enlightenment was curtailed by the stern interdictions of the persecutory object.

In this manner the patient selectively emitted cues to the secret bizarre object, while simultaneously distancing herself from the analyst by attacking all communicative links in the form of comments and interpretations. For example, while remaining seemingly receptive to my comments regarding the "keeper," when I asked her what I said, she became blank and said that she could not remember. "I was falling though space while you were talking." My tentative interpretations and questions became dangerous, invasive objects to be negated through attacks on linking. Even after years of therapy, my interventions with this patient were still premature.

Again, to avoid this impasse with psychotic patients, the best confessional outcome is likely to accrue when the analyst assumes a silent, unintrusive, receptive stance. Confession is fostered in an atmosphere of symbiotic relatedness minimally disturbed by the analyst's interventions, which become independent objects to be attacked.

RENEWAL REVISITED

The third step in confession, *renewal*, enables patients to cast old objects into new forms. Confession thereby becomes a restitutive vehicle for object transformation.

Confession connotes a maturational step in which the patient retrieves, synthesizes, and risks sharing a profound communication with the analyst, who may represent a new narcissistic selfobject deemed safe and worthy of such communications or a positive transference figure evocative of the loving, trustworthy parents. Alternatively, in the capacity of the new object, the analyst may be designated in fantasy as the rescuer (*redemption* aspect of confession) and/or avenger of parental slights on the patient's behalf.

Even when the therapist is viewed in fantasy or reality as a new object, old objects are clearly present transferentially. Patients' articulation of confession brings past objects into the sweep of the present. As patients explore the nature of confession, they become engaged in an educational enterprise in which they are literally "led out of" historically seclusive, narrow object relations into wider, more flexible ways of relating to these objects.

In the final stages of confession—redemption/renewal—the patient may choose to forgive the self and parental objects in the realization of "accountability without blame" (Mitchell, 1981, p. 396). Both the self and object are thereby salvaged from fantasized ruin or destruction. Alternatively, the patient may redefine the parents as villainous bad objects only some of the time in "re-viewing" these objects as tragic figures who did not always know better rather than as Machiavellian persecutory objects totally devoid of positive attributes.

Wagner and Fine (1980) note that the new object relationship allows for a decrease in libidinal ties to internalized bad objects. The analyst can help the patient fend off and triumph over bad objects in the quest for autonomy and the acquisition of self-initiated ego activities.

This function reminded me of my patient John, a 27-year-old highly successful salesman, who confessed that he felt totally inept and unintelligent. "I don't even know if I blow my nose correctly. In every aspect of my life, I'm afraid to miss any detail. I see all the little details, but am afraid that I might miss the big picture. With my nephew I'm different. I encourage him to try to tie his own shoelaces."

John and I explored his memories regarding his learning to tie his shoelaces. John sighed and then remarked, "It was a big embarrassment. My parents probably thought it was easier just to tie my shoes for me. In second grade we had to change from our shoes to sneakers. I stayed behind and asked the teacher to tie my shoes." John felt robbed of the ability to think or reason for himself. As an adult he continued to see all the details so that he would not have to make choices and exercise independent judgement. John's relationship with me and the analytic process itself facilitated the steady emergence of problem-solving and general thinking skills, as the patient was forced to choose material—a task he initially strenuously resisted by asking me what we should talk about and requesting that I summarize the salient points at the end of the session.

Exploration of the meaning of these requests in the context of a new relationship in which I encouraged and mirrored self-initiated thought endowed this patient with the courage to risk both confession and related problem-solving and synthesizing functions. John was able to effect this transition as his attachment to me allowed him gradually to withdraw from the entrenched bond with the internalized parental objects. John's confession helped him come to terms with the limitations of past objects as well as of the analyst, who was not able to produce an immediate change in his reliance on others and his emphasis on details to offset the need to make major decisions.

A common type of "object-related confession" is one in which the patient assumes a unidimensional view of the parents as villains and the child/patient as a martyr who was made to feel guilty, ashamed, unworthy, or unloved after an alleged wrongdoing was discovered. This perspective can undergo decentering (Piaget, 1962/1977) when, through the working through of the transference, the patient comes to see the parents and self as possessing other cognitive-affective dimensions, as well.

Such statements as, "I guess they were loving, too; they operated out of ignorance; I tried my best, but had no power," while no doubt indicative of rationalization in some patients, in other patients represent a reevaluation of the self and objects in multidimensional terms. Such reevaluations are reparative to both the self and the objects as the patient attempts to complete the contours of self and object relations by adding cognitive-affective aspects to his or her previous unidimensional focus (Piaget, 1962/1977) or by moving from splitting to ambivalence (Klein, 1975).

Patients are able to effect these changes, in part, because the analyst serves as an object whose real qualities, such as professional abilities and ideals (Blum, 1981), suggest new alternatives for relatedness. Further, the analyst as transferential object enables good and bad aspects of past objects to be brought to light, examined, and worked through in the context of specific confessions.

Regarding the redemptive aspect of confessions, Sandler and Sandler (1978) and Sandler (1981) set forth the thesis that patients strive to reenact a particular unconscious wished-for role relationship in the therapeutic object relationship to gain reassurance. It has been my experience that when patients confess, they simultaneously wish for a repetition of a parental response and hope for a reprieve and reconstruction. This reconstruction literally becomes a rebuilding in which both patient and analyst have the opportunity to interact in a way that alters the situation and the players in the situation so that the patient can extract those wished-for parental qualities in the analyst and add those longed-for qualities missing in the archaic objects.

Let us look at a typical confession. A little boy hits his sister and blackmails her into giving him more of her candy. The parents, upon discovering his secret, send him to his room without dinner, and revoke his allowance. As the patient discloses his secret, he remembers how he then saw his parents as totally unfair, bad objects.

During therapy the patient repeats his secret by cashing an insurance check that accidentally went to the patient instead of the analyst. The patient's secret wish to gain attention through adopting an attitude of entitlement was acted out to mold the analyst reconstructively to adopt parental traits of attentiveness, firmness, and limit setting.

Still the patient does not desire the analyst solely to repeat parental attitudes and behavior, but also selectively to modify such traits in order to renew the relationship; that is, the patient literally wishes to salvage the positive aspects of archaic objects, while adding new dimensions to heal the splits in self and objects. For example, in the aforementioned confession, the analyst as new object explores meanings and motives rather than summarily meting out punishment. Yet, like the archaic parents, the analyst also sets limits on what the patient can and cannot do.

Confession takes place in an interpersonal context in which patients attempt to strike a balance between seeking after the object and deriving autonomy from the object. In many instances of confession, the object relationship with the analyst is a wished-for repetition as well as a rebuilding in which select aspects of historical objects are retained while new elements in the self and object are explored and selectively added.

11
Ethical and Legal Dilemmas

There was a time, not so long ago, when diligent psychotherapists learned theories of development and principles of technique and practiced psychotherapy without worrying about ethical or legal considerations. For many years Freud set anxious analysts' minds to rest by espousing the doctrine of scientific objectivity as the sole permissible analytic value. In the famous passage from the 35th introductory lecture, Freud (1933) said, "Psychoanalysis in my opinion is incapable of creating a *Weltanschauung* of its own. It does not need one; it is a part of science and can adhere to the scientific *Weltanschauung*" (p. 181).

Nonetheless, while the issue of values and ethics has often been minimized or ignored in psychoanalysis, there have been notable exceptions (Hartmann, 1962; London, 1964). London, in particular, has championed the notion that the moral stance (conscious and unconscious) of both therapist and patient must be acknowledged and reckoned with if therapy is to remain a viable medium of communication. In London's (1964) words, "Some problems are inevitably moral ones from the perspective of either client or therapist" (p. 6).

Not all confessions comprise strictly intrapsychic or interpersonal problems. Some involve macrolevel religious, political, economic, or sociocultural issues whose outcome may have a direct impact on the patient as well as on society. The celebrated Tarasoff case cogently demonstrated to therapists that the therapeutic domain of confidentiality could no longer be separated from larger societal concerns.

While ethics and the law are not always twin handmaidens of the psychoanalytic process, they must now be taken into account by both patient and therapist when the patient makes a confession. As Gerald Johnson once remarked, "To equate ethics with legality is to adopt the morality of a scoundrel." The therapy couple nevertheless is subject to both legal and ethical imperatives.

Ethical "oughts" and legal "musts" have intruded into the privacy of psychotherapeutic treatment. Therapists or patients who attempt to eschew ethical and legal issues or who hide behind the cloak of so-called neutrality or scientific objectivity may find themselves vulnerable to legal and/or ethical battles. In such instances patient and therapist may undergo even greater embarrassment by public exposure of confessions that might never have advanced so far were the patient and therapist more cognizant of their liability under the law.

Because of concerns about the legal liability, free associations no longer can be indiscriminately free. Originally free association was implemented by Freud to lower the patient's moral compunctions. Today legal injunctions, including the therapist's "duty to warn," along with suggested informed consent guidelines (Hare-Mustin et al., 1979; Everstine et al., 1980; Berger, 1982), heighten an already resistant patient's reticence to risk confession.

Confessions, for example, that involve such issues as drug trafficking, child abuse, or sexual perversion present an overtly ethical and/or legal dimension. The therapist is best able to handle such confessions by being aware of the laws pertaining to confidentiality and privilege, and paying close attention to his or her own countertransferential reactions, including fear, repulsion, revulsion, dismay, disapproval, or even envy (if such confessions evoke the therapist's own forbidden secret desires).

These countertransferential affective reactions themselves sometimes constitute silent confessions of the therapist's own disavowed wishes, thoughts, or feelings, which can aid in the empathic understanding of the patient's confession. Empathy, however, requires that the therapist not defensively cut himself or herself off from the information conveyed by these feelings. Counter-transference, distilled in the person of the therapist, can likewise represent a generalized societal reaction to a confession in which the collective other (the community at large) is threatened.

Thus the therapy couple no longer simply faces the host of objects from the patient's and therapist's internal and external worlds, but also impersonal social forces, including the ethical guidelines of professional organizations, insurance companies, and legal codes. These additional elements have irrevocably altered the rules and ambience of treatment.

One nonsolution to a confession that poses an ethical dilemma is to avoid the issue. In this case the therapist is colluding with the patient by acting in bad faith in invoking the illusory concept of therapeutic neutrality. This same therapist may either rationalize that he or she has no authority to act otherwise or pray that the patient will leave with his or her confessional albatross. The therapist's disavowal or avoidance of such confessions serves as a mirror for the patient to disavow or avoid direct confrontation of a potentially central, or even life-threatening matter.

An example of an increasingly common confession with inescapable moral overtones concerns disclosures by heterosexual and homosexual patients of sexual episodes with homosexuals, which they fear will have future repercussions. The therapist who adopts a so-called morally neutral stance, and discusses genetic and current origins of such fears, as well as transferential implications, is still hard put to avoid these patients' real concerns. For example, the patient may be concerned with such religious-philosophical questions as: "Why did my friend die? Why not me? Why did AIDS appear at this point in history?"

Whatever the therapist's degree of activity or inactivity in such interchanges, he or she will still be transferentially invested with a moral position by the patient. Further, even a therapist's nonverbal stance may be seen as a libertarian position. In this light the therapist is viewed as advocating a laissez-faire, noninterventionist approach to *any* confession—whether or not larger societal forces are at stake. Finally, because an increasing number of therapists are now speaking out publicly on social concerns, patients may already be privy to therapists' publicly disclosed values.

THE TARASOFF CASE: CONFIDENTIALITY AND THE "DUTY TO WARN"

Since 1969 (the year of the Tarasoff case[1]), a number of states[2] have mandated that a psychotherapist must make public, under certain circumstances, what a patient has confided, no matter how deeply personal that confession might have been. The precedent-setting case was as follows: On August 20, 1969, a student outpatient named Poddar confessed to his therapist that he intended to murder his girlfriend, Tatiana Tarasoff, when she returned to the University of California at Berkeley after her vacation. The psychotherapist contacted the campus police, who took Poddar into custody, but later released him. Poddar subsequently terminated therapy.

On October 27, Poddar killed Tarasoff. Neither Tarasoff nor her parents were warned. Her parents filed suit against the university, certain employees at Cowell Memorial Hospital (where Poddar was an outpatient), the chief of the campus police and four officers, and the psychologist. The case was dismissed by the lower court, but on appeal, the California Supreme Court ruled that the psychologist and his supervisor failed to provide an adequate warning of Poddar's intended homicide to either the victim or her parents. Rejecting a defense based on patient-therapist confidentiality, the court wrote, "The protective privilege ends when the public peril begins."

The rule announced in the Tarasoff case was subsequently codified. The California Evidence Code of 1965 thus contains the following exception to patient-therapist privilege: "There is no privilege…if the psychotherapist has reasonable cause to believe that the patient is in such a mental or emotional condition as to be dangerous to himself or to the person or property of another and that disclosure of the communication is necessary to prevent the threatened danger" (cited in Everstine et al., 1980, p. 836). The Tarasoff decision demonstrates that the need for disclosure and warning can outweigh the confidentiality between therapist and patient.

Implications of the Tarasoff Decision

With trust as a prerequisite for satisfactory parent–infant interactions as well as for the subsequent therapeutic relationship, exceptions to confidentiality somewhat erode the patient's trust. Freud would enjoin his patients to say whatever came to mind in

---

[1] *Tarasoff v. Regents of University of California*, 17 Calif. 3d 425, 551 P. 2d 334 (1976).

[2] See *Harvard Law Review* article entitled "Developments—Privileged Communications" 98:1450–1666 (1985) for a detailed discussion of this issue. While I am utilizing the generic term "psychotherapist," it is important to note that certain therapy practitioners (e.g., nurses) are not protected by privilege.

free association, but no longer are all confessions treated equally, nor would the patient be on safe grounds were he or she to follow the rule of free association to the letter.

The therapist, in turn, must now function as a "double agent," selectively splitting his or her role as the patient's private confessor with that of public citizen charged with assessing the "larger benefit" wrought by disclosure of patients' confessions. Uncertainty about how to balance these two, often incompatible, roles can affect the therapist's treatment capacity, particularly if anxiety and fear of censure interfere with his or her professional attitude.

Certain recommendations have been made by the American Psychological Association's Committee on Scientific and Professional Ethics (Hare-Mustin et al., 1979; Everstine et al., 1980; Hall & Hare-Mustin, 1983) in an attempt to safeguard therapists, as well as patients, from the legal consequences of indiscriminate confession on the patient's part and legal uncertainty impinging on professional confidence on the therapist's part.[3] One especially cogent recommendation is that the therapist know the laws pertaining to privilege and confidentiality, and that therapists contact ethics committees of state organizations or colleagues with expertise in these areas to consult with and determine a course of action.

Therapists must now add legal acumen to the arsenal of skills they must possess in order to conduct treatment successfully and prudently. Freud, in *The Question of Lay Analysis* (1925–1926), anticipated the need for a broad knowledge base as a valuable asset for psychotherapists. Due to the ever-increasing reach of the law into the therapeutic realm, therapists may thus find themselves mired in a legal morass. In particular, *Tarasoff* raised such questions as under what circumstances therapists should exercise their "duty to warn." Many confessions contain violent content, and some patients will even routinely express the desire to kill or maim a significant object in their lives. Moreover, many therapists welcome, and may indeed encourage, the expression of "forbidden" aggressive content (e.g., Klein, 1975; Spotnitz, 1976; Kernberg, 1976). In the majority of cases, however, therapists are able to discern that these confessions are products of patients' fantasies.

With one of the major goals of psychoanalytic and expressive-emotive therapies being the expression of forbidden, often socially

[3] See Hare-Mustin and Hall (1981) for a clear description of the procedures adopted by the American Psychological Association to respond to ethical complaints. Similar ethical concerns have been codified by the American Psychiatric Association and the National Association of Social Workers.

unacceptable material, the therapist may be faced on a daily basis with confessions that go beyond therapeutic scrutiny into the legal domain. But therapists' predictions of violence are notoriously inaccurate, with false positives approaching 80 or 90 percent (Gurevitz, 1977; Monahan, 1981).

Therapists are thus faced with the legal and ethical dilemma of curtailing patients' expectations of confidentiality in order to prevent assaultive acting out in a few cases. Lane and Spruill (1980) maintain that when patients have prior histories of violent acting out, it may be more appropriate to breach confidentiality to prevent future violence.

If therapists do not warn victims, they may find themselves guilty of failing to carry out their duty to warn. Alternatively, if they do warn, they may be sued for breach of confidentiality. In this latter instance, if the therapist warns a third party, and the patient fails to carry out the threat, the therapist may be held liable for the violation of the patient's privacy and reputation. Lane and Spruill (1980) recommend that legislation be enacted to protect therapists from liability in such situations. Of equal import is that the patient be protected from therapists' capricious disclosure of the patient's private confessions to public scrutiny.

Hare-Mustin et al. (1979) and Everstine et al. (1980), in reporting on the American Psychological Association's ethics committee's recommendations, mention the use of contracts and informed consent.[4] These forms supply the patient with information about what confessions are inadmissible in therapy along with an explanation of the therapist's "duty to report" certain confessions, such as cases of child abuse in New York State. This approach is designed to educate the patient/consumer, but it can also result in either timidity regarding disclosure or the dismissal of therapy altogether as a viable medium for open communication.

Knapp and Vandecreek (1982) make two additional recommendations to help both therapist and patient live with the *Tarasoff* decision: the use of social or environmental manipulations, including asking patients to rid themselves of weapons, as well as informing them of the limits to confidentiality if serious threats continue; and the recording of management options that have been considered as a protective strategy should the therapist's decision ever be questioned.

George Orwell's predictions already began to be realized well before 1984, as therapists increasingly have been forced to assume

---

[4] The problems of informed consent are discussed in a subsequent section of this chapter.

social control functions. As Big Brother in the form of national health insurance, PSROs, peer review, and private insurance companies, as well as of computers, data banks, and automated information systems, continues to intrude into the therapy space, confessions become an ever-greater risk. Patients now not only must deal with their idiosyncratic anxieties and troubled world of internal and external objects, but also must face the legal limits imposed on the confidentiality between therapist and patient.

With the advent of third-party payments, we can sometimes ask where the therapist's loyalty lies. Is the payer or the patient the therapist's major concern? While the therapist will increasingly be called upon to balance confidentiality with the public interest, the therapist's social control function becomes dangerous if he or she acts in an omnipotent or omniscient way. Countertransferential feelings are thus heightened when the therapist manipulates or controls patients in this fashion.

From the patient's perspective, major resistance can arise from the fear that confessions will adversely affect his or her employment status. Some patients may actually forgo insurance to assuage these fears. Rather than being summarily rationalized as justifiable by the therapist, this stance can be analyzed and worked through. The therapist's countertransferential problems, in turn, may take the form of shielding patients from the third party by writing favorable reports. But sanitized reporting practices conflict with the therapist's standards of honesty in therapeutic treatment.

Another specialized group of patients who are often especially reluctant to confess all are analysts in training. Would-be analysts may resist free association in the fear that disclosed confessions will prevent them from graduating, being appointed to the faculty, or receiving patient referrals from the faculty. These patients' expectations focus on rejection, punishment, criticism, or loss following confession.

Widiger et al. (1984) point out that there have been few malpractice suits dealing with negligence in the psychotherapeutic relationship, in part because it is difficult to assess emotional harm. Notable exceptions are cases that involve sexual exploitation as in *Roy v. Hartogs* (1975), in which the psychiatrist induced a disturbed young woman to engage in sexual intercourse during 13 months of treatment,[5] and physical assault, as in *Hammer v. Rosen* (1960), in which a psychiatrist beat a patient repeatedly.[6]

[5] *Roy v. Hartogs*, 85 Misc. 2d 891, 381 N.Y.S. 2d 587 (1975).
[6] *Hammer v. Rosen*, 7 N.Y. 2d 376, 165 N.E. 2d 756, 198 N.Y.S. 2d 65 (1960).

Patients as consumers must be aware of the therapist's duty to warn in select instances of confession, and also must be cognizant of their right to expose their therapist if their integrity is being violated. Because the therapist is often seen as an expert or authority, patients may be reluctant publicly to disclose misgivings regarding treatment. This reluctance stems both from the shame and anxiety involved in public exposure and possible additional interrogation and from uncertainty about their own perceptions and ethical culpability.

The patient, transferentially cast into a trusting and dependent relationship, relies on the therapist/parent to know how to handle the treatment situation and to contain any untoward actions of the patient in the capacity of a concerned, protective object. Hare-Mustin et al. (1979) thus maintain that safeguarding patients' rights rests primarily with the therapist. Since many patients enter therapy unaware of its goals, procedures, and policies, it is the therapist in the role of professional and parent who is ethically and educationally endowed with the skills and knowledge that enable him or her to set limits and provide a structure for the emergence and treatment of confessions.

When therapists flagrantly abuse this relationship, patients, or those close to them, may find themselves virtually forced to confess. For example, in *Zipkin v. Freeman* (1979),[7] a therapist who took part in a nudist swimming party and overnight trips with his patient also advised her to divorce her husband, sue her brother, and invest $14,000 in a farm he wanted to buy. He further suggested that she move in with him and release her hostility by breaking into her husband's home and stealing a desk, two beds, a television set, and some suits. This example speaks to the importance of educating the patient/consumer not only about exceptions to privilege predicated on the therapist's duty to warn, but also about the possibilities of therapists' misdeeds that may call for legal consultation and eventual public disclosure to disengage the patient from the exploitative relationship.

As Schwartz (1984) states, "To behave in an ethically responsible fashion, one must first claim, own, or know one's personal history and one's self. Disowning the unconscious is self-deception, and self-deception blocks self-control and freedom" (pp. 566–567). The patient's decision to risk confession confronts him or her with the responsibility of weighing ethical possibilities within a framework of choice. Because most confessions address matters that would not endanger the community, acknowledgement of the secret

[7] *Zipkin v. Freeman*, 436 S.W. 2d 753 (1968).

enables the patient to choose his or her own program for dealing with the consequences of the confession extratherapeutically. While the psychodynamic features of the confession are worked through in the transference, the patient's acceptance of responsibility confronts him or her with additional extratherapeutic choices, such as overt actions of restitution, apology, or alteration of the nature of relationships.

WHEN THE THERAPIST CONFESSES "TOO MUCH"

Disclosure of patients' confessions outside of therapy is an accepted practice for purposes of consultation, evaluation, or supervision. The ethics of such interventions are built into therapy for pedagogical and training purposes. Patients may be acutely aware of the supervisor's influence when they note alterations in their therapist's habitual speech patterns and interpretations related to the unseen overseer incorporated into the dyadic relationship. These reactions are nonetheless considered normative grist for the mill.

While the flow of confessions from patient to therapist to supervisor is an expected occurrence, therapists at times extend the parameters of extratherapeutic relationships by disclosing patients' confessions to the media or to colleagues socially. Two cases (cited in Hall and Hare-Mustin [1983]) that deal with the therapist's need for self-aggrandizement through unauthorized confessions of confidential material are particularly noteworthy in this regard. In the first case, a therapist interviewed by a Midwest newspaper named famous people who were his patients. He then went on to identify the personality characteristics of each. The psychologist was censured by the American Psychological Association's ethics committee for his casual, unprofessional approach to confidentiality.

The second case concerned a nationally publicized murder trial during which a psychologist, who had seen the accused for evaluation purposes, described the personality profile of the suspected murderer to a local newspaper. The APA ethics committee informed her that her behavior was unethical, since no release had been provided by the person evaluated.

In these instances the therapists used patients to enhance their own narcissistic self-evaluation, as well as possible social status in the community, by disclosing the patients' confidences. Just as some parents are known to boast of living through their children, such therapists derive feelings of enhanced esteem by viewing their patients as selfobject extensions. The development of such idealizing countertransferences may even blind the therapist from acknowledging that such behavior is ethically questionable or detrimental to the patient.

The social use of patients' confessions as gossip ethically, although not necessarily legally, violates the canons of confidentiality. With regard to the gossiping psychoanalyst, Olinick (1980) writes, "The fulcrum of the gossiper's leverage is access to a secret that he wants to exploit with others....To have a secret is to have a secret power over others..." (p. 440). Such therapists can be seen as enacting idealizing "selfobject countertransferences" (Wolf, 1979; Köhler, 1984/1985) by sharing in their patients' fame or notoriety.

The gossiping therapist consciously attempts to navigate between guarding patients' confidentiality and inadvertently disclosing their identity, but sufficient cues are usually provided to enable the audience to piece together the identities of famous patients. The major motives in such violations of patient confidentiality include exhibitionism, envy resulting in derogation of the envied patient, and oedipal rivalry incurred in professional one-upmanship. Such "prosocial aggression" (Berkowitz, 1962) may increase the number of the therapist's admirers and enhance social standing, while simultaneously providing an outlet for hostility indirectly leveled at the patient.

These disguised confessions, while affording a social avenue for collegial repartee, are also ethically questionable, especially in instances in which the therapist's veiled confession contains sufficient cues that enable the listener to discern the patient's identity. This sort of confessional process is often unconsciously initiated by the therapist to gain the attention and admiration of other professionals or friends, and thus achieve self-aggrandizement at the patient's peril.

Further, should the therapist's countertransferential feelings of envy eventuate in the revelation of secrets that publicly derogate or discredit the patient, the spreading of such confessions can result in potential public exposure of the patient in the media. Thus the therapist's disclosure of a confessional tidbit for any reason other than consultation or supervision can have devastating social, and even legal consequences, if the secret should fall into the hands of professional "exposé-mongers."

In abstracting a series of principles from the various codes, standards, statutes, and regulations governing psychiatry, social work, and psychology, Berger (1982) notes that patients have a right to a therapist committed completely to promoting the patient's best interests and welfare. One of the corollary responsibilities of the therapist in this regard is "to avoid gratifying his or her needs at the patient's expense" (p. 82). Gratification of therapists' needs include not only flagrant sexual acting out, but also feelings of power and grandiosity derived from disseminating patients' confessions to eager audiences.

PRIVILEGE AND EXCEPTIONS TO PRIVILEGE

Confidentiality and privilege, while intertwined concepts, are not equivalent. Confidentiality pertains to the therapist's ethical obligation to maintain privacy reinforced in law by the therapist–patient contract. Privilege is a legal right belonging to the patient that permits the patient to prevent the therapist from disclosing confidential information unless the privilege is waived by the patient or statute. If the patient waives the privilege, the psycho-therapist cannot refuse to testify.

Two major theoretical rationales have been put forth to justify privilege.[8]

Utilitarian

Under this rationale the privilege is deemed necessary to pro-tect society's interest by encouraging patients to confess freely to their therapists.

The patient's rights here coincide with society's interest. This utilitarian justification derives from the psychoanalytic model in which full disclosure is deemed essential for effective treatment. Freud (1938) emphasized the importance of full disclosure in the following celebrated passage: "We pledge him to obey the *fundamental rule* of analysis, which is henceforward to govern his behavior toward us. He is to tell us not only what he can say intentionally and willingly, what will give him relief like a confession, but everything else as well that his self-observation yields him, everything that comes into his head, even if it is *disagreeable* for him to say it, even if it seems to him *unimportant* or actually nonsensical" (p. 174).

In fact a patient no longer can indiscriminately confess when the danger exists that such revealed information could be disclosed extratherapeutically. For example, when New York State required

---

[8] *Op. cit., Harvard Law Review*, 1542–1544.

physicians to report to a state agency all patients using narcotic medications, some patients discontinued treatment or obtained these medications in other states. This turn of events suggests that some patients in psychotherapy might likewise terminate treatment rather than risk the stigma of public disclosure of private confessions. Critics of the utilitarian approach maintain that no empirical evidence supports the notion that privilege is necessary to promote trust between patient and therapist and that most patients are unaware that privilege exists.

Privacy

This alternative rationale views privilege as necessary not so much to protect the privacy of the therapeutic relationship, but to shield the patient from a courtroom appearance that threatens public disclosure of confidential information.

In confessions of rape or child molestation, for example, a court grilling may reevoke the trauma, and, in itself, constitute a trauma by revictimizing the victim in what Symonds (1980) terms the "second injury." In cases of child abuse, children below the age of ten who are placed on the stand are often disoriented, confused, and traumatized by cross-examination. Serious questions arise in this context about the benefits of such disclosures versus the advisability of privacy. One method to mollify the harsh realities of courtroom disclosure in child abuse cases, for example, is to limit the number of persons present and to exclude the public. In so doing, the rights of patients to privacy are not further eroded by subjecting them to excessive scrutiny.

Dekraii and Sales (1982) present a detailed account of exceptions to privilege. An outline of these exceptions include:

1. If the patient is determined to be dangerous to the self or others, society ought to be protected by allowing disclosure. Unfortunately the prediction of violence is notoriously difficult to make (Monahan, 1981). Further, patients might be impeded from expressing aggressive or other forbidden content for fear of legal repercussions.

2. When the patient brings a malpractice claim against the therapist, the therapist can defend himself or herself by making confessions public. This exception can be abused, however, if the therapist threatens to disclose embarrassing confessions if the patient sues. Dekraii and Sales (1982) recommend *in camera* proceedings in which spectators are excluded from the

courtroom and records of the hearing are sealed from the public.

    3. When the therapist is appointed by the court to conduct a psychological examination, the authors recommend that the patient know beforehand that his or her confessions have to be revealed.

    4. When the psychotherapist determines that the patient is in need of hospitalization for mental disorder, in some states the privilege is waived. The authors suggest that the privilege be revised to exclude disclosure if the therapist advises commitment for more general reasons.

    5. When the patient utilizes his or her mental condition as a defense in a legal proceeding, Dekraii and Sales recommend that private confessions can here be revealed, since the disclosure is within the patient's control and is a product of the patient's actions.

Everstine et al. (1980) cite two other situations in which therapists in some states are required by law to disclose information obtained during therapy:

    1. When a court issues a subpoena.
    2. When the patient is under 16, and the therapist believes the patient has been the victim of a crime in which the therapist judges such disclosures to be in the patient's best interest.

The *Harvard Law Review* article on privilege (1985) adopts a conciliatory middle course. It advocates a scheme of privilege and exceptions to privilege that would salvage patients' privacy and confidence with the knowledge that laws exist that, in most cases, favor patients' interests over those of the state. The exceptions, in turn, would ensure that the courts would have access to needed information when the costs of lost information are assessed as especially high.

    An example of this attempt to balance privacy and public disclosure is evidenced by the Massachussetts Supreme Court decision in *Commonwealth v. Kobrin* (cited in Fisher, 1985a). This ruling protected those portions of the patient's records concerned with what the court terms the "psychotherapeutic dialogue," reflecting the patient's intimate thoughts, feelings, wishes, and intentions. Fees, diagnosis, treatment plans, and accounts of the patient's medical and psychiatric hospitalizations, history, including earlier hospitalization, were, however, subject to subpoena in cases of alleged payment fraud. While the decision was seen by some as a victory for the defenders of privilege, the state still is given access to highly sensitive information, including prior hospitalization and symptoms of neurosis or psychosis.

Everstine et al. (1980) and Hare-Mustin et al. (1979) recommend using consent forms to apprise the patient of exceptions to the rule of confidentiality, and thus partially to alleviate anxiety by informing the patient and setting limits on categories of confessions that do not fall solely within the therapeutic domain. Informed consent is thus construed as serving an educational and protective function.

Three problems inherent in informed consent indicate the benefits and risks of confession (Widiger et al., 1984). First, not all patients have the capacity to understand informed consent forms and, in fact, might panic and bolt from therapy altogether. Second, therapists may not be able to provide the necessary information beforehand because the risks and consequences of treatment are sometimes complex. Finally, informed consent forms increase the risk of legal action against the therapist if the patient, in our increasingly litigious society, perceives that the outcome has not been achieved.

When the patient's right to privacy conflicts with society's need to be warned about certain acts or intentions, patients who are cognizant of legal developments no longer will feel free to confess whatever comes to mind. Alternatively, patients who are uninformed of these legal developments and do confess material deemed risky to society at large may experience disillusionment in the therapist, who may be transferentially perceived as analogous to the patient's punitive parents. Warnings not to reveal certain material, in turn, make patients self-conscious about the propriety of their disclosures and may escalate resistance to confessions in general.

In every therapeutic encounter, then, both therapist and patient are faced not only with interpersonal and intrapsychic issues, but also with the invisible hand of the law casting a pall on the proceedings. Thus each must be aware of the broader sociolegal implications of confessions and "counterconfessions" (the therapist's confessions to patients, discussed in Chapter 12) in relation to the broader societal matrix.

VALUES AS ETHICAL CONCERNS

Suppose a therapist is confronted by a patient whose confession involves one of the following value-laden issues:

1. The patient confesses to feelings of inadequacy due to his newfound fear of heights, which prevents him from rejoining his bomber crew and dropping bombs effectively.

2. A physician's eyesight is so bad that the therapist notices that several times she has walked into the therapist's closet instead of out the door.

3. A patient who works for an "escort agency" confesses how much he enjoys the power involved in beating up women to "keep them in line."

In these instances even the most traditional "blank screen" therapist would be hard put to maintain a noncommittal attitude since all three ethical dilemmas involve the lives and well-being of others and/or the patient. Many questions may run through the therapist's mind. Should I simply explore the psychodynamic meaning and implications of these confessions? Should I adopt an educational approach and explain the personal and/or societal consequences of these actions? Alternatively, if I encourage the patient to become aware of and adhere to what he or she wants, am I not becoming a collusive "partner in crime?"

These three hypothetical cases illustrate that patient and therapist cannot ignore the ethical dimension in human interaction. Faced with value-laden issues such as these, the therapist as a first step ought to consult supervisors, more experienced colleagues, and/or ethics committees of state organizations. Further, therapists would do well to pay close attention to their own values as well as any countertransferential reactions evoked in them by the confession. Therapists who experience the red light of ethical disquietude can best serve the patient and protect themselves by squarely confronting their own as well as the patient's values that arise in the treatment situation.

Another confession that forces therapists out of their so-called neutrality concerns the patient's admission of having engaged in sex with a previous therapist. Sex between patient and therapist offends ancient notions of what is proper in a professional relationship. The Hippocratic Oath states that "Into whatever houses I enter I will go into them for the benefit of the sick and will abstain from every voluntary act of mischief and corruption, and further from the seduction of females or males, of freeman and slaves" (quoted in Braceland, 1969). Today virtually all of the major associations charged with regulating and administering psychotherapy have included in their ethical guidelines the principle that sexual activity with a patient is unethical.

Barnhouse (1978) advocates the following threefold approach for treating patients who became sexually involved with their therapists:

1. Rebuild trust by condemning the previous therapist's behavior.
2. Acknowledge that the patient has been victimized without aggravating the feelings of helplessness or avoiding ways in which the patient may have unconsciously colluded with the therapist.
3. Attempt to distinguish points of convergence and divergence between the original problems and problems arising specifically out of the sexual incident.

While Barnhouse offers a treatment approach to deal with such confessions, further value-laden elements that intrude into the therapeutic process must also be addressed. For example, therapists might unconsciously side with the former therapist to solidify professional and/or male (or female) loyalty bonds, or refuse to consider even the slightest culpability on the patient's part in order to consolidate the tendency to identify with the victim. This situation is sometimes complicated by legal ramifications. In Minnesota, for example, the Vulnerable Adults Act requires therapists who are informed by their patients of sexual involvement with a prior therapist to report their colleague to the licensing board. While the law was enacted to benefit patients, it might also conceivably harm patients if its enforcement would require the patient to undergo confrontation by the previous therapist, questioning by investigators, and the rigors of a trial.

In either instance it is important for the therapist to work with the patient in sorting out fantasy elements from reality without indiscriminately taking sides. The more therapists are able to monitor their values and are cognizant of the pertinent laws, the less likely they are to find themselves in ethical and/or legal dilemmas.

By being attuned to value resistances and counterresistances, the therapist can more effectively function as a benign superego to facilitate the patient's development of an autonomous value system.[9] There is an important distinction, however, between being aware of one's values and making one's values explicit. The thera-

[9] Major segments of this section are extracted from my paper "The Therapist's Seduction by the Feminist Resistance," *Dynamic Psychotherapy* 2[1]:31–41 (Spring/Summer 1984).

pist who has a need (conscious or unconscious) to proselytize and resocialize the patient is engaging in a counterresistance that blocks the working through of the confession in the transference.

Freud (1904b) advises against the analyst indoctrinating the patient and compares the analyst's task to that of the sculptor, who proceeds *per via di levare*; that is, the marble is chipped away until the statue comes into view. The patient is thereby freed to develop a value system based on the integration of unconscious perceptions and multiple identifications with the conscious sociocultural forces met up with in later developmental stages. The therapist who is cognizant of his or her values is less likely to become a Pygmalion molder of a Galatean patient.

How do value resistances and counterresistances become manifest in confessions? Values become especially obvious in confessions of patients' intentions or deeds involving larger scale sociological issues. Suppose a patient confesses to having painted a swastika on a subway wall as a child and having the urge to do so again as an adult. He subsequently confesses to fantasies of defacing or bombing synagogues.

A number of treatment and ethical issues are immediately raised. Can this confession be treated on a strictly psychodynamic level of transference and countertransference to avoid the moral/social implications altogether? Alternatively, while the patient may be expressing hostility toward the Jewish therapist/parent, might his intentions not also endanger a large subgroup of the population?

With the "rule" of confidentiality no longer sacrosanct, therapists will increasingly be faced with the ethical and legal dilemmas of deciding which situations call for disclosing patients' confessions. The balance between the patient's rights to privacy and the public's right to be protected does not carry a long list of legal precedents to guide patient and therapist in this decision. Since precedents are being set on a case-by-case basis, confessions are helping to shape history, as the traditional codes of confidentiality are being challenged.

Again, the therapist's awareness of what constitutes his or her own values and ideology mutes the possibility of substituting rhetoric for analysis in instances in which a patient's confession touches on or conflicts with the therapist's own unresolved value-laden secrets. In a previous paper (Hymer, 1984c), I especially singled out the feminist resistance, which I defined as "the politicalization of unconscious and conscious conflicts by acceding to a feminist value system that affixes moral and behavioral expectations to such conflicts." This same issue applies in all other therapies predicated on explicit values, such as Marxist therapy, "metaphysical" therapy, and gay therapy.

When the patient's confessions are treated by therapists who utilize an advocacy-educational model in which explicit political values (e.g., feminism) are substituted for prior values, the patient is not given the opportunity to struggle with formulating his or her own values, which may conflict with the therapist's ideology. Such explicit therapies often include the sharing of confessions by the therapist to promote a peer modeling and mirroring experience. Again, such free-flowing, mutual confessions are designed to emphasize similarities and the espousal of explicitly "appropriate" moral goals in lieu of fostering the emergence of the patient's own values, which may be anathema to those of the therapist.

An illustration of how therapists may attempt to balance being directive with a consideration of patients' perceptions and capacity for choice is provided by Huston's (1984) approach to battered women. In addressing the question of whether a woman who confesses to having been battered should be encouraged to leave her abusive relationship, Huston takes the stance that if she is found to be limited in her ability to make competent decisions about her relationship, then a "weak paternalistic stance" (p. 830) is ethically justifiable.

She justifies such a directive approach by concluding that:

1. Persons with limited competence are unable to make rational judgements because of physical or mental impairment brought on by learned helplessness or immobilizing depression.

2. There is no misuse of the therapist's position of power or transference feelings because treatment does not force the woman to leave her relationship but encourages the change.

Such an approach, however, always shifts the transference dynamics in substituting a new authority for an old one. We know that, transferentially, even a question can be construed as a command, so that encouragement could indeed unconsciously be seen as a strong exhortation to do the therapist's bidding.

The therapist here becomes a benign Big Brother utilizing a social control function to determine the outcome of a patient's confessions. Confessions no longer are open-ended exploratory issues in such a system, but are data that "gently" force the patient to conform to a social agenda that may not be beneficial.

Such confessions, moreover, often play into therapists' countertransferential rescue fantasies, which may, in turn, mask further fantasies of omnipotence and aggrandizement. Therapists also may be unconsciously participating vicariously in their own rescue mission by symbolically slaying their family dragons in the process. While Huston is careful to mention that encouragement rather than force is exacted by the therapist who suggests that the battered woman leave her husband, and that respect for the woman's autonomous decision making thereby persists, such autonomy at best is watered down and represents a rationalization of the choice that often accrues with less directive therapy.

A number of ethical issues can be raised at this juncture. Should all such disclosures be uniformly treated by the therapist in the "woman's best interest" or might a nondirective approach be effective with less impaired women? Perhaps a frank admission that many such patients cannot be treated within a traditional transference model is called for, since, in Huston's approach, the double message is transmitted that patients are both free to make choices and sufficiently incompetent to need "encouragement" from the therapist to leave their husbands.

Because every form of therapy contains an implicit value system and every therapist has an acquired set of personal values, therapists must be cognizant of countertransferential value possibilities in the treatment of patients whose values clash with those of the therapist. For example, female therapists, in particular, whether feminist in viewpoint or not, have acknowledged to me their annoyance with, hatred of, or contempt for male patients who confessed to abusing women physically or deliberately humiliating them. These therapists must be particularly aware of their values that impinge on the ethical domain.

One colleague found herself in an unusual ethical bind when one of her patients confessed that he was so angry at the woman who had given him herpes that he frequented bars every weekend and deliberately infected other women. In this confession not only are countertransferential feelings evoked, but also the very real ethical dilemma of how best to treat such a patient without resorting to the educative politicalization of the treatment process via willful or inadvertent consciousness raising. One can further speculate as to whether, in the future, the duty to warn might not take this confession into the larger societal arena, as well.

Feminist therapists might deal with such confessions on a conscious sociopolitical level by utilizing a consciousness-raising approach. This directive approach, in which the therapist is strictly interpersonal in orientation, minimizes unconscious value conflicts on the part of both patient and therapist.

When a patient's confession is dealt with solely on a macrolevel sociocultural plane, such therapy bypasses the patient's unconscious values along with the adaptive ego functions inherent in allowing the patient to make choices that adhere to an evolving value system. The ego in conflict, bereft of autonomy, succumbs to the charismatic therapist's value system. Should absolution for confession be contingent upon adoption of the therapist's brand of morality, the therapist becomes little more than a secular priest preaching a new gospel.

12

Transference and Counter-transference

Be an opener of doors for such as come after thee and do not try to make the Universe a blind alley.

—Ralph Waldo Emerson

As early as 1895, Freud compared the therapeutic situation to "the unlocking of a locked door, after which opening it by turning the handle offers no further difficulty" (p. 328). Concurrent with the excavational approach to confession, Freud made the momentous discovery of the transference in the case of Dora. Confession was now seen not simply as a matter of strangulated ideation or affect seeking expression, but also as a reconstructive and constructive phenomenon contingent upon the relationship established with the analyst. Indeed, although Freud viewed transference as resistance, he subsequently considered positive transference to be a valuable tool in overcoming resistances (1912a). The object relationship thereby became a crucial factor in facilitating confession.

Today we know that the transference–countertransference interchange involves not only passive imprints of historical material, but also active addenda and alterations that transform confessions in the light of maturation and the present-day experience. In Piagetian terms confessions involve both assimilation (reconstruction)—the fitting of genetic material into the habitual context of experience—and accommodation (construction)—the transformation of historical material through interpretation.

A great deal of emphasis has been placed on the analyst as real object (Adler, 1980), new object (Blum, 1982; Loewald, 1968/1980), ally (Greenson, 1967), and/or collaborative participant (Chrzanowski, 1980). It is also important to note, however, that the patient likewise becomes a new object to the self and others in the light of cognitive and developmental changes evoked by experiences in and out of the therapeutic relationship. The self-in-transformation is further consolidated as the analysis of transference continues to free the self from stereotypical relationships with archaic objects. (See Chapter 9 for an extended discussion of aspects of self in relation to confession.)

Confession is thus never faithfully evoked, but undergoes creative alterations. Many analysts (notable among these being Langs [1978]; Racker [1976]; Gill [1979]; Searles [1979]; Chrzanowski [1979]; and Schafer [1982]) have emphasized the interlocking, dynamic nature of transference and countertransference. Both patient and analyst contribute to the emergence, exploration, and working through of the confession in the transference—countertransference.

Awareness and resolution of transference (Gill, 1979) are often the most zealously guarded secrets in therapy. Countertransference issues likewise often remain rationalized, minimized, or acted out as long as analysts are not willing to acknowledge the profound impact that such reactions exert upon the treatment process. Just as some patients are apprehensive about revealing their contempt, envy, rage, or hatred directed at the analyst for fear of repercussions, many analysts are wary about acknowledging their analogous feelings toward patients. In these instances an intertwined conspiracy of silence is likely to develop. The therapy situation thereby replicates environmental failures to meet the patient's needs and the treatment is stymied as crucial confessions are blocked.

The transference itself is a form of silent confession to the analyst about critical affective and cognitive secrets that now become more accessible. The interpretation of transference, in turn, gives a voice to the silent confession, which now can be further scrutinized.

The pattern of confessions aids in the evaluation and treatment of the transference situation and vice versa.[1] Just as one can chart the patient's progress on a number of criteria, one can note the vicissitudes in the patient's confessional output, in part as a function of the evolving transference relationship. The linking of the confession with the *in vivo* object relationship endows it with greater immediacy and relevance regardless of the secret's historical time frame.

The analyst's inadvertent or deliberate countertransferential reactions to the patient's confessions will influence both the outcome of the confession and the pattern of the patient's subsequent confessional output. The more the analyst is aware of his or her own reactions to confessions, the more he or she is likely to pay attention to these responses in order to understand the interactional frame better. In so doing the analyst is less likely to respond detrimentally to the patient.

To reiterate, the transference is often the best-kept secret. But what are the components of this secret? The transference alludes to secrets that pertain not only to the self and objects in the patient's life history, but also to the patient's core characterological themes. As Blum (1982a) points out, the addict becomes extremely dependent on the therapist; the depressive may seek absolution from unconscious guilt by openly confessing; and so on. Thus direct or indirect confessions conveyed transferentially or extra-transferentially enable the analyst to begin to discern and further explore the confession with the patient.

While transference enters into all relationships when a present object consciously or unconsciously represents some aspect of a significant past object (Chrzanowski, 1979; Stolorow & Lachmann, 1984/1985; Singer, 1985), it is only in the therapy situation that significant secrets experienced with historical objects become crystalized and interpreted. The repetitive cycle is thus curtailed as the patient is gradually able to distinguish between past and present and to process the confession in a new way devoid of many of the entanglements of the past (*redemption/renewal* aspect of confession). The patient thus is no longer unconsciously condemned transferentially to repeat a secret relationship in a no-exit cycle of repetition.

---

[1]Even though I emphasize the interlocking nature of transference and countertransference phenomena, I shall discuss distinct features of each under separate headings. The reader should note, however, that whenever transference and countertransference are discussed separately, reciprocal processes can be adduced.

Stolorow and Lachmann's (1984/1985)[2] categorizations of transference can serve as a springboard for understanding how confession operates in select transferential schema. With regard to the notion of transference as regression, Stolorow and Lachmann remark, "In all cases, the analytic stance toward the emergence of archaic modes of organization should be to promote their integration with other, more mature modes, thereby enriching psychological functioning, rather than to insist on their renunciation or elimination" (p. 22). Many patients are afraid they will be censured for regressing, or become self-critical about "thinking or acting childishly." Such preludes to confession connote the reticence, as well as the desire, to confess a wish or action that the patient believes ought to be renounced.

That the analyst does not match the patient's critical expectations gives the patient the courage to risk further confession. Stolorow and Lachmann's views on regression in some respects resemble Piaget's stage concepts in which the acquisition of later stages does not negate the continuing usefulness of the attainments of earlier stages. Take the example of a patient who engages in some playful, animistic behavior of the type that characterizes Piaget's preoperational stage. Suppose this patient begs a bowling ball to turn around and not go into the gutter. This patient may be reticent to confess to this behavior for fear that the analyst/parent will consider it pathological. The analyst, in turn, must be able to appreciate patients' playful natures without anxiety or censure, recognizing that earlier developmental activities need not always be nullified, but may become functional additions to the adult repertory.

A second category of transference is that of displacement from past targets to present ones, thus enabling discharge to occur. A confession containing the kernel of a life theme is never simply displaced onto the analyst, who thereby becomes a passive recipient of a product. Both patient and analyst actively work together to make sense of the confession in the light of the "here-and-now" experience.

The use of transference as projection or projection identification was popularized by the Kleinians and post-Kleinians notably Racker (1976) and Kernberg (1975). In projective identification (see Chapter 10 for a further discussion), bad self and object

---

[2]For a detailed review of conceptions of transference, I recommend Stolorow and Lachmann's (1984/1985) article, "Transference: The Future of an Illusion," *Annual of Psychoanalysis* 12–13:19–37 (1984/1985).

images are externalized (Kernberg, 1975, 1976) or disavowed aspects of self are projected into external objects for safekeeping, control, and so on (Klein, 1975; Bion, 1977). Projective identification is a particularly cogent means of expressing confessions in a veiled manner. The analyst as container can process disavowed aspects of the patient's self or objects in such a way so as to feed them back to the patient in an empathic, palatable form. If the analyst remains unaware of his or her own forbidden feelings toward the patient, or, worse still, impulsively confesses them to the patient, a toxic rather than relieving atmosphere is maintained.

The fourth position mentioned by Stolorow and Lachmann entails transference as distortion of reality (e.g., Sullivan's [1953] parataxic distortion). The analyst's "objectivity" becomes one of the designated tools in correcting the patient's distortions. Stolorow and Lachmann advocate multiple perspectives to understand transference dynamics. They make the assumption that the analyst is not, and cannot be, a dispassionate, neutral, objective observer.[3]

With regard to multiple perspectives, transference interpretations need not be couched in the adversarial framework of the analyst's versus the patient's realities, but can constitute a collaborative product in which pooled data and shared empathy enable interpretations to reflect the combined efforts of analyst and patient. For many patients confessions are most likely to be forthcoming in an atmosphere in which the analyst is seen as a concerned partner "in the patient's court" rather than as an objective, aloof purveyor of interpretations.

RESISTANCE

Loewald (1968/1980) views the transference neurosis as a creative act in that while transference manifestations are repetitive responses that can occur with any person, the transference neurosis is a "creation of the analytic work done by the analyst and patient" (p. 310). It is creative and new because the analyst does not respond so as to feed and ensure the neurotic processes inherent in unanalyzed repetition of the confession. The patient, in turn, completes the process of renewal by working through rather than statically reviving the same material.

To return to the redemption/renewal aspect of confessions,

[3]The topic of analytic neutrality will be further delineated in the section entitled "Should the Analyst Confess?"

patients, in concert with the analyst, are able gradually to save themselves from the no-exit situation of the past. Change becomes possible as new editions of past confessional configurations emerge. New possibilities for thinking, feeling, and relating surface that enable the patient to relate to a new, more flexible object. A new relationship is given the opportunity to evolve in which the analyst, as a noninstinctually invested object, abstains from repeating the parents' unempathic responses. The patient thus can more readily individuate in slowly relinquishing libidinal or narcissistic involvement with parental objects.

THE TEMPORAL DIMENSION:
HERE-AND-NOW VERSUS THERE-AND-THEN

Racker (1976) presented a case for time fusion and compression uniting the past with the present in the transference. Viewing transference as a projection of internal objects, Racker (1976) wrote, "The 'past' is not felt as such but as present and the danger, therefore, is also felt as something present...if the past is felt as something present, the past and present images fuse into one: to the unconscious, the analyst *is* the father and the father *is* the analyst. Making something conscious always involves a change in the relationship with the analyst too, for transference, in essence, is nothing but a manifestation of the relationships with internal objects....Hence in 'remembering' too the resistance is directed against the re-experience of a dangerous object relationship" (p. 78).

This quote underscores the notion that past and present meet in the person of the analyst. Thus the fear of confessing involves not only the patient's connection with the subject matter of the confession, but also the patient's relationship with the analyst, who becomes transferentially equated with the archaic parents.

Heidegger's monumental work *Being and Time* (1962) advances the concept that time is both directional and relational. In this schema the past exists in the now as "from whence" and the future exists in the now as "to whence" possibilities. The transference may thus be seen as both regressive and progressive. Schafer (1982) maintains that the transference is circular rather than unidimensionally retrospective in that genetic reconstructions raise questions concerning the present transference, and vice versa. Blum (1983) likewise points to the mutually explanatory and synergistic nature of reconstructions and here-and-now transference analysis.

Stone (1981) discusses the concealed transference in which "analytic situation residues" (Gill, 1979) involving extraanalytic experiences can be viewed as veiled disclosures of the transference. Extratherapeutic references to people and events in the patient's life represent confessional compromise formations. Here the patient both conceals and reveals aspects of the ongoing relationship with the analyst that he or she is not ready to disclose directly.

Many schizoid and borderline patients cannot tolerate transference interpretations during early phases of treatment. With borderline patients, for example, clinging tendencies, reinforced by transference interpretations, can result in an abrupt swing toward distancing and withdrawal. Thus here-and-now transference interpretations must be approached with caution or postponed. The gradual exploration of historical confessions without repercussions engenders feelings of trust that enable these patients to venture slowly into the riskier domain of the here-and-now transference. To confront one's invisible demons is seen as less risky than to meet them head on in the analyst. Thus the importance of past reconstructions remains incontrovertible (Stone, 1981; Schafer, 1982; Blum, 1983).

Gill (1979, 1982, 1984) is one of the strongest advocates of bringing hidden allusions into the current transference. Langs (1978) also recommends analysis of the interactional level before analysis of genetic material. While the patient may view historical confessions as relieving and acceptable data for the "good patient" to expose, feelings toward the analyst may be zealously guarded in an effort to maintain the status quo; that is, the patient's conception of what therapy "should be." Other patients eschew direct transferential confessions in order to protect the analyst from their hateful or destructive feelings. By not confessing, these patients also see the analyst as blocked from executing retaliatory castration or other punitive measures.

PREOEDIPAL CONFESSIONS

For patients whose core issues are primarily preoedipal (see Chapter 8), I have found that many view their secret life as a separate, split-off entity to be zealously kept from the retaliatory analyst. Still others, in psychotic identifications, may fuse with the analyst, and thereby expose their most feared secrets, in the absence of a defensive structure. Patients may split off their transferential feelings toward the analyst, either to protect themselves from the overpowering, destructive preoedipal mother (Chasseguet-Smirgel, 1976) or to protect the analyst from the patient's fantasized destructive power.

Discomfort with awareness of transference (Gill, 1979) is often a major resistance when preoedipal issues of control are involved. For patients with controlling, retaliatory parents, to become aware of transference attachments can sometimes be equated with losing control and risking punishment at the hands of the analyst/surrogate parent.

Again, preoedipal secrets involving primal issues of separation, control, and punishment are especially likely to be split off by patients in the transference, since the confession of such primal involvement is likely to reevoke feelings of vulnerability and possible loss. When patients identify with the archaic powerful parents, it is often easier for them to risk confessing such affectively charged material. The analyst's induced countertransference, in turn, may help recapture some of the disavowed feelings of vulnerability experienced by the preoedipal child/patient.

Issues revolving around death and fragmentation are core preoedipal concerns with often unforeseen and complicated confessional transference manifestations. Tina, a 41-year-old patient, confessed, in a voice quivering with sorrow and despair, that she was convinced that I had died. Although she had discussed over several months her own preoccupation with death, all further associations resulted in stalemate.

Tina informed me that she had found a diary dating from the period when she became obsessed about my death and asked to bring it to her next session. Tina's diary traced the outbreak of her confessional conviction regarding my death to the time when I was forced to return to Canada due to my mother's prolonged illness. While I mentioned that I had to leave owing to a personal family matter, Tina discerned further significance to this message. She told me that she was sure that my mother had died.

At this point the transference dynamics become quite complicated. This patient, whose mother suffered from emphysema and heart disease, was convinced that she would die before her mother did, or immediately after her mother's death. That Tina was convinced that my mother had died therefore sealed my demise as well, in her eyes.

"Transsymbiotic links" were evidenced in the patient's fantasized parallel connection between the two mother–child pairs (patient's and therapist's) and the third crossover tie between the patient and myself (the third mother–child dyad). Hence the *idée fixe*, "If the analyst's mother dies, she will die. If she dies, I must die. Death is surrounding me." The diary served as a protective buffer to help the patient introduce the confession and put chaotic preoedipal feelings into words.

Finally, patients whose issues are not primarily preoedipal nevertheless at times reclaim preoedipal issues that have not been acknowledged and assimilated into their subsequent experiential repertory. One such patient was Tracy, a 37-year-old advertising executive, who one day vehemently exclaimed, "I don't like looking at the fish on your wall" (referring to my Escher print "Three Worlds"). I remained silent. After several moments of reflection, Tracy continued, "I'd like to remove it from the wall and smash it to pieces. It's funny, but it feels as though the fish has taken over your seat—like Charlie the Tuna, and I'm alone. You're gone."

Tracy shuddered and went on, "I don't want to sound paranoid, but the fish has evil eyes. As though it were a witch. But who really is the witch? You or me or my mother?"

While this vignette, taken out of context, might appear to place the patient in a predominately preoedipal life space, suffice it to say that Tracy's principal thematic and transferential makeup was oedipal. What is of interest here is that Tracy was able to make use of an external art source to lessen her transference resistance and to disclose secrets of high affective intensity.[4]

Two preoedipal secrets emerged transferentially:

　　　1. The patient's dependence on the analyst and sense of vulnerability in being alone.
　　　2. The magical and omnipotent witchlike powers of the analyst/mother and potentially, via projective identification, of the patient as well.

Once Tracy was able to risk the initial confession with the aid of the art source, she was able to explore its ramifications further without feeling further hampered by the constraints of "propriety." That I did not wince or rebuke her for wanting to destroy my painting gave her a feeling of power and determination to continue to experience this strength through confession.

───────

[4]The therapeutic uses of art references in self-reparation and the diminution of resistance is taken up in my article "The Therapeutic Nature of Art in Self Reparation," *Psychoanalytic Review* 70[1]:57–68 (Spring 1983).

OEDIPAL CONFESSIONS

Oedipally based confessions are sometimes unconsciously offered by patients to seduce or excite the analyst. (See Chapter 8.) Patients who harbor sexual or matrimonial fantasies may utilize confessions to entice the analyst to acquiesce to their secret wishes. Other patients, wishing to kill the intrusive analyst/parent, may disclose confessions intended to shock or symbolically get rid of the authoritarian object. Some of my patients have, in fact, prefaced their confessions by saying (jokingly), "When you hear this, it might kill you." Others have said, "Alright, I'm going to let you have it." Exploration of these prefatory comments revealed that these patients harbored unconscious fears and wishes relating to my demise. By making offhand, "joking" remarks to preface their confessions, patients were able both to kill me symbolically and to protect themselves from retaliatory action by verbally "softening the blow."

For many patients the riskiest confession involves these secret sexual and aggressive wishes directed toward the analyst. Moreover, for analysts who have incompletely resolved their own oedipal secrets, the patient who directly discloses this material may arouse counterresistances.

These counterresistances may take the form either of deflecting the patient's aggressively or sexually charged confessions to less risky, more distant historical confessions, or of retaliating by disclosing raw, unresolved, "forbidden" feelings rationalized as "confrontational interpretation." The analyst, in this latter instance, may have unconsciously adopted the stance of the historical parents vis-à-vis the child/patient. In the analyst's so doing, the patient's secret fears of retaliation, which prevented confessions from being forthcoming in the first place, are now realized. As such, the transference–countertransference reproduces a vicious cycle of repetition in lieu of producing therapeutic transformations.

Oedipal confessions may induce anxiety in the analyst to parallel the patient's anxiety. But instead of empathically processing this anxiety the better to understand and offer interpretations to the patient, the analyst's own unacknowledged subjective countertransference may impel him or her to voice unattuned interpretations prematurely.

Still another unacknowledged countertransferential reaction takes the form of narcissistic overstimulation that gratifies the analyst at the expense of the patient. One of the most common examples of oedipal confessions that function in this way concerns the patient's profession of undying love for or sexual interest in the analyst. Should the analyst yield to such flattery, or commit the still more grievous offense of succumbing sexually to the patient's requests, the patient is exploited and betrayed. The patient's secret oedipal wishes are temporarily gratified, only to be supplanted by the larger trauma in which the childhood cycle of longing, disappointment, and/or victimization is now repeated rather than relieved.

Another oedipal resistance in which the patient is able to avoid confessing directly to the analyst about the analyst occurs when the patient unconsciously reverses the confessional process. Patients sometimes assume the role of private detective in attempting to decode the secrets of the analyst's life. Clues are sought in the analyst's waiting room and in perceptions of family members who might occasionally appear if the office is located in the analyst's home. Some patients even do external research to find out the analyst's degrees, school attendance, birth date, and so on.

In so doing the patient may feel more privileged in becoming privy to "classified information" or more in control. Other patients, particularly those in the same field, have related that they feel closer to me since they perceive me to be more like them. Still other patients who attempt to extract confessions through extra-therapeutic research refer to envy experienced toward their parents or toward me. Sometimes only months or years later do they gather the courage to tell me that they acquired information about me from directories, professional affiliations, and so on.

These confessions are especially useful in elucidating oedipal material, since issues revolving around the patient's voyeuristic curiosity emerge in relation to the patient's engagement in scopophilic activities to extract the oedipal parent's/analyst's secrets. The patient's acting out is interpreted, but it is not condemned. That the patient is successful in the discovery of secrets, and is not punished for confessions to this effect, empowers the patient and gives the patient the courage to risk further confessions.

NARCISSISTIC CONFESSIONS

In Chapter 10 I discussed Sandler's (1981) conception of patients who attempt to evoke responses from the analyst to protect and affirm them. My patient Adrienne, a 26-year-old dancer, missed her appointment and called me to let me know that she had been there at noon (45 minutes earlier) and had left after half an hour. Adrienne remarked, "I didn't want to disturb you by knocking on your door, and thought you might be sleeping on the couch. I did start to read a letter out loud, hoping you would hear me, but I didn't think it would be right to knock on your door."

From earliest childhood Adrienne had been afraid to seek her parents' attention directly for fear that they would get angry or "go crazy" (her mother had had a breakdown and her father drank and had unpredictable fits of rage). She would, however, try to sing in a low voice—transferentially translated by her reading a letter out loud outside my door—in the hope that her parents would respond affirmatively. That they did not berate her or fly into rages at these times gave Adrienne the sense that she was safe and "within earshot"—a feeling paralleled by my not going into the waiting room and scolding her for reading a letter out loud.

Adrienne did, in fact, find that I responded in the wished-for role-appropriate way (Sandler, 1981). Yet she also unconsciously laid the groundwork for the confession of split-off feelings of concomitant disappointment and rage at not being allowed to express herself fully and receive more direct attention. That she was able to make the connection between the current transference event and its genetic equivalent (related to me with much embarrassment) strengthened the selfobject transference. As this transference became increasingly solidified, Adrienne felt readier to risk revealing the hitherto split-off feelings of rage and disillusionment in the safety of the mirroring transference.

Concerning the idealizing transference, many patients are most likely to risk confessing their disavowed feelings toward the analyst when feelings of devaluation surface. Since the patient is jolted out of the former blissful feelings of idealization, feelings of anxiety and dis-ease are often directed at the perceived source of these feelings.

My patient Gerald, a 31-year-old banker, came to a session and almost immediately began to perspire and breathe unevenly. When I asked him what the matter was, he blurted out, "You are, because you're not perfect. Last session, you admitted to not knowing about a 50-cent coin that was not pure silver. You should know about these things. If you didn't know about this, I can just imagine all the others things you are ignorant about. And I can only trust someone who is competent." Gerald's panic reactions impelled him to confess his feelings of devaluation toward the imperfect, nonomniscient analyst.

Empathic acknowledgment and mirroring of the patient's disappointment often spontaneously evoke historical confessions focusing on disillusionment with imperfect parents. The patient often weaves back and forth between genetic and transferential confessions in an effort to restore narcissistic equilibrium when the transference becomes too heated for the vulnerable self to tolerate.

It is most important that the analyst not become entangled in either conciliatory acquiescence or unleashed rage at the patient's alleged ingratitude. Both countertransferential reactions may result in the analyst's either "rationally" trying to dissuade the patient from the "unreality" of these feelings or engaging the patient in a battle of the wills that recreates a no-win situation in which the patient may again retreat from openly confessing.

To this end Kohut (1982) concludes, "Knowledge values and independence values have been the leading values of the psychoanalyst, and...they have guided him toward selective perception and selective action within the psychological field" (p. 399). He goes on to say that these values have interfered with "the analyst's ability to allow his analysands to develop in accordance with their nuclear program and destiny" (p. 399). Thus, in the above-mentioned examples, if the analyst's hidden agenda had involved either dispelling Adrienne of her "unrealistic" dependency needs or correcting Gerald's faulty "knowledge base" regarding his "illusory quest" for perfection in self and others, the analyst would be inflicting her own values on the patient without regard for the patient's current developmental needs. Confrontational interpretations in the absence of attunement to developmental deficits may disclose the analyst's need to be "right" rather than attuned. The analyst's blanket adherence to correct analytic technique may mask selfobject countertransferential difficulties (Wolf, 1979).

(Major related aspects of narcissistic confessions are discussed in Chapter 4.)

SELFOBJECT COUNTERTRANSFERENCE

Wolf (1979) coined the term selfobject countertransference to describe a configuration in which the patient becomes selfobject to the analyst; that is, the analyst experiences the patient as an extension of self. Wolf sees these countertransferences as positive when controlled empathy is employed in the service of treatment.

When a patient discloses a narcissistic injury, for example, the empathic analyst might help the patient recognize the legitimacy of feeling outraged over the injury and threat to the self. The analyst would not be helpful, however, if he or she allowed uncontrolled archaic empathy to emerge in the form of encouraging the patient's acting out in order also to assuage the analyst's deeply buried narcissistic rage in the process.

There are times when analysts' selfobject needs blind them to patients' selfobject needs. One common confession revealed to me by several analysts was an occasional tendency to respond to patients with their own agendas. Whether this agenda consists of the analyst's unconscious archaic needs or conscious cognitive interests, the analyst is disregarding the patient's experience at that moment. As one colleague noted, "Now that I'm studying separation-individuation, I see all my patients' problems as separation-individuation issues, and interpret accordingly."

Kohut (1971) has outlined several selfobject countertransferences, including becoming bored, sleepy, or disengaged; resentment at being treated as a mirror rather than as a whole person; and dissolution of the self in reaction to the patient's merger wishes. These forms of countertransference are some of analysts' best-kept secrets from themselves, since to acknowledge these reactions is to experience one's professional self in an undesirable light.

Still another aspect of selfobject countertransference that most analysts are unwilling or unable to acknowledge is the ethically, and sometimes legally, questionable use of patients for self-aggrandizement or personal gain. The analyst's cupidity or unbridled narcissism not only erodes any semblance of neutrality, but also may border on betrayal. Thus, for example, analysts in the grips of countertransferential feelings of entitlement may finagle stock tips or attempt to become media consultants by utilizing patients whose positions in these fields ensure the analyst access to needed information for self-advancement.

Köhler (1984/1985) points out that in idealizing selfobject countertransferences, the analyst feels exalted if he or she analyzes a gifted or successful patient. (For a discussion of the ethical and/or legal consequences of these acted-out selfobject countertransferences, see Chapter 11.) These countertransferential reactions, in turn, affect the patient's transference. Patients may feel that they can never fail for fear of making the analyst/archaic mother anxious. The secret collective grandiosity of the dyad, remaining unacknowledged and uninterpreted, thereby replicates rather than transforms the childhood drama.

Köhler next mentions the alter-ego countertransference especially prevalent in training analyses in which the training analyst unconsciously expects the candidate to hold the same ideals, and even sociocultural convictions. Should the training analyst only convey by a "gleam in the eye" a sense of pleasure when the candidate adheres to the analyst's values, the candidate, in the transference, may become a compliant clone in order to please the training analyst/parent.

Further, the candidate may develop secrets regarding values or ideologies that differ from those of the analyst. In this instance secrets may connote the patient's adaptive attempt to separate and develop an autonomous identity. They may also serve as a reality-based, expedient measure to protect the self from vulnerabilities stemming from the analyst's real power over the candidate's immediate professional future. The training analyst, in turn, may not be able to acknowledge the countertransferential need to use the candidate to "carry the torch" in the role of faithful son or daughter.

In mirror countertransferences the analyst needs the patient to confirm that he or she is a good analyst by showing improvement. Köhler points out that, in extreme instances, the analyst may develop a secret savior complex. Negative aspects of redemption in the confessional process emerge as the analyst foists his or her own redemptive needs onto the patient. The patient then is impeded from developing his or her own self-reparative processes in the service of growth and renewal.

SHOULD THE ANALYST CONFESS?

Epictetus once remarked, "Nature has given men one tongue but two ears, that we may hear from others twice as much as we speak." This maxim might well become the analyst's guiding principle when in doubt about how much to reveal.

A major controversy exists around the issue of whether confessions should be engaged in by both patient and analyst or undertaken solely by the patient. In a revealing letter about countertransference written to Binswanger in 1913, Freud stated, "What is given to the patient should indeed never be a spontaneous affect, but always consciously allotted, and then more or less of it as the need may arise. Occasionally, a great deal, but never from one's own unconscious....To give someone else too little because one loves him too much is being unjust to the patient and a technical error" (cited in Spotnitz, 1976, p. 51).

Freud (1912b), however, in the main advised against the analyst's sharing confessions with patients because, by arousing the patient's curiosity, one might inspire the patient to attempt to reverse the confessional process. Freud (1938) continued to maintain a primary posture revolving around the analyst's controlling self-disclosures when he wrote, "However much the analyst may be tempted to become a teacher, model, and ideal for other people and to create men in his own image, he should not forget that this is not his task in the analytic relationship, and indeed that he will be disloyal to his task if he allows himself to be led on by his inclinations. If he does, he will only be repeating a mistake of the parents who crushed their child's independence by their influence, and he will only be replacing the patient's earlier dependence by a new one" (p. 175).

While experimental studies and clinical reports are almost unanimous in citing the level of a patient's disclosure as a predictor of successful therapeutic results (Jourard, 1964; Truax & Carkhuff, 1965; Cozby, 1973), the data are much less certain on the effects of the analyst's disclosures. Since much of the disclosure literature focuses on confessions made in time-limited groups with undergraduate students or with inpatient schizophrenics, the generalizability of these findings is suspect. I shall therefore confine the discussion to the major clinical positions.

Kernberg (1965) has summarized the dominant countertransferential positions as follows:

> 1. The "totalistic" approach embodied in Heimann's (1950) and Racker's (1976) work concerning the totality of the analyst's psychological responses.
>
> 2. The classical position of Freud (1912b, 1938) and Annie Reich (1951, 1960a) on the analyst's unconscious reactions to the patient's transference.

The classical position maintains that the analyst must refrain from confessing countertransferential feelings. Advocates of the totalistic approach suggest that analysts utilize their countertransference to understand the patient better, while not necessarily disclosing these feelings.

To assess the question of whether the analyst should confess, we must first ask, "Confess what?" We can delineate three broad countertransferential categories:

> 1. *Intrapsychic level:* In this category we find the unresolved subjective countertransference (Winnicott, 1949/1975; Spotnitz, 1976) in which the analyst's own unacknowledged secrets emerge in response to the patient's transferential confessions.
>
> 2. *Interpersonal level:* Here we find the analyst's induced

feelings prompting silent understanding or objective counter-transferential responses (Winnicott, 1949/1975; Spotnitz, 1976) in response to the patient's transference. "Controlled confessions" on the part of the analyst are designed to feed back to the patient disavowed thoughts and affects that become more acceptable in mirrored form. Intrapsychic factors enter into the interpersonal equation as the analyst's unconscious resonates with the patient's unconscious in processing the patient's material.

3. *Sociocultural level:* Here we find conscious, deliberate disclosures made by the therapist. "Sharing," in the form of disclosures about the therapist's values, pastimes, interests, defects, and predilections, becomes an integral part of explicit therapies, such as feminist and Marxist therapy.

To summarize, we can cite four major positions regarding whether the analyst should confess countertransferential reactions or conscious material for proselytizing purposes.

1. *Never* (e.g., Freud and A. Reich). The classical position holds that the analyst should control his or her countertrans-ference and never confess to the patient. "The physician should be impenetrable to the patient and, like a mirror, reflect noth-ing but what is shown to him" (Freud, 1912b, p. 124).

2. *No, but* (e.g., Gill and Schafer). The analyst should, in general, utilize the countertransference silently. Confessions only should be made prudently in order to avoid turning the-rapy into a mutual confessional.

3. *Yes, but* (e.g., Spotnitz and Racker). It is appropriate for the analyst to feed back to the patient, in measured doses, material emanating from induced feelings in the analyst. The patient can thereby understand and assimilate the confession in a new form. Contaminating influences from the subjective countertransference, however, should be controlled.

4. *Yes* (e.g., Jourard and explicit therapies). Confession enhances mutuality and the therapist's humanness (Sullivan's concept that we are more human than anything else). Jourard (1964) sees withholding of authentic disclosure in therapists as resistance. In proselytizing therapies sharing encourages mod-eling of both the therapist and the therapy's explicit philosophy as embodied in the therapist.

The resurgence of interest in countertransference began in the 1950s. Both Heimann (1950) and Spitz (1956) acknowledged the usefulness of the countertransference in understanding the patient, but cautioned against disclosure of countertransferential reactions. Heimann anticipated subsequent interactional emphases in conceptualizing countertransferential feelings as the patient's creation; that is, transference induces countertransference, and vice versa. Little (1951) was one of the first analysts to recommend judicious confession of countertransferential feelings in seriously disturbed patients to enable the patient to establish genuine contact with someone. Spotnitz and Searles have also advocated therapists' selective disclosure of feelings induced in them by schizophrenic and borderline patients.

The notion of the neutral analyst onto whom the patient can unidirectionally project confessions has come under increasing fire in recent times (Langs, 1978; Searles, 1979; Chrzanowski, 1980; Fisher, 1985b). Chrzanowski has pointedly argued that we cannot be analytic observers without to some extent modifying the patient —a notion that has also been demonstrated in the physical sciences. However, disclosures of the analyst's subjective emotions or capricious experiences should not be made. Chrzanowski mentions sensitivity, tact, and self-restraint as analytic attributes to be utilized in decisions regarding disclosure.

Greenberg (cited in Fisher [1985]) advocates that analysts gear their disclosures to resonate to the patient's world of object relations. Greenberg views the silence of the classical position as promoting inclusion of the analyst in the patient's internal object world. A more active, self-disclosing posture, in turn, establishes the analyst as a new object. For example, patients who are frightened of their transference fantasies may need the analyst to make some basic disclosures in order to be reassured that the analyst will experience the impact of the transference differently from their parents. With these patients the analyst's aloofness and anonymity may actually confirm the patient's sense of having harmed the analyst. Greenberg maintains, however, that analysts who offer personal revelations to increase the patient's trust or identification with them are likely to limit the expression of the negative transference.

Especially problematic is the countertransference that remains unacknowledged, and therefore may be acted out through intrusive, unattuned disclosures or extratherapeutic disclosures (e.g., the "gossiping psychoanalyst" engaged in selfobject countertransference). When the analyst identifies with the patient's confessions, an unconscious collusive pact might develop between patient and analyst to avoid dealing with anxiety-provoking secrets they share in common (Giovacchini, 1981; Arlow, 1985).

Intrusive and premature interpretations are likely to be made when the analyst cannot contain the patient's transferential rage or devaluation, or when the analyst resonates with analogous unresolved, forbidden material in his or her history. In these instances the analyst may attempt to achieve premature closure to avoid more direct confessional confrontation and exploration. Interpretation here becomes a medium for the emergence of self and other-deception under the guise of elucidation of truth.

The analyst who has not come to terms with certain secrets in his or her own therapy may find these secrets transposed into the therapeutic realm. The redemptive aspect of confession concerns the patient's reparation to self, and possibly others, contingent upon the disclosure, exploration, and working through of hidden material in connection with the analyst. The analyst's unacknowledged need to save the patient and self by proxy becomes an undesirable, contaminating countertransferential reaction that unwittingly reinforces dependency in the patient.

"THE ANALYST SHOULD CONFESS" POSITIONS

Few analysts would advocate indiscriminate or unequivocal confession to patients. Still there exists a range of positions pertaining to when such disclosure is indicated, as well as to what kinds of confessional interventions should be made.

Prado (1980) and Bollas (1983), from somewhat different theoretical perspectives, maintain that the analyst can make disclosures to the patient when he or she knows that these confessions emanate from some part of the patient. Prado, in accordance with Bion's, Racker's, and Klein's theoretical concepts, views the psychotic transference as a tool that enables the analyst to understand the patient's preverbal language and acting out.

If we accept the plausibility of Klein's and Bion's contention that we all possess a psychotic core aspect to our natures, the psychotic countertransference can help the analyst tease out and verbalize hitherto inaccessible preverbal material for the patient. Because the analyst may experience induced countertransferential identifications that include envy, hatred, and rage toward the patient, it is often easier for the analyst to focus on the patient's hidden transference than to acknowledge his or her own "forbidden" countertransference. In focusing solely on one half of the interactional equation, the analyst avoids the inescapable interlocking and reciprocal nature of transference–countertransference.

Bollas (1983) emphasizes intersubjectivity as the process that enables the analyst interpretively to "give back to the patient either what he has lost, or bring those parts of himself to his attention that he may never have known" (p. 8). The analyst as intersubjective partner facilitates retrieval of hidden or lost information that becomes available through interpretation.

Interpretation can be seen as a vehicle for bringing potential confessions to light. An attuned interpretation can often elicit formerly undisclosed genetic material that resonates with the interpretation. When the analyst risks intersubjective interpretations emerging out of the transference–countertransference interchange, the patient often feels freer to risk elaborating upon the interpretation.

The principal arguments that have been advanced for self-disclosure[5] are that:

1. It promotes modeling: The therapist's disclosures facilitate identification. Modeling plays a major role in humanistic and directive explicit therapies, and has been found to be particularly promising with troubled adolescents (Vondracek & Vondracek, 1971). However, from the perspective of psychoanalytic psychotherapy, modeling dilutes unconscious processes and developmental needs for mirroring and idealization, and thereby weakens the development of autonomy.

2. It promotes participation in the analytic process: The establishment of a therapeutic alliance facilitates the patient's examination of the therapist's disclosures in the interest of learning more about his or her own disavowed aspects of self. The therapist's disclosures can serve as a mirror for the examination of the patient's disowned or unresolved confessions.

3. It dissolves transference resistances: Patients who see authority figures as aloof and moralistic, and who therefore eschew confessing, may benefit from prudent disclosures made by the therapist.

4. It increases the relevance of the here-and-now setting: Disclosures pertaining to transference–countertransference material are more helpful in enabling patients to face their own secrets than disclosures of the therapist's personal extratherapeutic experiences that deflect from the patient's material.

---

[5]For summaries of indications and contraindications for the therapist's disclosures, see Curtis (1981) and Glazer (1981).

"THE ANALYST SHOULD NOT CONFESS" POSITIONS

The unresolved subjective countertransference in part comprises secret intergenerational issues that continue when the analyst unconsciously adopts his or her analyst's/parent's dis-ease with aggression or any other affect-laden issue. In the current transference–countertransference dyad, these feelings remain unacknowledged or are deflected. It is not the existence per se of the subjective countertransference that is deleterious, but the analyst's unwillingness or defensive incapacity to acknowledge these reactions that adversely affect the patient's treatment.

The major arguments against self-disclosure[6] are that:

1. It promotes modeling: The therapist's disclosures set up expectations about how the patient "should be." Polansky (1967) maintains that the hidden message in these situations becomes "to do like me is to be normal, healthy and virtuous" (p. 578).

2. It engenders gratification: Disclosure is therefore especially contraindicated for acting-out or acting-in patients whose need for gratification far outstrips the desire for self-scrutiny or understanding.

3. It erodes the therapeutic relationship: The therapist's intimate revelations color the relationship and can seriously contaminate the transference by, for example, contributing to erosion of idealization.

4. It elicits narcissistic supplies: If self-disclosure is instituted to bolster the therapist's self-esteem, a competitive confessional element is introduced that is especially countertherapeutic for patients whose vulnerable selves need support. By staying within the patient's frame of reference, the therapist "holds" the patient through the confessional process.

SHOULD THE ANALYST CONFESS?
SOME CLOSING THOUGHTS

An old wag once stated that the psychologist's favorite statement is, "It depends." Lest I sound too equivocal in giving equal time

[6]For a detailed account of contraindications for self-disclosure, see Polansky (1967), Kaslow and Cooper (1979), Curtis (1981), and Glazer (1981).

to all positions, I shall mention what I consider to be some of the essential ingredients in the analyst's decision regarding self-disclosure.

In deliberating the question, it is first important to consider the kind of patients to whom we are making disclosures. For most patients intimate, extratherapeutic revelations gratify the analyst's narcissism while deflecting from the patient's disclosures. In general the analyst's confessions, when they are made, should be used in the service of the patient to facilitate the further elicitation and working through of patients' confessions. The more these confessions emanate from "objective" countertransferential feelings induced in the analyst by the patient, the more the patient is likely to be stimulated through shared curiosity to work on his or her own confessions. These confessions can now be studied by the patient from still another perspective in the transference–counter-transference interchange.

Even for the most severely disturbed patients, the analyst who is able to detoxify the patient's projective identifications and feed them back in palatable form can help him or her to assimilate hitherto disavowed material better. For neurotic or narcissistic patients with intrusive, demanding parents, any disclosure may be viewed as disruptive in reinstituting competitive oedipal rivalries or parental demands for attention.

This last point speaks to the importance of comprehending the patient's history of object relations before deciding how active or inactive to be in disclosing countertransferential reactions or other material. The more the patient's parents were perceived as critical and invasive, the more prudent the analyst should be in making disclosures. The more distant and emotionally unavailable the patient's parents were perceived to be, the more treatment-related disclosures might be seen as caring and productive. The analyst here becomes a new object to whom confessions can be offered without repercussions by transforming rather than repeating the childhood cycle of object relations.

A third criterion to be taken into account is the patient's level of self-development. The patient with a vulnerable self is more likely to benefit initially from benign abstinence on the analyst's part. The analyst who silently mirrors these patients helps fill in developmental deficits. Since even minor interventions are sometimes seen as criticisms by narcissistic patients, the analyst who abstains from all disclosures during the early stages of treatment is most likely to contribute to the consolidation of the patient's self. The more robust the patient's self, the more the patient is able to benefit from the exploration and assimilation of countertransferential disclosures.

From a drive perspective, any disclosure is counterproductive for impulse-ridden patients whose quest for ceaseless gratification is met rather than transformed by the analyst's disclosures. Such disclosures would also be contraindicated for many neurotic patients who equate confessions with seduction, competitive control, or aggressive retaliation. Since these feelings are likely to arise in some form in the transference, the analyst's additional disclosures may overstimulate these patients (Gedo, 1979).

Confessions, to be effective, help the patient to recognize and assimilate unacknowledged secrets. These disclosures can also encourage the patient to risk further confessions. The evocation, exploration, and working through of confessions in the transference–countertransference help the patient to develop the trust and confidence necessary to risk confession and stay with the material throughout the confessional process.

EPILOGUE

Confessions present a paradox. In the public consciousness, they tend to evoke either religious or forbidden, *outre* associations. I believe that confessions have rarely been examined as a significant therapeutic phenomenon, for two reasons:

1. Religious connotations die hard. Many therapists are unable or unwilling to acknowledge the pervasive influence of secular confessions in therapy.

2. Many therapists view all therapy as confessional, and do not understand how confessions differ from any other discourse.

It is particularly to the second point that I have addressed this book. The major characteristics of confessions are set forth, including exclusivity, affective and dramatic intensity, greater perceived risk, specialness, discontinuity, and greater identity investiture.

Confessions were destined to be an integral part of psychotherapy, not only because of the nature of the therapeutic process, but also because of a confluence of historical factors. With the decline in religious belief and practice, people had to seek comfort elsewhere. While the family doctor, cab driver, and hairdresser have always had ancillary confessional functions, in a world of inconstancy the therapist provides both continuity and constancy.

The therapeutic relationship radically altered the nature of confessions. The "quick fix approach" gave way to a process that granted neither absolution nor moral formulas to structure reparation. Insight, relatedness, and transformation as aspects of the therapeutic process surpassed the primary cathartic function of confessions in extratherapeutic settings.

The following principal points have been introduced:

1. The therapist can maximally benefit from a thorough knowledge of theory and praxis concerning confessions in psychotherapy. Ethical, theoretical, and practical treatment problems have been discussed in order to help the therapist understand and evaluate the myriad issues encompassing confessions.

2. Confessions alter the course of self and object relations, as disavowed aspects of self and objects come to be acknowledged, expressed, and worked through. Patients bring their own behavioral style to confessions. The manner of disclosure or concealment is itself revealing of patients' conflicts with objects and the self.

3. Confessions provide an arena for studying transference and extratransference relationships. The struggle between dependency on and separation from the object has been explored.

4. The therapist, as often exclusive confessional object, must be attuned to the patient's discourse filtered through the here-and-now interaction. The important active and receptive qualities that the therapist can adopt to facilitate and enhance patients' confessions have been underscored.

5. Therapists should pay particular attention to linguistic clues that provide valuable information about confessions. For example, prefatory phrases such as "You're never going to believe this" or "This is really disgusting, but" are often proffered to narcissistically safeguard patients from feelings of vulnerability.

6. Confessions can help patients build trust and intimacy in the therapeutic relationship. Therapist and patient can then

explore ways to transfer these gains to extratherapeutic relationships.

THE PROCESS

Confession is not an isolated act, but an evolving process in
which the patient's whole being is bound up. In the confessional
process, the patient's self, object relations, and historicity are all
swept into the present therapeutic interchange.

I have delineated a three-step confessional process consisting of
risk—relief—redemption/renewal.

1.*Risk:* Confessions begin with risk. That the therapist is a
low risk confessor who ensures confidentiality and acceptance
distinguishes this relationship from high-risk relationships in
which confessions to friends, family or romantic partners are
more likely to result in repercussions. (See chapter 11 for
exceptions to the rule of confidentiality.)

2. *Relief:* The cathartic aspects of confessions traditionally
have been singled out and overemphasized. Confession is an
ongoing, transformational process with crucial cognitive and
behavioral, as well as affective, components. The act of sharing
one's secret with the affirming therapist in time results in
catharsis. Even though some patients might initially experience an exacerbation of shame or guilt or become more resistant immediately following confession, relief is the final,
although not only, affective outcome of the confessional process.

3. *Redemption/renewal:* Patients' confessions save them
from the darker, disavowed aspects of their own nature. The
transformation of self and object that accrues from the interpretation of transference, as well as from extratransferential
aspects of the therapeutic interaction, results in renewal.

Redemption contains implicit value issues. Is redemption
made possible through the patient's quest for autonomy (e.g.,
Freud) or can it be achieved solely within the domain of self object
relations (e.g., Kohut)?

I contend that we are now undergoing a creative synthesis
(especially emphasized in recent object relations approaches) in
which the individual can be focused upon within an object rela-

tional framework. The patient is saved from the "no-exit" situation of the past by a collaborative therapeutic effort. Extratherapeutic support from significant others also can be sought to consolidate therapeutic progress.

Confessions underscore the twin goals of autonomy and relatedness. In undertaking the confessional journey with the therapist, the patient can paradoxically come to realize Nietzsche's imperative, "Follow not me, but you."

References

Abelin, E. (1975). Some further observations and comments on the earliest role of the father. *International Journal of Psychoanalysis, 56*(3), 293–302.

Abraham, K. (1924). A short study of the development of the libido, viewed in the light of mental disorders. In *Selected papers in psychoanalysis* (pp. 418–501). New York: Brunner/Mazel.

Adams, V. (1983, June). Testimony as therapy. *Psychology Today,* 84–85.

Adler, G. (1980). Transference, real relationship and alliance. *International Journal of Psychoanalysis, 61*(4), 547–558.

Ainsworth, M. (ed.) (1966). *Deprivation of maternal care: A reassessment of its effects.* New York: Schocken Books.

Ainsworth, M., & Bell, S. (1970). Attachment, exploration, and separation. *Child Development, 41,* 49–68.

American Psychological Association (1981a). *Ethical principles of psychologists.* Washington, D.C.: Author.

American Psychological Association (1981b). *Rules and procedures of the committee on scientific and professional ethics and conduct.* Washington, D.C.: Author.

Amsterdam, B., & Leavitt, M. (1980). Consciousness of self and painful self-consciousness. *Psychoanalytic Study of the Child, 35,* 67–83.

Apfelbaum, B. (1965). Ego psychology, psychic energy, and the hazards of quantitative explanation in psychoanalytic theory. *International Journal of Psychoanalysis, 46,* 168–182.

Arlow, J. (1985). Some technical problems of countertransference. *Psychoanalytic Quarterly, 54,*(2), 164–174.

Atkins, N. (1970). The Oedipus myth, adolescence and the succession of generations. *Journal of the American Psychoanalytic Association, 18*(4), 860–875.

Atwood, G. (1983). The pursuit of being in the life and thought of Jean-Paul Sartre. *Psychoanalytic Review, 70*(2), 143–162.

Bakan, D. (1954). A reconsideration of the problem of introspection. *Psychological Bulletin, 51,* 105–118.

Balint, M. (1979). *The basic fault.* New York: Brunner/Mazel.

Barnhouse, R. (1978). Sex between patient and therapist. *Journal of the American Academy of Psychoanalysis, 6*(4), 533–546.

Bartlett, F. (1967). *Remembering: A study in experimental and social psychology.* Cambridge, England: Cambridge University Press. (Original work published 1932.)

Bellow, S. (1975). *Humboldt's gift.* New York: Viking Press.

Berger, M. (1982). Ethics and the therapeutic relationship. In M. Rosenbaum (ed.), *Ethics and values in psychotherapy: A guidebook* (pp. 67–95). New York: Free Press.

Berkowitz, L. (1962). *Aggression: A social-psychological analysis.* New York: McGraw-Hill.

Berne, E. (1964). *Games people play: The psychology of human relations.* New York: Grove Press.

Bernfeld, S. (1951). The facts of observation in psychoanalysis. *Journal of Psychology, 12,* 289–305.

Bernstein, A. (1976). Freud and Oedipus: A new look at the Oedipus complex in the light of Freud's life. *Psychoanalytic Review, 63*(3), 393–407.

Bettelheim, B. (1950). *Love is not enough.* New York: Free Press.

Bibring, E. (1954). Psychoanalysis and the dynamic psychotherapies. *Journal of the American Psychoanalytic Association, 2,* 745–770.

Bion, W. (1967). Notes on the theory of schizophrenia. In *Second thoughts: Selected papers in psychoanalysis* (pp. 23–35). New York: Jason Aronson. (Original paper presented in 1953.)

Bion, W. (1967). On hallucination. In *Second thoughts: Selected papers in psychoanalysis* (pp. 65–85). New York: Jason Aronson. (Original work published 1958.)

Bion, W. (1967). A theory of thinking. In *Second thoughts: Selected papers on psychoanalysis* (pp.110–119). New York: Jason Aronson. (Original work published 1962.)

Bion, W. (1977). *Seven servants.* New York: Jason Aronson.

Blake, W. (1974). The marriage of heaven and hell. In *The portable Blake* (pp. 249–266). New York: Penguin Books. (Original work published 1903.)

Blanck, G. (1984). The complete Oedipus complex. *International Journal of Psychoanalysis, 65,* 331–339.

Blos, P. (1962). *On adolescence: A psychoanalytic interpretation.* New York: Free Press.

Blos, P. (1974). The genealogy of the ego ideal. *Psychoanalytic Study of the Child, 29,* 43–88.

Blum, H. (1977). The prototype of preoedipal reconstruction. *Journal of the American Psychoanalytic Association, 25*(4), 757–785.

Blum, H. (1981). Some current and recurrent problems of psychoanalytic technique. *Journal of the American Psychoanalytic Association, 29*(1), 47–68.

Blum, H. (1982a). The transference in psychoanalysis and in psychotherapy: Points of view past and present, inside and outside the transference. *Annual of Psychoanalysis, 10,* 117–137.

Blum, H. (1982b). Theories of the self and psychoanalytic concepts. Discussion. *Journal of the American Psychoanalytic Association, 30*(4), 959–978.

Blum. H. (1983). The position and value of extratransference interpretation. *Journal of the American Psychoanalytic Association, 31*(2), 587–617.

Bohart, A. (1980). Toward a cognitive theory of catharsis. *Psychotherapy: Theory, Research and Practice, 17*(2), 192–201.

Bollas, C. (1983). Expressive uses of the countertransference. *Contemporary Psychoanalysis, 19*(1), 1–34.

Boss, M. (1962). 'Daseinsanalysis' and psychotherapy. In H. Ruitenbeek (ed.), *Psychoanalysis and existential therapy* (pp. 81–89). New York: Dutton.

Boswell, J. (1981). *The life of Johnson.* New York: Penguin Books. (Original work published 1791.)

Bowlby, J. (1969). *Attachment.* New York: Basic Books.

Bowlby, J. (1977a). The making and breaking of affectional bonds. 1. Etiology and psychopathology in the light of attachment theory. *British Journal of Psychiatry, 130,* 201–210.

Bowlby, J. (1977b). The making and breaking of affectional bonds. 2. Some principles of psychotherapy. *British Journal of Psychiatry, 130,* 421–431.

Braceland, F. (1969). Historical perspectives on the ethical practice of psychiatry. *American Journal of Psychiatry, 126,* 230–237.

Bromberg, P. (1983). The mirror and the mask: On narcissism and psychoanalytic growth. *Contemporary Psychoanalysis, 19*(2), 359–387.

Bronfenbrenner, U. (1974). The origins of alienation. *Scientific American, 321,* 53–61.

Brown, N. O. (1959). *Life against death.* Middletown, Conn: Wesleyan University Press.

Brown, R. M. (1973) *Rubyfruit jungle.* New York: Bantam Books.

Broyard, A. (1982, March 14). Kafka and Prague in New York. *New York Times,* 47.

Bruner, J. (1956). Freud and the image of man. *American Psychologist, 11,* 463–466.

Brunswick, R. Mack (1940). The preodipal phase of the libido development. *Psychoanalytic Quarterly, 9,* 293–319.

Buber, M. (1937). *I and thou.* Edinburgh: T. & T. Clark.

Buber, M. (1965). Elements of the interhuman. In M. Friedman (ed.), *The knowledge of man* (pp. 72–88). New York: Harper/Torch Books.

Buber, M. (1965). Guilt and guilt feelings. In M. Friedman (ed.), *The knowledge of man* (pp. 121–148). New York: Harper/Torch Books.

Budge, E. A. W. (ed.). (1965). *The Egyptian book of the dead.* New York: Dover Publications.

Burgess, A. (1983). *This man and music.* New York: Avon/Discus.

Camus, A. (1956). *The fall.* New York: Vintage Books.

Canaday, J. (1964). *Mainstreams of modern art.* New York: Holt, Rinehart & Winston.

Cassimatis, E. (1985). The "false self": Existential and therapeutic issues. *International Review of Psychoanalysis, 11*(1), 69–77.

Chasseguet-Smirgel, J. (1976). Freud and female sexuality: The consideration of some blind spots in the exploration of the "Dark Continent." *International Journal of Psychoanalysis, 57*(3), 275–286.

Chrzanowski, G. (1979). The transference-countertransference transaction. *Contemporary Psychoanalysis, 15,* 458–471.

Chrzanowski, G. (1980). Collaborative inquiry, affirmation and neutrality in the psychoanalytic process. *Contemporary Psychoanalysis, 16*(3), 348–366.

Clance, P. (1985). *The impostor syndrome.* Atlanta, Ga.: Peachtree Press.

Coleridge, S. (1977). Letter to Thomas Poole. In I. A. Richards (ed.), *The portable Coleridge* (pp. 219–221). New York: Penguin.

Conger, J. (1981). Freedom and commitment: Families, youth, and social change. *American Psychologist, 36,* 1475–1484.

Coppolillo, H., Horton, P., & Haller, L. (1981). Secrets and the secretive mode. *Journal of the American Academy of Child Psychiatry, 20*(1), 71–83.

Cozby, P. (1973). Self disclosure: A literature review. *Psychological Bulletin, 79,* 73–91.

Curtis, J. (1981). Indications and contraindications in the use of therapist's self-disclosure. *Psychological Reports, 49*(2), 499–507.

Dali, S. (1968). *The secret life of Salvador Dali* (3rd ed.). (H. M. Chevalier, trans.) London: Vision. (Original work published 1904.)

Dekraii, M., & Sales, B. (1982). Privilege communications of psychologists. *Professional Psychology, 13,* 372–388.

Descartes, R. (1969). *The essential Descartes.* New York: American Library. (Original work published 1628.)

Diamond, M. (1984, November). Conversation with Marian Diamond. *Psychology Today,* 62–73.

Dickinson, E. (1969). No rack can torture me. In C. Coffin (ed.), *The major poets: English and American* (2nd ed., p.408). New York: Harcourt, Brace & World. (Original work published 1862.)

Dostoevsky, F. (1927). *Crime and punishment.* (C. Garnett, trans.) New York: Grosset & Dunlap. (Original work published 1866.)

Dostoevsky, F. (1957). *The brothers Karamazov.* New York: Signet. (Original work published 1881.)

Du Maurier, D. (1938). *Rebecca.* London: V. Gollancz.

Eisnitz, A. (1980). The organization of the self-representation and its influence on pathology. *Psychoanalytic Quarterly, 49*(3), 361–392.

Eliot, G. (1965). *The mill on the floss.* New York: Signet. (Original work published 1860.)

Eliot, T. S. (1950). *The cocktail party.* New York: Harvest/Harcourt, Brace, Jovanovich.

Elkin, H. (1972). On selfhood and ego structures in infancy. *Psychoanalytic Review, 59,* 389–416.

Ellenberger, H. (1966). The pathogenic secret and its therapeutics. *Journal of the History of the Behavioral Sciences, 2*(1), 29–42.

Emerson, R. W. (1965). Circles. In W. Gilman (ed.), *Selected writings of Ralph Waldo Emerson* (pp. 295–306). New York: Signet. (Original work published 1841.)

Erard, R. (1983). New wine in old skins: A reappraisal of the concept "acting out." *International Review of Psychoanalysis, 10*(1), 63–73.

Erikson, E. (1959). Identity and the life cycle. *Psychological Issues, 1*(1) (Monograph no. 1).

Erikson, E. (1962). *Young man Luther: A study in psychoanalysis and history.* New York: Norton.

Erikson, E. (1963). *Childhood and society* (2nd ed.). New York: Norton.

Erikson, E. (1968). *Identity, youth and crisis.* New York: Norton.

Evers, H. (1970). *The art of the modern age.* New York: Crown.

Everstine, L., Everstine, D., Heymann, G., True, R., Frey, D., Johnson, H., & Seiden, R. (1980). Privacy and confidentiality in psychotherapy. *American Psychologist, 35*(9), 828–840.

Fairbairn, W. (1943). The repression and the return of bad objects (with special reference to the "war neuroses"). *British Journal of Medical Psychology, 19,* 327–341.

Fairbairn, W. (1954). *An object relations theory of the personality.* New York: Basic Books.

Fenichel, O. (1945). *The psychoanalytic theory of neurosis.* New York: Norton.

Fenichel, O. (1946). On acting. *Psychoanalytic Quarterly, 15,* 144–160.

Ferenczi, S. (1926). Psycho-analysis of sexual habits. In *Further contributions to the theory and technique of psycho-analysis* (pp. 259–297). London: Hogarth. (Original work published 1925.)

Ferenczi, S. (1930). The principle of relaxation and neocatharsis. *International Journal of Psychoanalysis, 11,* 428–443.

Fisher, K. (1985a, October). Court protects talk within therapy session. *APA Monitor,* p. 32.

Fisher, K. (1985b, November). In defense of analyst neutrality. *APA Monitor,* p. 24.

Fisher, M. (1982). The shared experience: A theory of psychoanalytic psychotherapy. In M. Fisher & G. Stricker (eds.), *Intimacy* (pp.115–125). New York: Plenum.

Flamm, J. (1985, June). The evocation of unseen forces. What Picasso learned from the primitives. *The Sciences,* p. 53.

Flaubert, G. (1965). *Madame Bovary.* New York: Penguin. (Original work published 1856.)

Forster, E. M. (1950). *A passage to India.* New York: Penguin. (Original work published 1924.)

Foucault, M. (1980). *History of sexuality* (Vol. 1). New York: Vintage Books.

Frank, J. (1959). Dynamics of the psychotherapeutic relationship: Determinants and effects of the therapist's influence. *Psychiatry, 22,* 17–39.

Frank, J. (1963). *Persuasion and healing.* New York: Schocken.

Frank, J. (speaker) (1981). *Therapeutic components shared by all psychotherapies* (Cassette Recording no. 1-113-81). Washington, D.C.: American Psychological Association.

Freeman, L., & Roy, J. (1976). *Betrayal.* New York: Stein & Day.

Freud, A. (1958). Adolescence. *Psychoanalytic Study of the Child, 13,* 255–278.

Freud, S. (1950) *The origins of psychoanalysis.* New York: Basic Books. (Original work published 1887–1902.)

Freud, S. (1953). The interpretation of dreams. In J. Strachey (ed. and trans.), *The standard edition of the complete psychological works of Sigmund Freud* (Vols. 4 & 5). London: Hogarth Press. (Original work published 1900.)

Freud, S. (1963). Freud's psychoanalytic method. In P. Rieff (ed.), *Freud. Therapy and technique* (pp. 63–76). New York: Collier Books. (Original work published 1904a.)

Freud, S. (1953). On psychotherapy. In J. Strachey (ed. and trans.), *op. cit.* (Vol. 7, pp. 257–268). (Original work published 1904.)

Freud, S. (1953). Fragment of an analysis of a case of hysteria. In J. Strachey (ed. and trans.), *op. cit.* (Vol. 7, pp. 3–122). (Original work published 1905a.)

Freud, S. (1953). Three essays on the theory of sexuality. In J. Strachey (ed. and trans.), *op. cit.* (Vol 7, pp. 7–125). (Original work published 1905a.)

Freud, S. (1957). The future prospects of psychoanalytic therapy. In J. Strachey (ed. and trans.), *op. cit.* (Vol 11, pp. 77–88). (Original work published 1910.)

Freud, S. (1958). The dynamics of the transference. In J. Strachey (ed. and trans.), *op. cit.* (Vol. 12, pp. 105–116). (Original work published 1912a.)

Freud, S. (1958). Recommendations for physicians on the psychoanalytic method of treatment. In J. Strachey (ed. and trans.), *op. cit.* (Vol. 12, pp. 117–126). (Original work published 1912b.)

Freud, S. (1958). Totem and taboo. In J. Strachey (ed. and trans.), *op. cit.* (Vol. 13, pp. 1–161). (Original work published 1912–1913.)

Freud, S. (1957). On narcissism: An introduction. In J. Strachey (ed. and trans.), *op. cit.* (Vol. 14, pp. 73–102). (Original work published 1914a.)

Freud, S. (1958). Remembering, repeating and working-through. In J. Strachey (ed. and trans.), *op. cit.* (Vol. 14, pp. 145–156). (Original work published 1914b.)

Freud, S. (1957). Mourning and melancholia. In J. Strachey (ed. and trans.), *op. cit.* (Vol. 14, pp. 237–260). (Original work published 1917a.)

Freud, S. (1963). Introductory lectures on psycho-analysis. In J. Strachey (ed. and trans.), *op. cit.* (Vols. 15 & 16). (Original work published 1917b.)

Freud, S. (1955). A childhood recollection from *Dichtung und wahrheit.* In J. Strachey (ed. and trans.), *op. cit.* (Vol. 17, pp. 145–156). (Original work published 1917c.)

Freud, S. (1955). Group psychology and the analysis of the ego. In J. Strachey (ed. and trans.), *op. cit.* (Vol. 18, pp. 69–143). (Original work published 1921.)

Freud, S. (1955). Two encyclopedia articles. In J. Strachey (ed. and trans.), *op. cit.* (Vol. 18, pp. 235–254). (Original work published 1922a.)

Freud, S. (1955). Medusa's head. In J. Strachey (ed. and trans.), *op. cit.* (Vol. 18, pp. 273–274). (Original work published 1922b.) 1922b.)

Freud, S. (1961). The ego and the id. In J. Strachey (ed. and trans.), *op. cit.* (Vol. 19, pp. 3–66). (Original work published 1923.)

Freud, S. (1961). The dissolution of the oedipus complex. In J. Strachey (ed. and trans.), *op. cit.* (Vol. 19, pp. 172–179). (Original work published 1924.)

Freud, S. (1959). Moral responsibility for the content of dreams. In J. Strachey (ed. and trans.), *op. cit.* (Vol. 19, pp. 131–134). (Original work published 1925a.)

Freud, S. (1959). An autobiographical study. In J. Strachey (ed. and trans.), *op. cit.* (Vol. 20, pp. 3–74). Original work published 1925b.)

Freud, S. (1962). The question of lay analysis. In J. Strachey (ed. and trans.), *op. cit.* (Vol. 20, pp. 179–250). (Original work published 1925–1926.)

Freud, S. (1964). Humor. In *Collected papers* (Vol. 5, pp. 215–221). New York: Basic Books. (Original work published 1928.)

Freud, S. (1961). Civilization and its discontents. In J. Strachey (ed. and trans.), *op. cit.* (Vol. 21, pp. 64–145). (Original work published 1930.)

Freud, S. (1961). Female sexuality. In J. Strachey (ed. and trans.), *op. cit.* (Vol. 21, pp. 225–243). (Original work published 1931.)

Freud, S. (1964). New introductory lectures on psychoanalysis. In J.

Strachey (ed. and trans.), *op. cit.* (Vol. 22, pp. 5–182). (Original work published 1933.)

Freud, S. (1959). A disturbance of memory on the Acropolis. In *Collected papers* (Vol. 5, pp. 302–312). New York: Basic Books. (Original work published 1936.)

Freud, S. (1964). Constructions in analysis. In J. Strachey (ed. and trans.), *op. cit.* (Vol. 23, pp. 255–269). (Original work published 1937.)

Freud, S. (1964). An outline of psychoanalysis. In J. Strachey (ed. and trans.), *op. cit.* (Vol. 23, pp. 141–206). (Original work published 1938.)

Freud, S., & Breuer, J. (1966). *Studies in hysteria.* New York: Avon. (Original work published 1895.)

Gedo, J. (1979). *Beyond interpretation.* New York: International Universities Press.

Gill, M. (1979). The analysis of the transference. *Journal of the American Psychoanalytic Association, 27,* 263–288.

Gill, M. (1982). Analysis of the transference: 1. Theory and technique. *Psychological Issues* (Monograph no. 53).

Gill. M. (1983). The interpersonal paradigm and the degree of the therapist's involvement. *Contemporary Psychoanalysis, 19,* 200–237.

Gill, M. (1984). Psychoanalysis and psychotherapy. A revision. *International Review of Psychoanalysis, 11*(2), 161–179.

Gilligan, C. (1982). *In a different voice.* Cambridge, Mass.: Harvard University Press.

Giovacchini, P. (1981). Countertransference and therapeutic turmoil. *Contemporary Psychoanalysis, 17*(4), 565–594.

Glazer, M. (1981). Anonymity reconsidered. *Journal of Contemporary Psychotherapy, 12*(2), 146–153.

Godwin, G. (1983). A diarist on diarists. In J. C. Oates (ed.), *First person singular* (pp. 24–29). Princeton, N. J.: Ontario Review Press.

Goffman, E. (1955). On face-work: An analysis of ritual elements in social interactions. *Psychiatry, 18,* 213–231.

Goffman, E. (1959). *The presentation of self in everyday life.* New York: Anchor Books.

Goleman, D. (1985). *Vital lies, simple truths.* New York: Simon & Shuster.

Görg, J., & Schmidt, H. (eds.). (1970). *Ludwig van Beethoven.* Hamburg: Deutsche Grammophon Gesellschaft mbH.

Green, H. (1964). *I never promised you a rose garden.* New York: Holt, Rinehart & Winston.

Greenacre, P. (1954). The role of the transference: Practical considerations in relation to therapy. *Journal of the American Psychoanalytic Association, 2*, 671–684.

Greenacre, P. (1957). The childhood of the artist. Libidinal phase development and giftedness. *Psychoanalytic Study of the Child, 12*, 47–772.

Greenacre, P. (1958). The family romance of the artist. *Psychoanalytic Study of the Child, 13*, 9–36.

Greenacre, P. (1959). Play in relation to creative imagination. *Psychoanalytic Study of the Child, 14*, 61–80.

Greenberg, J., & Mitchell, S. (1983). *Object relations in psychoanalytic theory.* Cambridge, Mass.: Harvard University Press.

Greenson, R. (1967). *The technique and practice of psychoanalysis.* New York: International Universities Press.

Gross, A. (1951). The secret. *Bulletin of the Menninger Clinic, 15*, 37–44.

Grotstein, J. (1981). *Splitting and projective identification.* New York: Jason Aronson.

Grotstein, J. (1982). New perspectives on object relations theory. *Contemporary Psychoanalysis, 18*(1), 43–91.

Guntrip, H. (1969). *Schizoid phenomena, object relations and the self.* New York: International Universities Press.

Gurevitz, H. (1977). Tarasoff: Protective privilege vs. public peril. *American Journal of Psychiatry, 134*(3), 289–292.

Hall, J., & Hare-Mustin, R. (1983). Sanctions and the diversity of ethical complaints against psychologists. *American Psychologist, 38*, 714–729.

Hare-Mustin, R., Maracek, J., Kaplan, A., & Liss-Levenson, A. (1979). Rights of clients, responsibilities of therapists. *American Psychologist, 34*,(1), 3–16.

Hartmann, H. (1962). *Psychoanalysis and moral values.* New York: International Universities Press.

Hartmann, H. (1964). Comments on the psychoanalytic theory of the ego. In *Essays on ego psychology* (pp. 113–141). New York: International Universities Press.

Hartmann, H. (1964). *Essays on ego psychology.* New York: International Universities Press.

Hartmann, H., & Lowenstein, R. (1962). Notes on the superego. *Psychoanalytic Study of the Child, 17*, 42–81.

Harvard Law Review Staff (1985). Developments—Privileged communications. *Harvard Law Review, 98*, 1450–1666.

Hawthorne, N. (1962). *The scarlet letter.* Columbus, Ohio: Ohio State University Press. (Original work published 1850.)

Heidegger, M. (1962). *Being and time.* (J. Macquarrie & E. Robinson, trans.) New York: Harper & Row.

Heimann, P. (1950). On countertransference. *International Journal of Psychoanalysis, 31,* 81–84.

Heimann, P. (1952). A contribution to the re-evaluation of the Oedipus complex. *International Journal of Psychoanalysis,33,* 84–92.

Hoyt, M. (1978). Secrets in psychotherapy: Theoretical and practical considerations. *International Review of Psychoanalysis, 5*(2), 231–241.

Huston, K. (1984). Ethical decisions in treating battered women. *Professional Psychology, 15,* 822–832.

Hymer, S. (1982). The therapeutic nature of confessions. *Journal of Contemporary Psychotherapy, 13*(2), 129–143.

Hymer, S. (1983). The therapeutic nature of art in self reparation. *Psychoanalytic Review, 70*(1), 57–68.

Hymer, S. (1984a). Narcissistic friendship. *Psychoanalytic Review, 71*(3), 423–439.

Hymer, S. (1984b). The self in victimization: Conflict and developmental perspectives. *Victimology, 9*(1), 142–150.

Hymer, S. (1984c). The therapist's seduction by the feminist resistance. *Dynamic Psychotherapy, 2*(1), 31–41.

Hymer, S. (1985). Absorption as a therapeutic agent. *Journal of Contemporary Psychotherapy, 15*(1), 93–108.

Hymer, S. (1986). The multidimensional significance of the look. *Psychoanalytic Psychotherapy, 3*(2), 149–157.

Jacobson, E. (1964). *The self and the object world.* New York: International Universities Press.

James, H. (1962). The beast in the jungle. In *The turn of the screw and the short novels* (pp. 404–451). New York: New American Library. (Original work published 1903.)

James, W. (1890). *The principles of psychology.* New York: Holt.

James, W. (1963). *The varieties of religious experience.* New Hyde Park, N.Y.: University Books. (Original work published 1902.)

Jones, E. (1953). *The life and work of Sigmund Freud* (Vol. 1). New York: Basic Books.

Jourard, S. (1964). *The transparent self.* Princeton, N. J.: Van Nostrand.

Jung, C. G. (1933). *Modern man in search of a soul.* New York: Harvest Books.

Jung, C. G. (1965). *Two essays in analytic psychology.* New York: Meridian Books. (Original work published 1943–1945.)

Jung, C. G. (1961). Therapeutic principles of psychoanalysis. In *The collected works of C. G. Jung* (Vol. 4, pp. 181–203). Princeton, N. J.: Princeton University Press/Bollinger Foundation.

Kafka, F. (1971). The metamorphosis. In N. Glatzer (ed.), *Kafka: The complete stories* (pp. 89–139). New York: Schocken Books. (Original work published 1915.)

Kaslow, F., & Cooper, B. (1979). Family therapist authenticity as a key factor in outcome. *International Journal of Family Therapy, 1*(2), 184–199.

Kernberg, O. (1975). *Borderline conditions and pathological narcissism.* New York: Jason Aronson.

Kernberg, O. (1976). *Object relations theory and clinical psychoanalysis.* New York: Jason Aronson.

Kernberg, O. (1979). Some implications of object relations theory for psychoanalytic technique. *Journal of the American Psychoanalytic Association, 27,* 207–240.

Khan, M. (1974). *The privacy of the self.* New York: International Universities Press.

Khan, M. (1983). *Hidden selves. Between theory and practice in psychoanalysis.* New York: International Universities Press.

Klein, M. (1975). On the theory of anxiety and guilt. In *Envy and gratitude* (pp. 25–42). New York: Delta. (Original work published 1948.)

Klein, M. (1975). *Envy and gratitude.* New York: Delta.

Knapp, S., & Vandecreek, L. (1982). Tarasoff: Five years later. *Professional Psychology, 13,* 511–516.

Kohlberg, L. (1969). Stage and sequence: The cognitive-developmental approach to socialization. In D. Goslin (ed.), *Handbook of socialization theory and research* (pp. 347–489). Chicago: Rand McNally.

Köhler, L. (1984/1985). On selfobject countertransference. *Annual of Psychoanalysis, 12/13,* 39–56.

Kohut, H. (1966). Forms and transformations of narcissism. *Journal of the American Psychoanalytic Association, 14*(2), 243–272.

Kohut, H. (1971). *The analysis of the self.* New York: International Universities Press.

Kohut, H. (1977). *The restoration of the self.* New York: International Universities Press.

Kohut, H. (1982). Introspection, empathy, and the semi-circle of mental health. *International Journal of Psychoanalysis, 63,* 395–407.

Kohut, H. (1984). How does analysis cure? Chicago: University of Chicago Press.

Kohut, H., & Wolf, E. (1978). The disorders of the self and their treatment. An outline. *International Journal of Psychoanalysis, 59,* 413–425.

Laing, R. D. (1960). *The divided self.* London: Tavistock.

Laing, R. D. (1962). Ontological insecurity. In H. Ruitenbeek (ed.), *Psychoanalysis and existential philosophy* (pp. 41–69). New York: Dutton.

Laing, R. D. (1970). *Knots.* New York: Pantheon.

Lamb, M. E. (1980). The development of parent-infant attachments in the first two years of life. In F. A. Pedersen (ed.), *The father-infant relationship* (pp.21–43). New York: Praeger.

Lampl-de Groot, J. (1946). The pre-oedipal phase in the development of the male child. *Psychoanalytic Study of the Child, 2,* 75–83.

Lampl-de Groot, J. (1952). Re-evaluation of the role of the Oedipus complex. *International Journal of Psychoanalysis, 33,* 335–342.

Lampl-de Groot, J. (1962). Ego ideal and superego. *Psychoanalytic Study of the Child, 17,* 94–106.

Lane, P., & Spruill, J. (1980). To tell or not to tell: The psychotherapist's dilemma. *Psychotherapy: Theory, Research and Practice, 17*(2), 202–209.

Langs, R. (1978). *Technique in transition.* New York: Jason Aronson.

Larson, K. (1985, February 4). Missed hit. *New York Magazine,* 64–65.

Leighton, A., & Leighton, D. (1941). Elements of psychotherapy in Navaho religion. *Psychiatry, 4,* 515–523.

Levenson, E. (1974). Changing concepts of intimacy in psychoanalytic practice. *Contemporary Psychoanalysis, 10,* 359–369.

Lewis, H. B. (1971). *Shame and guilt in neurosis.* New York: International Universities Press.

Lewis, H. B. (1984). (Review of J. M. Masson's *The assault on truth: Freud's suppression of the seduction theory.*) *Psychoanalytic Psychology, 1*(4), 349–355.

Lichtenberg, J. (1975). The development of the sense of self. *Journal of the American Psychoanalytic Association, 23,* 453–484.

Lichtenberg, J. (1979). Factors in the development of the sense of the object. *Journal of the American Psychoanalytic Association, 27,* 375–386.

Lichtenberg, J. (1980). Clinical application of the concept of a cohesive sense of self. *International Journal of Psychoanalytic Psychotherapy, 8,* 85–114.

Lichtenstein, H. (1964). The role of narcissism in the emergence and maintenance of a primary identity. *International Journal of Psychoanalysis, 45,* 49–56.

Lichtenstein, H. (1977). *The dilemma of human identity.* New York: Jason Aronson.

Lifton, R. J. (1979). *The broken connection.* New York: Simon & Shuster.

Little,M. (1951). Countertransference and the patient's response to it. *International Journal of Psychoanalysis, 32,* 32–40.

Loewald, H. (1980). On the therapeutic action of psychoanalysis. In *Papers on psychoanalysis* (pp. 221–256). New Haven, Conn.: Yale University Press. (Original work published 1957.)

Loewald, H. (1980). The transference neurosis: Comments on the concept and phenomenon. In *Papers on psychoanalysis* (pp.302–314). New Haven, Conn.: Yale University Press. (Original work published 1968.)

Loewald, H. (1980). Perspectives on memory. In *Papers on psychoanalysis* (pp. 148–173). New Haven, Conn.: Yale University Press. (Original work published 1972.)

Loewald, H. (1980). The waning of the Oedipus complex. In *Papers on psychoanalysis* (pp. 384–404). New Haven, Conn.: Yale University Press. (Original work published 1978.)

London, P. (1964). *Modes and morals of psychotherapy.* New York: Holt, Rinehart & Winston.

McGlashin, T., & Miller, G. (1980). The goals of psychoanalysis and psychoanalytic therapy. *AMA Archives of General Psychiatry, 39*(1), 377–388.

Mahler, M. (1968). *On human symbiosis and the vicissitudes of individuation.* New York: International Universities Press.

Margolis, G. (1966). Secrecy and identity. *International Journal of Psychoanalysis, 47,* 517–522.

Margolis, G. (1974). The psychology of keeping secrets. *International Review of Psychoanalysis, 1*(3), 291–296.

Masson, J. M. (1984). *The assault on truth: Freud's suppression of the seduction theory.* New York: Farrar, Straus & Giroux.

Masterson, J. (1976). *Psychotherapy of the borderline adult.* New York: Brunner/Mazel.

May, R. (1958). Contributions of existential psychotherapy. In R. May, E. Angel, & H. Ellenberger (eds.), *Existence* (pp. 37–91). New York: Basic Books.

May, R. (1959). The existential approach. In S. Arieti (ed.), *The American handbook of psychiatry* (Vol. 2, pp. 1348–1361). New York: Basic Books.

Meares, R. (1976). The secret. *Psychiatry, 39,* 258–265.

Meissner, W. (1976). Three essays plus seventy. *International Journal of Psychoanalysis, 57,*(1–2), 127–133.

Merleau-Ponty, M. (1962). *The phenomenology of perception.* London: Routledge & Kegan Paul.

Milgram, S. (1970). The experience of living in cities. *Science, 167,* 1461–1468.

Miller, Alice (1981). *Prisoners of childhood.* New York: Basic Books.

Miller, Alice (1983). *For your own good.* New York: Farrar, Straus & Giroux.

Miller, Arthur (1957). Introduction. In *Collected plays* (pp. 3–55). New York: Viking Press.

Miller, Arthur (1957). *Death of a salesman.* In *Collected plays* (pp. 130–222). New York: Viking Press.

Miller, R. F. (1984). Dostoevsky and Rousseau: The morality of confession. In R. L. Jackson (ed.), *Dostoevsky* (pp. 82–98). Englewood Cliffs, N.J.: Prentice-Hall.

Mishima, Y. (1958). *Confessions of a mask.* New York: New Directions.

Mitchell, S. (1981). The origin and nature of the "object" in the theories of Klein and Fairbairn. *Contemporary Psychoanalysis, 17*(3), 374–398.

Mitchell, S. (1984). Object relations theory and the developmental tilt. *Contemporary Psychoanalysis, 20*(4), 473–499.

Modell, A. (1975). A narcissistic defense against affects and the illusion of self-sufficiency. *International Journal of Psychoanalysis, 56,* 275–282.

Monahan, J. (1981). *The clinical prediction of violent behavior.* Rockville, Md.: National Institute of Mental Health.

Montaigne, M. (1965). *The complete works of Montaigne.* (D. M. Frame, trans.). London: Hamish Hamilton.

Morrison, A. (1983). Shame, ideal self and narcissism. *Contemporary Psychoanalysis, 19*(2), 295–318.

Mowrer, O. H. (1961). Psychopathology and the problem of guilt, confession and expiation. In W. Dennis (ed.), *Current trends in psychological theory* (pp. 208–229). Pittsburgh: University of Pittsburgh Press.

Mowrer, O. H. (1964). *The new group therapy.* Princeton, N.J.: Van Nostrand.

Nemiroff, R., & Colarusso, C. (1980). Authenticity and narcissism in the adult development of the self. *Annual of Psychoanalysis, 8,* 111–129.

Newirth, J. (1982). Intimacy in interpersonal psychoanalysis. In M.
    Fisher & G. Stricker (eds.), *Intimacy* (pp. 79–97). New York:
    Plenum.
Nietzsche, F. (1967). *Thus spake Zarathustra.* New York: Heritage.
    (Original work published 1885.)
Norton, R., Feldman, A., & Tofoya, D. (1974). Risk parameters
    across types of secrets. *Journal of Counseling Psychology, 21,*
    450–454.
Olinick, S. (1980). The gossiping psychoanalyst. *International
    Review of Psychoanalysis, 7*(4), 439–445.
O'Neill, E. (1940). *The iceman cometh.* New York: Random House.
Opler, M. (1936). Some points of comparison and contrast between
    the treatment of functional disorders by Apache shamans and
    modern psychiatrists. *American Journal of Psychiatry, 92,*
    1371–1387.
Oxford English Dictionary. (1971). Oxford University Press.
Packard, V. (1972). *A nation of strangers.* New York: David McKay.
Penfield, W. (1959). The interpretive cortex. *Science, 129,*
    1719–1725.
Perls, F., Hefferline, R., & Goodman, P. (1951). *Gestalt therapy.* New
    York: Delta.
Piaget, J. (1977). The language and thought of the child. In H.
    Gruber & J. J. Vonèche (eds.), *The essential Piaget* (pp. 65–
    88). New York: Basic Books. (Original work published 1923.)
Piaget, J. (1932). *The moral judgment of the child.* New York: Free
    Press.
Piaget, J. (1977). The role of imitation in the development of repre-
    sentational thought. In H. Gruber & J. J. Vonèche (eds.) *The
    essential Piaget* (pp. 508–514). New York: Basic Books. (Origi-
    nal work published 1962.)
Piaget, J. (1977). Moral feelings and judgments. In H. Gruber & J. J.
    Vonèche (eds.), *The essential Piaget* (pp. 154–158). New York:
    Basic Books. (Original work published 1966.)
Pine, F. (1984). *Developmental theory and clinical process.* New
    Haven, Conn.: Yale University Press.
Pinter, H. (1978). *Betrayal.* New York: Grove Press.
Plato (1932). *The republic.* (B. Jowett, trans.). New York: Random
    House.
Poe, E. A. (1965). William Wilson. In *The complete works of Edgar
    Allan Poe* (Vol. 3, pp. 299–325). New York: AMS Press. (Origi-
    nal work published 1839.)
Polansky, N. (1967). On duplicity in the interview. *American Jour-
    nal of Orthopsychiatry, 37,* 568–580.

Prado, M. (1980). Neurotic and psychotic transference and projective identification. *International Review of Psychoanalysis, 7*(2), 157–164.

Proust, M. (1981). *Remembrance of things past.* New York: Random House. (Original work published 1913–1927.)

Racker, H. (1976). *Transference and countertransference.* New York: International Universities Press.

Rangell, L. (1955). The role of the parent in the Oedipus complex. *Bulletin of the Menninger Clinic, 19,* 9–15.

Reich, A. (1951). On countertransference. *International Journal of Psychoanalysis, 32,* 25–31.

Reich, A. (1960a). Further remarks on countertransference. *International Journal of Psychoanalysis, 41,* 389–395.

Reich, A. (1960b). Pathological forms of self-esteem regulation. *Psychoanalytic Study of the Child, 15,* 215–231.

Reich, W. (1972). *Character analysis* (3rd ed.). New York: Farrar, Straus & Giroux.

Reik, T. (1959). *The compulsion to confess.* New York: Farrar, Straus & Cudahy.

Rexroth, K. (1964). *One hundred Japanese poems.* New York: New Directions.

Rich, A. (1979). *On lies, secrets and silence. Selected prose 1966–1978.* New York: Norton.

Rist, K. (1979). Incest: Theoretical and clinical views. *American Journal of Orthopsychiatry, 49*(4), 680–691.

Rosenfeld, H. (1983). Positive object relations and mechanisms. *International Journal of Psychoanalysis, 64*(3), 261–267.

Rothstein, A. (1979). Oedipal conflicts in narcissistic personality disorders. *International Journal of Psychoanalysis, 60*(2), 189–192.

Rousseau, J. J. (1977). *The confessions.* New York: Penguin. (Original work published 1781.)

Sachs, H. (1951). *The creative unconscious.* Cambridge, Mass.: Sci-Art Publishers.

Saint Augustine (1961). *Confessions.* New York: Penguin. (Original work written 398 A.D.)

Sandler, J. (1981). Character traits and object relationships. *Psychoanalytic Quarterly, 50*(4), 694–708.

Sandler, J., & Rosenblatt, B. (1962). The concept of the representational world. *Psychoanalytic Study of the Child, 17,* 128–145.

Sandler, J., & Sandler, A. (1978). On the development of object relationships and affects. *International Journal of Psychoanalysis, 59,* 285–296.

Sartre, J. P. (1949). *Existentialism.* New York: Philosophical Library.

Sartre, J. P. (1966). *The words.* New York: Fawcett Crest.

Sartre, J. P. (1971). *Being and nothingness.* New York: Citadel Press.

Schafer, R. (1960). The loving and beloved superego in Freud's structural theory. *Psychoanalytic Study of the Child, 15,* 163–188.

Schafer, R. (1968). *Aspects of internalization.* New York: International Universities Press.

Schafer, R. (1973). The idea of resistance. *International Journal of Psychoanalysis, 54*(3), 259–285.

Schafer, R. (1974). Problems in Freud's psychology of women. *Journal of the American Psychoanalytic Association, 22,* 459–485.

Schafer, R. (1977). The interpretation of transference and the conditions for loving. *Journal of the American Psychoanalytic Association, 25,* 335–362.

Schafer, R. (1982). The relevance of the "here and now" transference interpretation to the reconstruction of early development. *International Journal of Psychoanalysis, 63*(1), 77–82.

Schafer, R. (1983). *The analytic attitude.* New York: Basic Books.

Schneck, J. M. (1974). Oedipus revisited—An additional review. *Journal of the American Academy of Psychoanalysis, 2*(1), 63–70.

Schwartz, W. (1984). The two concepts of action and responsibility in psychoanalysis. *Journal of the American Psychoanalytic Association, 32*(3), 557–572.

Searles, H. (1959). Oedipal love in the countertransference. *International Journal of Psychoanalysis, 40,* 180–190.

Searles, H. (1979a). Jealousy involving an internal object. In J. Leboit & A. Capponi (eds.), *Advances in psychotherapy of the borderline patient* (pp. 344–403). New York: Jason Aronson.

Searles, H. (1979b). *Countertransference and related subjects. Selected papers.* New York: International Universities Press.

Sedler, M. (1983). Freud's concept of working through. *Psychoanalytic Quarterly, 52*(1), 73–98.

Shakespeare, W. (1958). *Hamlet.* New York: Washington Square Press. (Original work published 1603.)

Shakespeare, W. (1966). *Othello.* Waltham, Mass.: Blaisdell. (Original work published 1622.)

Shaw, G. B. (1919). *Mrs. Warren's profession.* In *Plays pleasant and unpleasant* (Vol. 1, pp. 165–245). New York: Brentano. (Original work published 1894.)

Siegman, A. (1964). Exhibitionism and fascination. *Journal of the American Psychoanalytic Association, 12,* 315–334.

Simmel, G. (1950). Secrecy. In K. Wolff (ed.), *The sociology of Georg Simmel* (pp. 330–344). New York: Free Press.

Singer, J. (1985). Transference and the human condition: A cognitive-affective perspective. *Psychoanalytic Psychology, 2*(3), 161–172.

Sircello, G. (1972). *Mind and art: An essay on the varieties of expression.* Princeton, N.J.: Princeton University Press.

Skeat, W. (1961). *Etymological dictionary of the English language.* Oxford: Clarendon Press.

Sophocles (1982). *Oedipus the king.* In M. Hadras (ed.), *Greek drama.* New York: Bantam Books. (Original work written 430 B.C.)

Spieler, S. (1984). Preoedipal girls need fathers. *Psychoanalytic Review, 71*(1), 63–80.

Spitz, R. (1956). Countertransference. *Journal of the American Psychoanalytic Association, 4,* 256–265.

Spitz, R. (1965). *The first year of life.* New York: International Universities Press.

Splitter, R. (1980). Proust's myth of artistic creation. *American Imago, 37*(4), 386–412.

Spotnitz, H. (1976). *Psychotherapy of preoedipal conditions.* New York: Jason Aronson.

Spotnitz, H. (1979). Narcissistic countertransference. *Contemporary Psychoanalysis, 15*(4), 545–559.

Steiner, J. (1985). Turning a blind eye. The cover for Oedipus. *International Review of Psychoanalysis, 12*(2), 161–172.

Stern, H. (1981). The "becoming question": A variation in responding to patients' queries. *Modern Psychoanalysis, 6*(2), 195–200.

Stevenson, R. L. (1925). The story of a lie. In *The strange case of Dr. Jekyll and Mr. Hyde* (pp. 167–179). New York: Scribner's. (Original work published 1879.)

Stevenson, R. L. (1925). Th strange case of Dr. Jekyll and Mr. Hyde. In *The strange case of Dr. Jekyll and Mr. Hyde* (pp. 1–89). New York: Scribner's. (Original work published 1886.)

Stolorow, R., & Atwood, G. (1979). *Faces in a cloud.* New York: Jason Aronson.

Stolorow, R., & Lachmann, F. (1980). *Psychoanalysis of developmental arrests.* New York: International Universities Press.

Stolorow, R., & Lachmann, F. (1984/1985). Transference: The future of an illusion. *Annual of Psychoanalysis, 12/13,* 19–37.

Stone, L. (1981). Some thoughts on the "here and now" in psychoanalytic technique and process. *Psychoanalytic Quarterly, 50*, 709–733.

Strachey, J. (1934). The nature of the therapeutic action of psychoanalysis. *International Journal of Psychoanalysis, 15*, 127–159.

Sullivan, H. S. (1953). *The interpersonal theory of psychiatry.* New York: Norton.

Sulzberger, C. (1953). Why it is hard to keep secrets. *Psychoanalysis, 2*(2), 37–43.

Suzuki, D. (1956). *Zen Buddhism.* New York: Doubleday.

Symonds, M. (1980). The second injury. In L. Kivens (ed.), *Evaluation and change: Services for survivors* (pp. 36–38). Minneapolis, Mn.: Minneapolis Medical Research Foundation.

Tertullian (1931). *De resurrectione mortuorum.* In *Apology* (T. Glover, trans.). New York: G. P. Putnam. (Original work published 1521.)

Tillich, P. (1952). *The courage to be.* New Haven, Conn.: Yale University Press.

Tillich, P. (1962). Existentialism and psychotherapy. In H. Ruitenbeek (ed.), *Psychoanalysis and existential philosophy* (pp. 3–16). New York: Dutton.

Tolpin, M. (1971). On the beginnings of a cohesive self: An application of the concept of transmuting internalization to the study of the transitional object and signal anxiety. *Psychoanalytic Study of the Child, 26*, 315–352.

Tolstoy, L. (1983). *Confession.* New York: Norton. (Original work published 1882.)

Tolstoy, L. (1975). The death of Ivan Ilyich. In *Leo Tolstoy. Short stories* (pp. 136–198). Moscow: Progress Publishers. (Original work published 1886.)

Truax, C., & Carkhuff, R. (1965). Client and therapist transparency in the psychotherapeutic encounter. *Journal of Counseling Psychology, 12*, 3–9.

Twain, M. (1940). *The adventures of Huckleberry Finn.* New York: Heritage Press. (Original work published 1885.)

Updike, J. (1985, September 2). Personal history. At war with my skin. *New Yorker,* 39–57.

Vogel, J. (1962). *Leos Janacek. His life and works.* London: Paul Hamlyn.

Vondracek, F., & Vondracek, F. (1971). The manipulation and measurement of self-disclosure in adolescents. *Merrill-Palmer Quarterly, 17*, 51–58.

Wagner, H., & Fine, H. (1980). Object relations and its clinical implications. *Psychoanalytic Review, 67*(2), 231–252.

Weigert, E. (1960). Soren Kierkegaard's mood swings. *International Journal of Psychoanalysis, 41*, 521–525.

White, M. (1980). Self relations, object relations and pathological narcissism. *Psychoanalytic Review, 67*, 3–23.

White, R. (1963). Ego and reality in psychoanalytic theory: A proposal regarding independent ego energies. *Psychological Issues, 3*(3) (Monograph no. 11).

Widiger, T., & Rorer, L. (1984). The responsible psychotherapist. *American Psychologist, 39*, 503–515.

Wilde, O. (1964). *The picture of Dorian Gray.* New York: Airmont. (Original work published 1890.)

Wilner, W. (1982). Philosophical approaches to interpersonal intimacy. In M. Fisher & G. Stricker (eds.), *Intimacy* (pp. 21–38). New York: Plenum.

Winnicott, D. (1975). Reparation in respect of mother's organized defense against depression. In *Through paediatrics to psycho-analysis* (pp. 91–96). New York: Basic Books. (Original work published 1948.)

Winnicott, D. (1975). Hate in the countertransference. In *Through Paediatrics to psycho-analysis* (pp. 194–203). New York: Basic Books. (Original work published 1949.)

Winnicott, D. (1975). Metapsychological and clinical aspects of regression within the psychoanalytic set-up. In *Through paediatrics to psycho-analysis* (pp. 278–294). New York: Basic Books. (Original work published 1954.)

Winnicott, D. (1965). The capacity to be alone. In *The maturational processes and the facilitating environment* (pp. 29–36). New York: International Universities Press. (Original work published 1958.)

Winnicott, D. (1965). The development of the capacity for concern. In *The maturational processes and the facilitating environment.* New York: International Universities Press. (Original work published 1963.)

Winnicott, D. (1965). *The maturational processes and the facilitating environment.* New York: International Universities Press.

Winnicott, D. (1971). The use of an object and relating through identification. In *Playing and reality* (pp. 86–94). London: Tavistock. (Original work published 1968.)

Winnicott, D. (1971). *Playing and reality.* London: Tavistock.

Winnicott, D. (1975). *Through paediatrics to psycho-analysis.* New York: Basic Books.

Wittkower, R., & Wittkower, M. (1963). *Born under Saturn.* London: Weidenfeld & Nicolson.

Wolf, E. (1979). Transferences and countertransferences in the analysis of the disorders of the self. *Contemporary Psychoanalysis, 15,* 577–594.

Wolfe, T. (1940). *You can't go home again.* New York: Scribner's.

Worthen, V. (1974). Psychotherapy and Catholic confession. *Journal of Religion and Health, 4*(3), 275–284.

Yankelovich, D. (1981). *New rules: Searching for self-fulfillment in a world turned upside down.* New York: Random House.

INDEX